COSMIC TRIGGER I

FINAL SECRET OF THE ILLUMINATI

'Tis an ill wind that blows no minds."

- Malaclypse the Younger, *Principia Discordia*

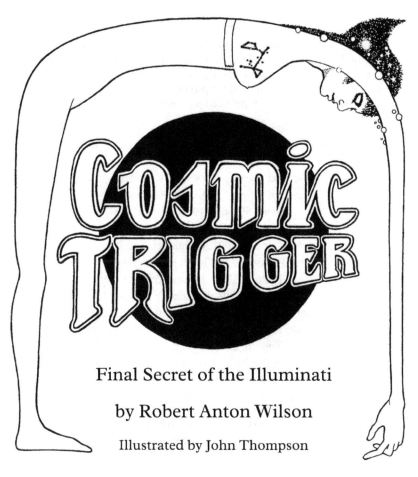

Final Secret of the Illuminati

by Robert Anton Wilson

Illustrated by John Thompson

Introduction by John Higgs
Forewords by Timothy Leary, Ph.D.

HILARITAS
⊚PRESS

International Standard Book Number: 13: 978-0692513972
Library of Congress Catalog Card Number: 77-89428
First Edition: 1977
Second Printing 1978, And/Or Press
Third Printing 1978, Simon & Schuster
Fourth Printing 1986, Falcon
Fifth Printing 1987, Sixth Printing 1989
Seventh Printing 1991, Eighth Printing 1992
Ninth Printing 1993, Tenth Printing 1995
Eleventh Printing 1996. Twelfth Printing 1997
Thirteenth Printing 1998, Fourteenth Printing 1999
Fifteenth Printing 2000, Sixteenth Printing 2001
Seventeenth Printing 2002, Eighteenth Printing 2004
Nineteenth Printing 2005, Twentieth Printing 2007
Twenty-first Printing 2008, Twenty-second Printing 2009
Twenty-third Printing 2011
Second Edition 2016, Hilaritas Press

Cover Design by amoeba
Book design by Pelorian Digital

Hilaritas Press, LLC.
P.O. Box 1153
Grand Junction, Colorado 81502
www.hilaritaspress.com

This book is dedicated to
  Ken Campbell and the Science Fiction
  Theatre of Liverpool, England
and to
  The Temple of the Hidden God,
  Houston, Texas

Appreciation for Light along the Way:
  Alan Watts,
  Timothy Leary,
  Parcifal,
  Malaclypse the Younger,
  The New Reformed Orthodox
    Order of the Golden Dawn,
  Dr. Israel Regardie

TABLE OF CONTENTS

INTRODUCTION

by John Higgs

Truly great books tend to have two things in common.

First, they are utterly of their time. They are so absorbed in their specific world that it is inconceivable that they could have come from any other time or place. They can define how we think about that period of history. Think of the work of Geoffrey Chaucer, or Jane Austen, or Charles Dickens.

And secondly, they transcend their time. They are universal, and capture something fundamental about the human experience. They speak to all people in all places at all times. Think again of the same work by Geoffrey Chaucer, Jane Austen, and Charles Dickens.

Cosmic Trigger, for all the wandering the author and his family do in the book, is about the counterculture's mid-1970s Northern California heartland. This was when psychedelic drug culture was being overtaken by a more cocaine-dominated culture. A period of absorbing wild new ideas was giving way to egos, certainty, and falling hard for your own delusions. It was as crazy as it gets, in other words. It was the edge. Western culture may never be more Out There, wild-eyed or full of crap.

We now take a certain pleasure from how deluded this culture was. History has not been kind to many of the speculative scientists Wilson discusses here. Nearly forty years after it was written, this is a book of failed predictions and gorgeously optimistic claims. Humanity is going to become an immortal interstellar race, it promises us, probably by the mid-1990s.

So Cosmic Trigger is a book utterly of its time. That is reason to think fondly of it, but it isn't reason enough to keep reading it. The reason why its flame still burns is that it is also a book for the ages. It is a story about becoming lost. It is about entering that psychological space where all your maps have run out, and the world refuses to make sense regardless of how you look at it. This is a universal story and its perfect setting is that extreme edge of the 1970s counterculture, because if you're telling a story about losing your anchor you want the bewilderment, craziness and paranoia to be as extreme as possible.

I won't spoil the book by detailing Wilson's account of his time in the Wilderness, but his refusal to fully believe the growing evidence for what part of him dearly wants to be true, and the point at the end where he finally plants his flag in the sand, are what makes this book relevant. Both for now, and for all time.

It affects people, this book. It can send your life off in strange directions. As an example, on 23 February 2014 I was in Mathew Street in Liverpool, England. I formed an ungainly attempt at a human pyramid with the writers Ian 'Cat' Vincent and Alistair Fruish underneath a bust of Carl Jung set about 10 feet up in the outside wall of a pub. This allowed the theatre director Daisy Eris Campbell to scramble up on our backs and place a pair of rainbow knickers on Jung's head. A wave of cheering and approval then came from the assembled crowd of 50 or so, cheering that only increased when a poor bewildered football fan, wearing a Liverpool shirt with the number '23' on his back, happened to wander past. All this probably needs a bit of explanation.

The statue and a nearby manhole cover are significant in Liverpool folklore thanks to a dream that Jung once had, it's impact on the Liverpool poet Peter O'Halligan, and their proximity to the Cavern Club where The Beatles emerged to change the world. Campbell, who was embarking on a theatrical adaptation of Cosmic Trigger, also viewed the location, the bust and the knickers as deeply meaningful, but for her own personal reasons. I too found it significant, in part because of its connections to a book about the 90s dance band The KLF I had just written. The Scottish artist, money burner and one half of The KLF Bill Drummond had recently spent 17 hours of his 60th birthday standing on the nearby manhole cover, for reasons that were meaningful to him. My book also mentions the musician and writer Julian Cope, who had busked under this same statue a year or so before, for reasons that made sense in his personal mythology.

Pretty much everybody considered the location meaningful, in other words, they just had differing reasons as to why.

This might sound problematic. When people disagree about what is meaningful, it rarely ends well. But the people assembled in Mathew Street had read Robert Anton Wilson, and they took it as read that others see things differently. They knew that this doesn't diminish what they find personally important. On the contrary, it reveals further pieces of the puzzle.

The many hundreds of people who were drawn to the November 2014 Cosmic Trigger play and accompanying 'Find The Others' festival, as cast, crew or audience, all had their own reasons for being there. They were very different people, with very different histories, prejudices, hopes and beliefs. There were new-age heads and materialist rationalists, American libertarians and British socialists, the focused and the vague, and the serious and the silly. The only thing they had in common was that they had read Robert Anton Wilson, and felt that their lives were better for his philosophy. And that was enough. That was enough for all their own personal stories to harmoniously mesh with all the others, into what we soon began calling the Ever-Thickening Mythos. The shared love of Cosmic Trigger was the grit around which a tribal pearl formed.

Cosmic Trigger is autobiographical, the story of one man. Yet it has become a glue which connects the personal mythologies of a wide network of people, all of whom add to a greater story which we only catch glimpses of.

In a short novel I wrote called The Brandy of the Damned, the characters find pages from an alternative bible. One reads:

If you apply meaning to a thing you have made, then you have art.

If you apply meaning to a person, then you have love.

If you apply meaning to the universe, then you have God.

Meaning is free.

There is an inexhaustible supply of meaning.

So what's the fucking problem?

The problem is, of course, that meaning is not fixed. It ebbs and flows like the tide. Sometimes you are drenched in the stuff, and life is self-evidently worthwhile and full of purpose and humour. And at others, it all drains away, and you are left with the horrors. In Cosmic Trigger, Robert Anton Wilson shows us how to navigate these waters, both when life is too meaningful and when all meaning is gone.

Wilson's own personal mythology, and what was meaningful to him, is great fun. What grey-faced soul does not enjoy a yarn about giant invisible rabbit spirits, the number 23 and 6000-year-old communications with the Dog Star Sirius? But, as Wilson would be the first to insist, just because these things were meaningful in his personal story does not mean that they should be equally meaningful in yours. Your own personal mythos will be equally idiosyncratic and peculiar, and it will always be more sustaining, rewarding and funny than anyone else's. And as Wilson once said, "humans live through their myths, and only endure their realities."

Wilson's refusal to insist that his reality tunnel has more validity than that of his readers is, I think, the great gift of this book. That is why it has become so loved: you can see your own potential in its pages. That is why it is one of the great books of the 1970s. And that why it is one of the great books of all time.

PREFACE

By the author, originally called *Preface to the New Edition,*
but it was not a new edition — merely a new publisher. – *Ed.*

Cosmic Trigger was originally published by And/Or Press
about ten years ago, and by Pocket Books shortly thereafter.
Although some of my novels have sold far better, in two dimensions at least it is my most "successful" book in human terms.

1. From the date of first printing to the present, I have received more mail about *Cosmic Trigger* than about anything else
I ever wrote, and most of this mail has been unusually intelligent
and open-minded. For some reason, many readers of this book
think they can write to me intimately and without fear, about
subjects officially Taboo in our society. I have learned a great
deal from this correspondence, and have met some wonderful
new friends.

2. On lecture tours, I am always asked more questions about
this book than about all my other works together.

This new edition presents an opportunity to answer the most
frequent questions and to correct the most persistent misunder-
standings.

It should be obvious to all intelligent readers (but curiously
is not obvious to many) that my viewpoint in this book is one
of agnosticism. The word "agnostic" appears explicitly in the
Prologue and the agnostic attitude is restated again and again
in the text, but many people still think I "believe" some of the
metaphors and models employed here. I therefore want to make
it even clearer than ever before that

I DO NOT BELIEVE ANYTHING

This remark was made, in these very words, by John Gribbin, physics editor of *New Scientist* magazine, in a BBC-TV debate with Malcolm Muggeridge, and it provoked incredulity on the part of most viewers. It seems to be a hangover of the medieval Catholic era that causes most people, even the educated, to think that everybody must "believe" something or other, that if one is not a theist, one must be a dogmatic atheist, and if one does not think Capitalism is perfect, one must believe fervently in Socialism, and if one does not have blind faith in X, one must alternatively have blind faith in not-X or the reverse of X.

My own opinion is that *belief is the death of intelligence.* As soon as one believes a doctrine of any sort, or assumes certitude, one stops thinking about that aspect of existence. The more certitude one assumes, the less there is left to think about, and a person sure of everything would never have any need to think about anything and might be considered clinically dead under current medical standards, where the absence of brain activity is taken to mean that life has ended.

My attitude is identical to that of Dr. Gribbin and the majority of physicists today, and is known in physics as "the Copenhagen Interpretation," because it was formulated in Copenhagen by Dr. Niels Bohr and his co-workers c. 1926-28. The Copenhagen Interpretation is sometimes called "model agnosticism" and holds that any grid we use to organize our experience of the world is a model of the world and should not be confused with the world itself. Alfred Korzybski, the semanticist, tried to popularize this outside physics with the slogan, "The map is not the territory." Alan Watts, a talented exegete of Oriental philosophy, restated it more vividly as "The menu is not the meal."

Belief in the traditional sense, or certitude, or dogma, amounts to the grandiose delusion, "My current model" — or grid, or map, or reality-tunnel — "contains the whole universe and will never need to be revised." In terms of the history of science and of knowledge in general, this appears absurd and arrogant to me, and I am perpetually astonished that so many people still manage to live with such a medieval attitude.

Cosmic Trigger deals with a process of *deliberately induced brain change* through which I put myself in the years 1962-76. This process is called "initiation" or "vision quest" in many traditional societies and can loosely be considered some dangerous variety of self-psychotherapy in modern terminology. I do not recommend it for everybody, and I think I obtained more good results than bad ones chiefly because I had been through two varieties of ordinary psychotherapy before I started my own adventures and because I had a good background in scientific philosophy and was not inclined to "believe" any astounding Revelations too literally.

Briefly, the main thing I learned in my experiments is that *"reality" is always plural and mutable.*

Since most of Cosmic Trigger is devoted to explaining and illustrating this, and since I have tried to explain it again in other books, and since I still encounter people who have read all my writings on this subject and still do not understand what I am getting at, I will try again in this new Preface to explain it ONE MORE TIME, perhaps more clearly than before.

"Reality" is a word in the English language which happens to be (a) a noun and (b) singular. Thinking in the English language (and in cognate Indo-European languages) therefore subliminally programs us to conceptualize "reality" as one block-like entity, sort of like a huge New York skyscraper, in which every part is just another "room" within the same building. This linguistic program is so pervasive that most people cannot "think" outside it at all, and when one tries to offer a different perspective they imagine one is talking gibberish.

The notion that "reality" is a *noun*, a solid thing like a brick or a baseball bat, derives from the evolutionary fact that our nervous systems normally organize the dance of energy into such block-like "things," probably as instant bio-survival cues. Such "things," however, dissolve back into energy dances — processes, or verbs — when the nervous system is synergized with certain drugs or transmuted by yogic or shamanic exercises or aided by scientific instruments. In both mysticism and physics, there is general agreement that "things" are constructed by our nervous systems and that "realities" (plural) are better described as *systems* or bundles of energy-functions.

So much for "reality" as a *noun*. The notion that "reality" is *singular*, like a hermetically sealed jar, does not jibe with scientific findings which, in this century, suggest that "reality" may better be considered as flowing and meandering, like a river, or interacting, like a dance, or evolving, like life itself.

Most philosophers have known, at least since around 500 B.C., that the world perceived by our senses is not "the real world" but a construct we create — our own private work of art. Modern science began with Galileo's demonstration that color is not "in" objects but "in" the inter-action of our senses with objects. Despite this philosophic and scientific knowledge of neurological relativity, which has been more clearly demonstrated with each major advance in instrumentation, we still, due to language, think that *behind* the flowing, meandering, inter-acting, evolving universe created by perception is one solid monolithic "reality" hard and crisply outlined as an iron bar.

Quantum physics has undermined that Platonic iron-bar "reality" by showing that it makes more sense scientifically to talk only of the inter-actions we actually experience (our operations in the laboratory); and perception psychology has undermined the Platonic "reality" by showing that assuming it exists leads to hopeless contradictions in explaining how we actually perceive that a hippopotamus is not a symphony orchestra.

The only "realities" (plural) that we actually experience and can talk meaningfully about are perceived realities, experienced realities, existential realities — realities involving ourselves as editors — and they are all relative to the observer, fluctuating, evolving, capable of being magnified and enriched, moving from low resolution to hi-fi, and do not fit together like the pieces of a jig-saw into one single Reality with a capital R. Rather, they cast illumination upon one another by contrast, like the paintings in a large museum, or the different symphonic styles of Haydn, Mozart, Beethoven and Mahler.

Alan Watts may have said it best of all: "The universe is a giant Rorschach ink-blot." Science finds one meaning in it in the 18th Century, another in the 19th, a third in the 20th; each artist finds unique meanings on other levels of abstraction; and each man and woman finds different meanings at different hours of the day, depending on the internal and external environments. This book deals with what I have called *induced brain change*, which Dr. John Lilly more resoundingly calls "metaprogramming the human bio-computer." In simple Basic English, as a psychologist and novelist, I set out to find how much rapid reorganization was possible in the brain functioning of one normal domesticated primate of average intelligence — the only one on whom I could ethically perform such risky research — myself.

Like most people who have historically attempted such "metaprogramming," I soon found myself in metaphysical hot water. It became urgently obvious that my previous models and metaphors would not and could not account for what I was experiencing. I therefore had to create new models and metaphors as I went along. Since I was dealing with matters outside consensus reality-tunnels, some of my metaphors are rather extraordinary. That does not bother me, since I am at least as much an artist as a psychologist, but it does bother me when people take these metaphors too literally.

I beg you, gentle reader, to memorize the quote from Aleister Crowley at the beginning of Part One and repeat it to yourself if at any point you start thinking that I am bringing you the latest theological revelations from Cosmic Central.

What my experiments demonstrate — what all such experiments throughout history have demonstrated — is simply that our models of "reality" are very small and tidy, the universe of experience is huge and untidy, and no model can ever include all the huge untidiness perceived by uncensored consciousness.

I think, or hope, that my data also demonstrates that **neurological model agnosticism** — the application of the Copenhagen Interpretation beyond physics to consciousness itself — allows one to escape from certain limits of mechanical emotion and robot mentation that are inescapable as long as one remains within one dogmatic model or one imprinted reality-tunnel.

Personally, I also suspect, or guess, or intuit, that the more unconventional of my models here — the ones involving Higher

Intelligence, such as the Cabalistic Holy Guardian Angel or the extraterrestrial from Sirius — are *necessary* working tools at certain stages of the metaprogramming process.

That is, whether such entities exist anywhere outside our own imaginations, some areas of brain functioning cannot be accessed without using these "keys" to open the locks. I do not insist on this; it is just my own opinion. Some people seem to get through this area of Chapel Perilous without such personalized "Guides." I know one chap who did it by imagining a super-computer in the future that was sending information backwards in time to his brain. More clever people may find even less "metaphysical" metaphors.

Ten years after the point at which this book ends, I do not care much about such speculations. Our lonely little selves can be "illuminated" or flooded with radical science-fiction style information and cosmic perspectives, and the source of this may be those extraterrestrials who seemed to be helping me at times, or the Secret Chiefs of Sufism, or the parapsychologists and/or computers of the 23rd Century beaming data backward in time, or it may just be the previously unactivated parts of our own brains. Despite the current reign of our New Inquisition, which attempts to halt research in this area, we will learn more about that as time passes. Meanwhile, agnosticism is both honest and becomingly modest.

In this connection, I am often asked about two books by other authors which are strangely resonant with *Cosmic Trigger* — namely *VALIS* by Philip K. Dick and *The Sirian Experiments* by Doris Lessing. *VALIS* is a novel which broadly hints that it is more than a novel — that it is an actual account of Phil Dick's own experience with some form of "Higher Intelligence." In fact, *VALIS* is only slightly fictionalized; the actual events on which it is based are recounted in a long interview Phil gave shortly before his death (See Philip K. Dick: *The Last Testament*, by Gregg Rickman.) The parallels with my own experience are numerous — but so are the differences. If the same source was beaming ideas to both Phil and me, the messages got our individual flavors mixed into them as we decoded the signals.

I met Phil Dick on two or three occasions and corresponded with him a bit. My impression was that he was worried that his experience was a temporary insanity and was trying to figure out if I was nutty, too. I'm not sure if he ever decided.

I interviewed Doris Lessing a few years ago for *New Age* magazine. She takes synchronicities very seriously, but was as agnostic as I am about the possibility that some of them are orchestrated by Sirians.

I heartily recommend all three volumes — *VALIS, The Last Testament* and *The Sirian Experiments* — to readers of this book. Unless you are locked into a very dogmatic reality-tunnel, you will have a few weird moments of wondering if Sirians *are* experimenting on us, and a few weird moments can be a liberating experience for those who aren't scared to death by them.

What is more important than such extra-mundane speculation, I think, are practical and pragmatic questions about what one *does* with the results of brain change experience. It is quite easy, I have discovered by meeting many New Age people, to use the techniques in this book and go stone crazy with them. Paranoid and schizophrenic cases are quite common among those who experiment in this area. Less clinical, but socially even more nefarious, are the leagues of self-proclaimed gurus and their equally deluded disciples, who have discovered, as I did, that there are many realities (plural), but have picked out one favorite non-Occidental reality-tunnel, named it Ultimate Reality or True Reality, and established new fanaticisms, snobberies, dogmas and cults around these delusions.

There is a great deal of lyrical Utopianism in this book. I do not apologize for that, and do not regret it. The decade that has passed since the first edition has not altered my basic commitment to the game-rule that holds that an optimistic mind-set finds dozens of possible solutions for every problem that the pessimist regards as incurable.

Since we all create our habitual reality-tunnels, either consciously and intelligently or unconsciously and mechanically, I prefer to create for each hour the happiest, funniest and most romantic reality-tunnel consistent with the signals my brain apprehends. I feel sorry for the people who persistently organize experience into sad, dreary and hopeless reality-tunnels, and try to show them how to break that bad habit, but I don't feel any masochistic duty to share their misery.

This book does **not** claim that "you create your own reality" in the sense of total (but mysteriously unconscious) psychokinesis. If a car hits you and puts you in the hospital, I do not believe this is because you "really wanted" to be hit by a car, or that you "needed" to be hit by a car, as two popular New Age bromides have it. The theory of transactional psychology, which is the source of my favorite models and metaphors, merely says that, once you have been hit by a car, the **meaning** of the experience depends entirely on you and the *results* depend partly on you (and partly on your doctors). If it is medically possible for you to live — and sometimes even if the doctors think it is medically impossible — you ultimately decide whether to get out of the hospital in a hurry or to lie around suffering and complaining.

Most of the time, this kind of "decision" is unconscious and mechanical, but with the techniques described in this book, such decisions can become conscious and intelligent.

The last part of this book deals with the worst tragedy of my life. I want to say, without self-pity (a vice I despise) that my years on this planet have included many other terrible and punishing experiences, starting with two bouts of polio when I was a child and including dozens of other things I don't want to complain about in public. When I write of creating a better and more optimistic reality-tunnel, of transcending ego games, and of similar matters, it is not because I have lived in an ivory tower. It is because I have learned a few practical techniques for dealing with the brutal conditions on this primitive planet.

People at my lectures and seminars usually ask me if I am still optimistic about civilian space programs and life extension. I am more optimistic than ever. Despite the seemingly terminal case of *rigidicus bureaucraticus* at NASA, I have reason to believe certain European countries will soon jointly launch the kind of space migration effort advocated here; and Reagan's SDI, for all its jingoism, means that more money will be spent on basic research than at any previous time in history.

On the life extension front, there have been several best sellers on the subject since this book first appeared; there is interest even in the most intellectually backward part of U.S. society (namely, the Congress); and scientists in the longevity field whom I have met recently all cheerfully say they are getting more money for research than in the 1970s. The breakthrough cannot be far away.

Finally, as a matter of some entertainment value, not all the mail I have received about this book has been intelligent and thoughtful. I have received several quite nutty and unintentionally funny poison-pen letters from two groups of dogmatists — Fundamentalist Christians and Fundamentalist Materialists.

The Fundamentalist Christians have told me that I am a slave of Satan and should have the demons expelled with an exorcism. The Fundamentalist Materialists inform me that I am a liar, charlatan, fraud and scoundrel. Aside from this minor difference, the letters are astoundingly similar. Both groups share the same crusading zeal and the same total lack of humor. charity and common human decency.

These intolerable cults have served to confirm me in my agnosticism by presenting further evidence to support my contention that when dogma enters the brain, all intellectual activity ceases.

Robert Anton Wilson
Dublin 1986

FOREWORDS

by Timothy Leary, Ph.D.

Robert Anton Wilson is a man whose time has come.

It is true of all good things — they are a long time coming.

Intelligence on this planet has evolved in metamorphic stages — long periods of quiescent preparation, then sudden, slam-bang flashes of change.

The personal evolution of Robert Anton Wilson has followed the same rhythm. It's always like that with sages, evolutionary operatives, Intelligence Agents.

It has been axiomatic since Haeckel that *ontology recapitulates phylogeny* — that the individual in Hir* development repeats, step-by-step, the evolution of the species.

♦

Editor's note: Dr. Leary prefers the forms SHe (she or he) and Hir (his or her) to the traditional habit of referring to the general human being as masculine.

♦

We now understand the mystery and the paradox of the great alchemists, philosophers, mystics, sages. They *pre-capitulate*. They prospectively live out in their own nervous systems the future of evolution, the stages which await in the future of the species. Their nervous systems get into communication (via reverse transcriptase) with DNA. They learn how to decode the genetic blueprint. They experience what is to happen in the future. This, surely, is the royal road to wisdom, the highway of evolution —

the two-way traffic between the Central Nervous System (CNS) and the DNA archives, via RNA messenger molecules.

Consider Lao-tse. In the 6th Century B.C., SHe realizes Einsteinian relativity, senses that all is flow and evolutionary change; anticipates (in the *I Ching)* what computer designers will understand 2,500 years later — that energy comes in the binary code of *yin-yang* (off-on); forecasts (in the *Ching* trigrams) what micro-geneticists will discover 2,500 years later — the triplicate function of amino-acid binding.

Now reflect on the poignant destiny of Lao-tse. SHe knows that SHe will not be around in biological form when Watson and Crick decipher the DNA code. The time-lag problem is solved by transtime neurogenetic signalry. Symbolism. The Intelligence Agent called Lao-tse teaches the *I Ching* codes to domesticated primates, injects some fortune-telling hocus-pocus and thus sends down the 2,500-year CNS-RNA-DNA teletype channel this basic code. SHe knows that the Confucians will distort the signal with Boy Scout moralisms (dutifully preserved in the inane Baynes-Wilhelm commentaries), knows that countless charlatans will peddle vulgar *I Ching* fortunes for a nickel in Oriental bazaars. But SHe knows, also, that when external technology catches up, 20th Century Intelligence Agents will receive the dot-dash trigram message and realize that binary codes and triplicate trigrams are genetic guide posts explaining the direction and molecular structure of evolution, from the terrestrial, ☷, earth, to the extraterrestrial, ☰, heaven.

Now consider the Buddha.

Also in the 6th Century B.C., SHe realizes that consciousness creates reality; that all is *maya,* i.e. an internal dance of neurons, an external dance of protons. SHe advises detachment from tribal imprints (local reality-tunnels), announces the octave nature of evolution (again knowing it will be corrupted by moralists into the 8-fold path of domesticated virtue and marketed eventually as the 8 x 8 chessboard). SHe knows that Mendeleyev and the octave division of quarks await 100 generations in the future.

We are awed by this unbroken chain of generational signalry. In each of the 100 generations since Buddha, a few Intelligence

Agents are born and spend their brief lives, detached from the hive, poring over the octaves. In response, we assume, to some RNA suggestion about the sequence of the eight periods of evolution-from heavy to light, from slow to fast, from water to fire, from terrestrial to post-terrestrial, from Kun ☷ to Chien ☰, from earth metals to noble gases.

Next, consider the plight of G.I. Gurdjieff, who, 40 years before the Apollo Lunar Landings and 50 years before the space shuttle, writes *Beelzebub's Tales to His Grandson*, predicting the post-terrestrial future of the species.

Recall the last lines of Aleister Crowley's Confessions, where he sadly recognizes that scientific experiments of the next generation will manifest precisely what his magical rituals could only internalize and ceremonially anticipate.

This book, *Cosmic Trigger*, and its author, Robert Anton Wilson, can best be understood as modern links in this unbroken chain of alchemical philosophers and Intelligence Agents who have systematically learned how to dial and tune their own nervous systems and (via internal biochemical auto-experiments) learned how to converse, via RNA, with their own DNA, decipher the genetic Rosetta Stone and get direct experiential knowledge of the evolutionary process.

Wilson describes 30 years of experimentation on and with his own brain. Most important, he recounts his attempts to correlate inner, subjective vision with the external, objective language of the energy sciences.

And here is the issue, the classic challenge of philosophy: to expand inner neurological reality and to link it with the outer realities measured by scientists. Intelligence evolves when the occult and magical become the objective-scientific.

I recall clearly my first conversation with Robert Anton Wilson in 1964. He was the first and lonely journalist who had actually read my writings and understood the steady development of my own research — from interpersonal psychology to interstellar neurogenetics.

Wilson's ability to open himself up and receive signals both from within his own expanding neurology and from the broadcasts of scientists defines him as one of the key personalities of modern neurological philosophy. He is becoming a major literary figure.

There are two words which always define a great writer-philosopher:

encyclopedic

and

epic.

Each civilization, we are told, produces at its high-water mark one or more encyclopedic works which summarize the knowledge, technology, culture, philosophy of the epoch. Such books are like neurogenetic manuals which summarize and explain a primitive planetary culture to an Intelligence Agent from another world. Dante, Boccaccio, James Joyce, Hesse. As American civilization moves from its adolescence into the final terrestrial stages of technological centralization preceeding Space Migration, it is beginning to produce such encyclopedic writings. For example, Thomas Pynchon's *Gravity's Rainbow*, the *Illuminatus* trilogy of Wilson and Shea, and the book you hold in your hand.

Please consult this book if and when you wish a modern, personal summary of such basic concepts as: the Illuminati conspiracy, the Sirius phenomenon, UFOs, mind-changing drugs, new experiential perspectives on Lee Harvey Oswald, Jim Garrison, Hugh Hefner, the 24 clones of Timothy Leary, the meaning of the number 23, Aleister Crowley, Aldous Huxley, Carl Sagan, Gurdjieff, Alan Watts, William Burroughs, immortality, Nikola Tesla, modern quantum theory, the physics of consciousness, the eight evolving circuits of the nervous system, etc.

In each of these academic references there is an anecdotal flash so that these important names and topics become alive on the page. This is good writing.

Cosmic Trigger is also an epic work.

An epic is a story of exploration, voyaging, adventurous search for meaning.

Cosmic Trigger is an odyssey recounting the personal quest of the author. He explores the labyrinthine regions of his own brain with drugs and many other neuro-activating methods. He experiments with magick, ritual, ESP, isolation. He continually consults his most treasured traveling companions — his beautiful red-haired wife, Arlen, and his sparkling, wise children.

Wilson realizes (as do all alchemists) that he must evolve as the work develops. He knows that the motto *solve et coagule* means that he, too, must accept personal dissolution, that he must vary his own temperature and pressure, test his own sanity in the crucible of change. He gives up a deluxe-sexy job and retreats to social isolation. He plunges unflinchingly into outcaste poverty. He becomes that most recklessly heroic person — the self-employed intellectual! He turns his back on faculty salary and establishment grant and lives by his wits and wisdom. Reading this book, we share his grinding Blakean poverty, his highs and lows.

Cosmic Trigger sparkles with humor, openness of mind, courage, understanding, tolerance. It is the epic adventure of a man who invites us to grow and change with him.

We thank you, Robert Anton Wilson, for this timely and timefull treasure.

Los Angeles, California
Summer, 1977

Prologue:

Thinking About the Unthinkable

Everything you know is wrong.

          – The Firesign Theatre

Thinking About the Unthinkable

As the late, great H.P. Lovecraft might begin this narrative: It is now nearly 13 years since the ill-fated day when I first began investigating the terrible legends surrounding the enigmatic Bavarian Illuminati, an alleged conspiracy that some people believe rules the world. Like a Lovecraft hero, I embarked on my research with no suspicion of the perils awaiting me: I thought I was just investigating a notable case of political paranoia and expected to find only some insight into the psychology which causes otherwise sane individuals to subscribe to such absurdly ridiculous conspiracy theories.

Eventually, in collaboration with Robert J. Shea, I wrote a three-volume satirical novel on the conspiracy, *Illuminatus!* Completing such an exhaustingly long book should have terminated my interest in the subject, but my researches continued nonetheless, evidently propelled by some mysterious momentum. *(Rising organ music, please.)* I had become psychically hooked to the Illuminati. Like a tarantula in the bed-sheets or the laugh of a woman you once loved, the accursed Illuminati simply could not be forgotten or ignored. This was most annoying to the Skeptic, who is one of the 24 selves who live within me and the only one who usually possesses veto power over all the others.

Eventually, my interest in the Illuminati was to lead me through a cosmic Fun House featuring double and triple agents, UFOs, possible Presidential assassination plots, the enigmatic symbols on the dollar bill, messages from Sirius, pancakes from God-knows-where, the ambiguities of Aleister Crowley, some mysterious hawks that follow Uri Geller around, Futurists, Immortalists, plans to leave this planet and the latest paradoxes of quantum mechanics. It has been a prolonged but never boring pursuit, like trying to find a cobra in a dark room before it finds you.

Briefly, the background of the Bavarian Illuminati puzzle is this. On May 1, 1776, in Bavaria, Dr. Adam Weishaupt, a professor of Canon Law at Ingolstadt University and a former

Jesuit, formed a secret society called the Order of the Illuminati within the existing Masonic lodges of Germany. Since Masonry is itself a secret society, the Illuminati was *a secret society within a secret society, a mystery inside a mystery, so to say.* In 1785 the Illuminati were suppressed by the Bavarian government for allegedly plotting to overthrow all the kings in Europe and the Pope to boot. This much is generally agreed upon by all historians. Everything else is a matter of heated, and sometimes fetid, controversy.

It has been claimed that Dr. Weishaupt was an atheist, a Cabalistic magician, a rationalist, a mystic; a democrat, a socialist, an anarchist, a fascist; a Machiavellian amoralist, an alchemist, a totalitarian and an "enthusiastic philanthropist." (The last was the verdict of Thomas Jefferson, by the way.) The Illuminati have also been credited with managing the French and American revolutions behind the scenes, taking over the world, being the brains behind Communism, continuing underground up to the 1970s, secretly worshipping the Devil, and mopery with intent to gawk. Some claim that Weishaupt didn't even invent the Illuminati, but only revived it. The Order of Illuminati has been traced back to the Knights Templar, to the Greek and Gnostic initiatory cults, to Egypt, even to Atlantis. The one safe generalization one can make is that Weishaupt's intent to maintain secrecy has worked; no two students of Illuminology have ever agreed totally about what the "inner secret" or purpose of the Order actually was (or is . . .). There is endless room for spooky speculation, and for pedantic paranoia, once one really gets into the literature of the subject; and there has been a wave of sensational "exposes" of the Illuminati every generation since 1776.[1] If you were to believe all this sensational literature, the damned Bavarian conspirators were responsible for everything wrong with the world, including the energy crises and the fact that you can't even get a plumber on weekends.

For instance, the first explosion of anti-Illuminati hysteria in this country, in the 1790s, was stirred up by fanatic Federalists and centered on the charge that Thomas Jefferson and the Democratic Republican party were pawns of the European Illuminati. The second major cluster of excited exposes came in the 1840s, and was circulated by the Anti-Masonic Party, who believed that the Illuminati still controlled the Masons and had infiltrated our government at all levels. In both of these instances, the Illuminati were portrayed as radical democrats or outright anarchists in the tradition of the ultra-left wing of the French Revolution. Current anti-Illuminati literature, which is mostly distributed through the anti-Semitic, paramilitary Right, portrays the Illuminati as the masters of both international Communism and international banking. A separate and weirder strain of anti-Illuminati theory, occasionally interacting with this political conspiracy literature, portrays the Illuminati as Nazis, black magicians, astral mind-fuckers and Satanists.

But these are only the major themes of the anti-Illuminati symphony. There are countless individuals who have tooted some be-bop riffs — e.g., Philip Campbell Argyle-Smith, editor of a bizarre journal called *High IQ Bulletin*, claims that the Illuminati, known as "Jews" on this planet, are actually invaders from Vulcan. I have also seen a book (author and title now forgotten, alas) which argued that the Illuminati are a Jesuit conspiracy which infiltrated Masonry and then took over the world, using the Masonic front to keep anybody from guessing that the real control actually comes from the Vatican, heh-heh-heh. Typical of the ingenuity of such conspiracy theories, the facts which most glaringly contradict it (namely, the anti-Masonic fulminations and excommunications by all the Popes for the last century, and the tons of anti-Catholic propaganda circulated by Masonic lodges) are explained as "part of the cover-up."

And, of course, anti-Illuminati diatribes of all schools somberly agree that "accidents have a way of happening to those who find out too much about the Bavarian Illuminati." (Let's have that rising organ music again, and an eldritch laugh, like The Shadow's on the old radio series.)

Once when I was appearing on a radio show on KGO-San Francisco, where listeners call in and talk to the guests, a woman phoned to say I knew so much about the Illuminati that I must be one of them.

I became whimsical. "Maybe," I said, "the secret of the Illuminati is that you don't know you're a member until it's too late to get out."

This was too metaphysical for the caller. "Furthermore," she said triumphantly, pursuing her own script, "you're the people who control the Federal Reserve and the Morgan and Rockefeller banks."

"Well," said the Writer of Satire, temporarily displacing the Skeptic, "I certainly won't deny that. It can't help but improve my credit rating."

That woman is probably still telling her friends how she got one of the Illuminati to confess right over the radio.

Actually, I no longer disbelieve in the Illuminati, but I don't believe in them yet, either. Let us explain that odd remark quickly, before we go any further in the murk. In researching occult conspiracies, one eventually faces a crossroad of mythic proportions (called Chapel Perilous in the trade). You come out the other side either a stone paranoid or an agnostic; there is no third way. I came out an agnostic.

Chapel Perilous, like the mysterious entity called "I," cannot be located in the space-time continuum; it is weightless, odorless, tasteless and undetectable by ordinary instruments. Indeed, like the Ego, it is even possible to deny that it is there. And yet, even more like the Ego, once you are inside it, there doesn't seem to be any way to ever get out again, until you suddenly discover that it has been brought into existence by thought and does not exist outside thought. *Every thing you fear* is waiting with slavering jaws in Chapel Perilous, but if you are armed with the wand of intuition, the cup of sympathy, the sword of reason and the pentacle of valor, you will find there (the legends say) the Medicine of Metals, the Elixir of Life, the Philosopher's Stone, True Wisdom and Perfect Happiness.

That's what the legends always say, and the language of myth is poetically precise. For instance, if you go into that realm without the sword of reason, you will lose your mind, but at the same time, if you take only the sword of reason without the cup of sympathy, you will lose your heart. Even more remarkably, if you approach without the wand of intuition, you can stand at the door for decades never realizing you have arrived. You might think you are just waiting for a bus, or wandering from room to room looking for your cigarettes, watching a TV show, *or reading a cryptic and ambiguous book.* Chapel Perilous is tricky that way.

I entered Chapel Perilous quite casually one day in 1971 while reading *The Book of Lies* by the English mystic Aleister Crowley.[2] Crowley aroused my interest because he had indubitably been a high adept of both yoga and occultism, was regarded as a Black Magician by many and as the Magus of the New Aeon by some, and had a contradictory reputation as heroic mountain climber, poet, bisexual pioneer Hippy, alchemist, sadistic prankster, worker of wonders and charlatan. I was especially charmed by the persistent legend that Crowley had once turned poet Victor Newburg into a camel, and the testimony of many that he had smashed a glass across a room by staring at it, in a demonstration at Oxford. All of Crowley's books are witty, paradoxical, brilliant, obscure and deliberately enigmatic in varying degrees, but *The Book of Lies* is by all odds the most mystifying of all, and hence a favorite of mine since I love to solve puzzles and mysteries.

Facing the title page of *The Book of Lies* is a nonchalant announcement informing the reader, "There is no joke or hidden meaning in the publisher's imprint." This seems to be a veiled warning about what will follow, but is actually the first lie in the book; occult historian Francis King has carefully determined the date on the imprint is inaccurate by at least a year. This type of perverse artistry is typical of Crowley's dealings with the reader, and I have enjoyed myself over the years deciphering his similarly gnomic jokes in other books. I always return to *The Book of Lies*, however, because Crowley claimed that somewhere in that book he had revealed the inner secret of freemasonry and Illuminism, coded so that only those with "spiritual insight" would be able to decipher it. In 1971, I had already read the book many times without finding the secret, but I was still trying, since Crowley is regarded as a ringleader of the Illuminati conspiracy by many writers[3] and, indeed, used the title "Epopt of the Illuminati," along with a few dozen other honorifics, when he was in the mood to put on some swank.

Suddenly, in a "blinding flash" or at least a mini-Satori, I knew Crowley's secret. It was in Chapter 69 and deals with Tantric Sex. It will be explained, you may be sure, at the appropriate place in our narrative. The effect on me was that I entered a belief system in which the anti-Illuminati authors I had studied so extensively were no longer seen by me as simple paranoids. They were looking at something quite real, I now felt, and were only misinterpreting it a little bit. They were those without the pentacle of valor who stand in terror outside the door of Chapel Perilous, trembling and warning all who would enter that the Chapel is really an Insect Horror Machine programmed by Death Demons and dripping fetidly with Green Goo.

I immediately determined upon a course of neuro-psychological experiments which would, I thought, demonstrate objectively whether or not I had really guessed the true secret. The principal results of these experiments are presented in this book. The outstanding result was that I entered a belief system, from July 1973 until around October 1974, in which I was receiving telepathic messages from entities residing on a planet of the double star Sirius.

I also began to find — sometimes by the most implausible coincidences — various documentary leads firmly tying the long, mysterious history of Illuminism to occult beliefs about Sirius. These "lucky coincidences" — or synchronicities as they are called in Jungian psychology — are commonplace among those who get involved with occult secret societies in general and Chapel Perilous in particular. As Neal Wilgus notes in *The Illuminoids*,

> From the beginning *The Illuminoids* was shaped by coincidence, from the discovery of Daraul's *Secret Societies* to the publication of Shea and Wilson's *Illuminatus* . . . A book by another Wilson — Colin Wilson's *The Occult* — was also discovered at just the right moment and often "fell open at the right page" just as Wilson says other references did for him.[4]

That last sentence is a fitting overture to the ambiguities we shall soon confront. Not even I am sure whether the last clause refers to me or to Colin Wilson.

After October 1974 (due to a meeting with Dr. Jacques Vallee, an extraordinarily erudite astronomer, cyberneticist and UFOlogist), I began to develop new belief systems to explain my Sirius experience, not necessarily involving the breathtaking assumption that I was literally receiving actual transmissions from an ESP-broadcaster in the Sirius star system.

Dr. Vallee has been concerned with UFOs since the early 1960s, when he saw two of the beasties. Over the years Vallee has broadened his investigations to include "psychic" experiences that relate in one way or another to the UFOs, such as my Sirius experiences. He believes that this whole area of otherworldly communications has been going on for centuries and will probably not turn out to be extraterrestrial. The extraterrestrial content of the experience these days, he says, is just an adaptation to 20th Century beliefs. The phenomenon took other and spookier forms, his data indicate, in other epochs.

This made perfect sense to me, since I had originally gotten in touch with "the entity" by means of Crowleyan occultism. The extraterrestrial explanation was not the *real* explanation, as I had thought; it was just the latest model for the Experience, as angels had been a model for it in the Middle Ages, or dead relatives speaking through mediums had been a model in the 19th century.

Then, on Sunday, March 13, 1976, a dispatch from Reuters News Service appeared in newspapers around the world. I read it in the *San Francisco Examiner-Chronicle* and it was like opening a door in my own house and finding Ming the Merciless shooting it out with Flash Gordon.

The dispatch concerned Robert K.G. Temple, a Fellow of the Royal Astronomical Society of England, a scientist of dignity and status, who was propounding a theory wild enough to come from the pages of von Daniken himself. Temple claimed that Earth had been visited by an advanced race from a planet in the system of the double star, Sirius, around 4500 B.C. Temple based this assertion on the fact that *definite and specific knowledge* of the Sirius system can be found in the mythology of the Baby-

lonians, the Egyptians, and some surviving African tribes —
knowledge which modern astronomy has only rediscovered with
the fantastically delicate instruments of the last two decades.

Now, anybody would be taken aback to see an astronomer
of Temple's status expressing such a Hearst Sunday Magazine
theory, but I was beyond surprise; I was discombobulated.

I mentioned the Reuters dispatch a few days afterward to a
friend, Saul Paul Sirag, a monstrously erudite physicist who usually knows more about any other science you mention than most
of the experts in that field.

"Oh, Temple's data aren't all new," Saul Paul said. "Anthropologists have known for years that several African tribes have
very advanced knowledge about the Sirius system. For instance,
some of them knew about the companion of Sirius — a dwarf
star — long before we discovered it with our telescopes."

"And how do the anthropologists explain that?" I asked.

"They don't," Saul Paul said with a Groucho Marx grin. "It's
regarded as a mystery." Saul Paul, who was a theologian before
he became a physicist, is also the author of a hilarious theolog-
ical-psychedelic novel called *Jumped by Jesus*. He is an even
more advanced case of Aggravated Agnosticism than your humble narrator, and loves data that won't fit into anybody's theories.

I quickly obtained a copy of Temple's book from England,
and was staggered by it[5] Temple's evidence, which we will summarize later, *could be interpreted* to indicate the arrival of people
from Sirius who had come here in a physical space ship around
4500 B.C. According to Temple, information about this had been
passed on through various initiatory orders in the ancient Mediterranean and in Africa to the present time. But the evidence
could also be interpreted to mean that methods of interstellar telepathy between Earth and the Sirius system had been discovered
back then and that many have been tuning in on that channel
ever since. In other words, through Crowley's secret teaching, I
might have tuned in on a nearly 6,500-year-old cosmic dialogue,
after all.

Chapel Perilous, as I said before, is tricky that way. When
you think you're out of it, you're just in another hall of illusions

painted to look like the safe forest outside; and when you think you're inside again, you'll suddenly discover you're actually walking on the road back home. As the traditional Zen saying sums it up:

First there is a mountain,
Then there is no mountain,
Then there is.

In this context, we don't expect anybody to believe in the Sirius transmissions just because the author seems like an honest guy. Richard Milhous Nixon once seemed like an honest guy, at least to the folks who voted for him. We are emphatically not competing for the True Believer Market with Nixon (or Erich von Daniken). We hope to show, with objective and documented evidence, that *something is going on. Something* more physical and palpable than hallucination.

The semanticist raises his eyebrows and mutters that the expression "something more physical and palpable than hallucination" does not convey a very precise idea; one might as well talk of *something more tangible and objective than reverie.* We will become more specific as we proceed, but at this stage we must define our god-awful ignorance explicitly before we dare to propound our speculations. It is important to state unambiguously that our data are not in conflict with "science," as the naive will imagine — in fact, we will provide several scientific explanations for all of it, in Part Two — but it is, grotesquely and awkwardly, *in total conflict with common sense.* It is perverse, paradoxical and preposterous. One might say, "It's *damned funny*" and if a child asked innocently, "Do you mean '*funny-haha*' or '*funny-peculiar*'?" I'd have to answer, "Both."

Let us illustrate with an example of the kind of mystery we will be confronting — the Case of the Pancakes from Outer Space. Like a pig with wings, this is definitely funny; we leave it to the reader to decide whether to consider it funny-haha or funny-peculiar.

Joseph Simonton of Eagle River, Wisconsin, claims that a flying saucer landed in his back yard one day and an extraterrestrial got out and gave him some pancakes.

There were no other witnesses to this remarkable occurrence, so it is certainly tempting to say that Simonton must have been hallucinating. There is no reason to think that he was consciously perpetrating a hoax, however. He has not tried to commercialize on his encounter in any way and seems to be baffled by the whole experience, just as you would be.

Dr. J. Allen Hynek, a skeptical astronomer, who explained other UFOs as "swamp gas," was sent by the Air Force to investigate the Simonton mindfuck. Dr. Hynek took some of the damnable pancakes back to the Dayton Air Force base, where the UFO investigation is headquartered, and scientists there determined that the pancakes were perfectly normal and contained nutritious wheat germ, perhaps indicating that the Space Brothers are Ralph Nader fans. Dr. Hynek himself says he thinks that Simonton was telling the truth, i.e., he believed in his experience.

Dr. Jacques Vallee also investigated this case and says that he too is convinced that Simonton is honest.

Simonton himself has no idea why he, of all the people on Earth, was singled out for this perplexing gift.[6]

If Simonton merely hallucinated the whole episode, *where did the accursed astral pancakes actually come from?* Answer me that, O ye skeptics. On the other hand, if the flying saucer was really there in the yard, why in the name of all the pot-bellied gods of Burma did the extraterrestrials decide on this occasion to present a human being with a gift of *pancakes?* The story is equally bizarre and unsatisfying however we interpret it.

Simonton's adventure is more characteristic of UFO contacts than readers who are unfamiliar with the subject will realize. The newspapers and TV generally cover only a tiny fraction of UFO reports and usually publicize only the contactees who establish quasi-religious movements around themselves, based on doctrines of peace and pop ecology allegedly transmitted by the UFOnauts. Such messianic accounts are comfortable reading, since most of us secretly would like to believe that benevolent Space Brothers are trying to save this planet from the various disasters that seem to threaten it, *but they are a minority. The Simonton pancakes are much more typical.*

One classic Contact involved two Naval Intelligence officers of high probity. There was also a "coincidental" (but highly mysterious) radar blackout of the whole area — almost as if Chapel Perilous in this case was using a technology that renders itself invisible to radar. The officers seemed to have contacted a benevolent being from the planet Uranus. The naive believer in loving Space Brothers will rejoice at such a yarn, especially since the communications received included the usual peace propaganda. The more analytical will detect the pig-with-wings element in the facts that (a) Uranus is almost certainly *incapable of supporting life* and that (b) the communicating entity gave a name which sounds suspiciously like a joke at the expense of any student of Cabala who studies the transcript. The name was "AFFA," which in a Cabalistic language called "angelic" means *nothing* or *the void*. The Contact, in this case, was 99% "telepathic," as in my Sirius experience, but the officers were given a view of *what looked like* a real spaceship outside their window at the climax of the experience. And that was the point in time when the radar blackout "coincidentally" occurred in the area.[7]

Others have had classic "hallucinatory" or "psychotic" experiences with the Space Brothers, such as meeting Jesus on a flying saucer or being taken a hundred light years and back in a half-hour; so that the hurried investigator would be inclined to dismiss such yarns as imaginary. Unfortunately, these people often have ambiguous but definite evidence that *something* happened — independent witnesses saw a UFO at the same time, or there were weird mechanical failures in the neighborhood; Once two people involved in different Contacts hundreds of miles away from each other and a year apart told the same absurd details. Each alleged a visit to a planet named "Lanalus," where all the natives are humanoid and go naked. This yarn was told by both a West Virginia salesman and a Washington, D.C. law student, *independently of each other*.[8] In such a case the most ardent reductionist can't reduce what happened to less than a *hallucination shared by telepathy*, which is staggering in itself. (How many independent witnesses have to be involved before any event can no longer be dismissed as shared hallucination? As Berkeley,

Hume and others have indicated, it is logically impossible to prove that our everyday experience isn't all fantasy. Since only telepathy can explain the shared space-journey in this particular case, data may be called shared hallucination by the determined skeptic even when witnesses are independent of each other. That way lies solipsism, if not paranoia.)

To claim that both witnesses were liars would be convenient, of course, but one has the uneasy feeling that it is a weird coincidence for two liars to independently invent the same lie. You could reject any data that way, including any laboratory experiments you don't like. For instance, those who reject even telepathy have reached the point where they are impugning either the honesty or the sanity of *several thousand* scientific researchers on *all major continents* over a period of *decades*. Such expedient ways of disposing of data are shared only by the most ardent anti-Evolutionists among the Fundamentalist sects.

Please note that we promised several scientific explanations of our data, not one explanation. There is, at this point, no single theory that will account for all of the Damned Things we are going to bring forth and parade for your inspection. To give you some perspective in advance, let us list a few of the ideas that have passed through this investigator's mind in the course of his journey into and out of Chapel Perilous.

Either . . .

(a) the evidence assembled here can be explained by Bell's Theorem, a breakthrough in physics suggesting a *basic indivisibility of all things.* Bell also allows for three sub-models we shall be discussing: (1) the observer-created universe; (2) parallel universes; (3) information-without-energy;

and/or

(b) some human beings of highly evolved psychic powers ("the Illuminati") are playing head-games with other human beings, sometimes passing themselves off as (c) or (d) below;

and/or

(c) we really are being contacted, experimented upon or otherwise manipulated by Higher Intelligences from Outer Space, probably from Sirius (or the Illuminati are creating a simulation of such extraterrestrials);

and/or

(d) we have always shared this planet with another intelligent species, which can either remain invisible or manifest to us in any form it chooses. UFO researcher John Keel calls these hypothetical entities "ultra-terrestrials." Earlier ages called them fairies, angels, demons, the weird people, etc.

and/or

(e) *we are all evolving into the use of new neurological circuits, which will make us superhuman in comparison to our present average state.* The activation of these new circuits creates a great deal of temporary weirdness until we learn to use them properly. This is the theory of such scientifically oriented yogis as Sri Aurobindo and Gopi Krishna, and of Dr. Timothy Leary.

and/or

(f) a combination or permutation of the above is going on simultaneously.

Some of our data fit one of the above theories better than another; some fit equally well into *two* or *three* theories; some don't fit any theory yet. The multi-theory approach (or, as it is called in physics, the multi-model approach) is the only way to deal adequately with all the facts. Any single-theory approach is premature and causes a truncation of our intelligence; it forces us to ignore or belittle parts of the data that might be crucial.

The multi-model approach began in sub-atomic physics and is chiefly due to Nobel laureate Niels Bohr. In dealing with certain mysterious entities on that quasi-astral plane, physicists had found hard evidence that these entities were particles. Good. Unfortunately, other evidence, equally persistent, showed that the entities were really waves. Not so good. Some physicists held to the particle theory, and insisted that all evidence supporting the wave theory would eventually be explained away. Others, however, accepted the waves and rejected the particles. Still others, somewhat facetiously, began talking of "wavicles." *Bohr suggested that the search for one correct model was medieval, pre-scientific and obsolete. We can best understand sub-atomic events, he said, if we accept the necessity of allowing for more than one model.* As Marshall McLuhan has pointed out, in *The Mechanical Bride* and other works, the multi-model approach has now influenced all the sciences and even appears in modern art (e.g., cubist paintings show several views at once; Joyce's Ulysses describes the same day in various styles — epic, dramatic, journalistic, subjective, naturalistic, etc.). McLuhan has even proclaimed, in his usual apocalyptic style, that the multi-model approach is the most important, and most original, intellectual discovery of the 20th century. Count Alfred Korzybski said that it marked the transition from Aristotelian civilization (dogmatic, monistic, authoritarian) to non-Aristotelian civilization (relativistic, pluralistic, libertarian).

For convenience, all of the models discussed above and to be discussed as we proceed can be summed into two metamodels. (1) It is all done by our own nervous systems. As we advance toward Higher Intelligence, our brains can increasingly affect the universe, by quantum inseparability, creating first coincidences, then Jungian synchronicities, then seemingly external Superhuman Beings, who are really masks of the greater selves we are evolving into. (2) It is *not* all done by our nervous systems. As we advance toward Higher Intelligence, our brains can increasingly contact other Higher Intelligences. By Bell's quantum monism, this includes contact with advanced adepts who are both human and inhuman terrestrial and extraterrestrial, and located temporally throughout what we call past, present and future.

But such Philosophical questions can best be postponed until after we have examined the chrono-log of my own adventures in Chapel Perilous. Remember: it is tricky in there. Some of the time we will not seem to be passing through the Gates of Mystery but merely wandering about in a Fun House at a rather seedy Amusement Park.

Part I:
The Sirius Connection

PART I : THE SIRIUS CONNECTION

IN THIS BOOK IT IS SPOKEN OF THE SEPHIROTH &
THE PATHS, OF SPIRITS & CONJURATIONS, OF GODS, SPHERES,
PLANES & MANY OTHER THINGS WHICH MAY OR MAY NOT EXIST.
IT IS IMMATERIAL WHETHER THEY EXIST OR NOT. BY DOING
CERTAIN THINGS CERTAIN RESULTS FOLLOW ; STUDENTS ARE
MOST EARNESTLY WARNED AGAINST ATTRIBUTING OBJECTIVE
REALITY OR PHILOSOPHICAL VALIDITY TO ANY OF THEM. CROWLEY

The Sirius Connection:

INTRODUCTORY FABLES
(Let's stretch those mental muscles a bit, fellers.)

From the Sufi:
Mullah Nasrudin once entered a store and asked the proprietor, "Have you ever seen me before?"

"No," was the prompt answer.

"Then," cried Nasrudin, "how do you know it is me?"

From the ancient Babylonian:
It was the sad time after the death of the fair young god of spring, Tammuz. The beautiful goddess, Ishtar, who loved Tammuz dearly, followed him to the halls of Eternity, defying the demons who guard the Gates of Time.

But at the first Gate, the guardian demon forced Ishtar to surrender her sandals, which the wise men say symbolizes giving up the Will. And at the second Gate, Ishtar had to surrender her jeweled anklets, which the wise say means giving up Ego. And at the third Gate, she surrendered her robe, which is the hardest of all because it is giving up Mind itself. And at the fourth Gate, she surrendered her golden breast-cups, which is giving up Sex Role. And at the fifth Gate, she surrendered her necklace, which is giving up the rapture of Illumination. And at the sixth Gate, she surrendered her earrings, which is giving up Magick. And finally, at the seventh Gate, Ishtar surrendered her thousand-petaled crown, which is giving up Godhood.

It was only thus, naked, that Ishtar could enter Eternity.

From the Zen tradition:
A monk who had meditated long in search of Illumination finally received a great flash of insight. Rushing to his roshi (Zen Master), the monk cried out, "I have it! I have it! That rock there is inside my head."

"You must have a big head," the Master replied, "to hold a rock that size."

The Door to Chapel Perilous

I was born into a working-class Irish Catholic family in Brooklyn at the brutal bottom of the Great Depression. As a child I seem to have had no odd psychic abilities and I remember no weird experiences. The only religious event of my childhood — my first Holy Communion — was a total failure; I experienced none of the rapture and contact with God which the nuns had promised me.

At 14 I became an atheist, and in college I majored originally in Electrical Engineering, switching later to Mathematics when I realized my basic temperament was analytical rather than practical. In my twenties I underwent three forms of psychotherapy in order to clear up the remaining conflicts between my atheistic hedonism and the Catholic indoctrination of my childhood.

Once at the age of 18 I had a strange experience of coming unstuck in time, like Billy Pilgrim in Vonnegut's *Slaughterhouse Five*. Again, at 24, I had a kind of spontaneous Satori, a sudden awakening to the immanent divinity of all things. I had regarded both of these experiences as hallucinatory and was so ashamed of them that I never discussed them with any of my three psychotherapists.

Then in 1962, at the age of 30, I began to experiment with mind-altering drugs. This area is only a little less controversial than nuclear power plants, to put it mildly, but let us remember that there are three schools of scientific thought about those chemicals.

I. Some regard these potions as *psychotomimetic*: that is, the altered consciousness they produce is considered an imitation (mime) of psychosis.

II. Some regard them as *hallucinogens*: that is, the new mental state created by ingestion is considered a hallucinatory experience, but not quite a psychosis.

III. Some regard them as *psychedelics* (a word coined by Humphrey Osmond, M.D.) or as *metaprogramming substances* (coined by John Lilly, M.D.); that is, the new state is considered one in which we can reorganize or re-imprint our nervous system for higher functioning.

Science will eventually determine which interpretation is most correct *through future research*. This decision will unfortunately not be reached by any amount of verbal debate or throwing the dissenters into jails, no matter how loud the denunciations or how many heretics are imprisoned. This is very inconvenient for the government, which always wants to settle every issue by outlawing disagreement, but that is not how science works.

I originally got interested in mind-altering drugs due to an article in the most conservative magazine in the U.S.A., the *National Review*, edited by Roman Catholic millionaire William Buckley, Jr. Later, of course, Buckley and his magazine would attack drug experiments with neo-Inquisitorial fury, but back in innocent '60 or '61, they naively printed an article, by conservative historian Russell Kirk, reviewing Aldous Huxley's *The Doors of Perception*, in which Huxley recounted how he had transcended time and space and experienced "Heaven."

Huxley did it under the influence of mescaline, a drug derived from the "sacred cactus," peyote, used in American Indian rituals. Russell Kirk thought this was good scientific evidence to support religiosity in general against the "liberal humanists," whom he regards as the prime villains in history. Kirk said, among other things, that "only the most dogmatic old-fangled materialist" would reject Huxley's report a priori without duplicating the experiment. Being a dogmatic old-fangled materialist at the time, I resented this and argued about it a lot inside my head over a period of months. It seemed that, as a materialist, I had to accept one aspect of Huxley's book that Kirk had not noted: the strong implication that *consciousness is chemical in nature and changes as its chemistry changes*. That *was* provocative.

The Materialist had his first drug trip on December 28, 1962, in an old slave-cabin in the woods outside Yellow Springs, Ohio.

With my wife, Arlen, and our four small children, I had rented the cabin from Antioch College for $30 per month and had an acre of cleared land to grow food on, 30 acres of woods to seek Mystery in. Farming was only partly supporting us; I was working as Assistant Sales Manager for a microscopic business, the Antioch Bookplate Company in Yellow Springs. But we had found (we thought) a way to escape the regimented urban hive without starving to death.

Before eating the first peyote button, the Materialist asked his supplier (a black jazz musician), "Is this stuff dangerous at all?"

"The fuck," he said. "The Indians been eating it every full moon for thousands of years."

"Oh, yeah, that's right," the Materialist said, remembering also Huxley's glowing description of his first trip. I quickly ate seven buttons and for the next 12 hours whirled through an unrehearsed and incoherent tour of the vestibule of Chapel Perilous — a most educational and transcendental experience.

A few years later, it would have been different, of course. The Materialist would have said, "But the newspapers claim that people sometimes go crazy on this stuff and flip out for months."

And the Supplier would have said, "The newspapers also say our troops are in Vietnam to help the Vietnamese. Man, don't believe any of the crap *they* say."

And, being of a curious and experimental nature, I would have gone ahead anyway, but with a lot of doubt, and that could easily have turned into anxiety or outright panic. We later saw exactly that happen to others, after the press really got into gear on this story and built up the hysteria to fever-pitch.

As it was, the Materialist simply suffered the usual delusion of the first trip: he thought he was reborn. After all, back then, he had Russell Kirk and the *National Review* — the certified sages of sanctified conservatism — on his side.

When, in the following weeks, it became sadly obvious that I was not entirely reborn, and that many neurotic, depressive and egotistic programs still remained in my central computer, I was somewhat disillusioned. But the trip had been so interesting and ecstatic . . . Like the Lady of Spain in the poem, I tried "again. And again. And again and again and again." By mid-1963, I had logged 40 trips to inner space and it was obvious that peyote was, indeed, a magical chemical, as the Indians claim, but that one had to be a shaman to know how to use it profitably.

We don't propose to enthuse about those 40 peyote voyages in technicolor prose. There was more than enough of that kind of writing in the 1960s. In Dr. Timothy Leary's terminology, each trip involved a transmutation of consciousness from the "symbolic" and linear terrestrial circuits of the nervous system to the somatic-genetic future circuits (Dr. Leary's circuit theories are explained in Part Two, "Models and Metaphors.") The Materialist learned to experience rapture and bliss, to transcend time. In each trip, the Body was Resurrected, Osiris rose from his tomb; I was godly and eternal for a while. Each time, the yo-yo effect (as Dr. Richard Alpert calls it) occurred within a day or so: I came down again. The next trip brought me back up, of course, but then, once more, I came down again; up-and-down, up-and-down — the yo-yo effect. It was alternately inspiring and exasperating.

But a change in my mind (my "neurological functioning,' Dr. Leary would say) was slowly and subtly, beginning to happen.

The Materialist frequently had the hallucination of telepathic communication with plants, both when flying on the wings of peyote and when he was straight. *Hallucination* was the judgment of his engineering-trained rational mind; it *seemed* real as all get-out each time it happened. But the Materialist knew too much to take it seriously . . . and he continued to know too much until later in the '60s, when Cleve Backster's research with polygraphs produced some hard evidence that human-plant telepathy may be occurring all the time, usually outside the conscious attention of the human participant.

Several times the Materialist contacted an Energy or an Intelligence that seemed to deserve the description superhuman. It was obvious to me that I could easily, with a less skeptical cast of mind, describe these trans-time dialogues as meetings with actual gods or angels. (Quanah Parker, the great Cheyenne war-chief, who was converted to pacifism by a peyote trip and later founded the Native American Church, used to say, "The white man goes into his church and talks *to* Jesus. The Indian goes into his tipi, takes peyote, and talks *with* Jesus.") I regarded the entities contacted as X's — unknowns — and tried, in each experiment and in reflections between experiments, to find a psychological, neurological, or even parapsychological explanation.

The strangest entity I contacted in those twenty-odd months of psychedelic explorations appeared *one day after* the end of a peyote trip, when I was weeding in the garden and a movement in the adjoining cornfield caught my eye. I looked over that way and saw a man with warty green skin and pointy ears, dancing. The Skeptic watched for nearly a minute, entranced, and then Greenskin faded away "just a hallucination . . ."

But I could not forget him. Unlike the rapid metaprogramming during a peyote trip, in which you are never sure what is real and what is just the metaprogrammer playing games, this experience had all the qualities of waking reality, and differed only in *intensity*. The entity in the cornfield had been more beautiful, more charismatic, more *divine* than anything I could consciously imagine when using my literary talents to try to portray a deity. As the mystics of all traditions say so aggravatingly, "Those who have seen, *know*."

Well, I had seen, but I didn't know. I was more annoyed than enlightened.

But that was not to be my last encounter with that particular critter. Five years later, in 1968, the Skeptic read Carlos Castaneda's *The Teachings of Don Juan*, dealing with traditional Mexican shamanism and its use of the sacred cactus. Castaneda, an anthropologist, saw the same green man several times, and Don Juan Matus, the shaman, said his name was Mescalito. *He was the spirit of the peyote plant.*[10] But the Materialist had seen him before he ever read a description of him. That was most perplexing to the Materialist.

A fairly plausible explanation is that Mescalito is an archetype of the collective unconscious, in the Jungian sense. He has been reported by many others besides Castaneda and me, and he always has the same green warty skin and is often dancing.[11]

However, might we dare consider that Mescalito may be just what the shamans (who know him best) always say he is — one of the "spirits" of the vegetation? Too silly an idea for sophisticates like ourselves? Paracelsus, the founder of modern medicine, believed in such spirits and claimed frequent commerce with them. So did the German poet Goethe and the pioneer of organic agriculture, Rudolph Steiner — and the ideas of Goethe and Steiner, once rejected as too mystical, are currently being seriously reconsidered by many ecologists.[12]

Or consider Gustav Fechner, the creator of scientific psychology and psychological measurement. Fechner lost his sight and then regained it, after which he asserted that with his new vision he saw many things normal people do not see — including auras around humans and other living creatures, and vegetation spirits just like Mescalito. George Washington Carver also claimed a link with spirits in the vegetation, and so did the great Luther Burbank. Thomas Edison became so convinced of their literal existence that he spent many years trying to develop a photographic process that would render them visible.[13]

Marcel Vogel (whose corporation, Vogel Luminescence, has developed the red color used in fluorescent crayons, and the psychedelic colors popular in 1960s poster art) has been studying plant consciousness and vegetative "telepathy" for ten years now. In one experiment, Vogel and a group of psychologists tried concentrating on sexual imagery while a plant was wired up with a polygraph to reveal its electrochemical ("emotional"?) responses to their thoughts. The plant responded with the polygraph pattern typical of excitement. Vogel speculates that talking of sex could stir up in the atmosphere some sort of sexual energy, such as the "orgone" claimed by Dr. Wilhelm Reich. If this is true, the ancient fertility rites in which humans had sexual intercourse in freshly seeded fields might indeed have stimulated the fertility of the crops, and the shamans are not as naive as we like to think.[14] Mescalito could be *both* an archetype of Jung's Collective Unconscious and an anthromorphized human translation of a persistent signal sent by the molecular intelligence of the vegetative world. Naturally, the ability to decode such orgonomic or neuro-electric signals would be eagerly sought by all shamans in societies dependent on agriculture. In other words, according to this model, Mescalito is a genetic signal in our collective unconscious, but activated only when certain molecular transmissions from the plant world are received.

This shamanic kind of selective attention, or special perception, has been duplicated in the modern world by Dr. Vogel, who has given many demonstrations before audiences, in which he accurately reads vegetative signals from plants. It is no more spooky than the selective yogic trance of the average city-dweller, which allows him to walk in mindless indifference through incredible noise, filth, pandemonium, misery, neurosis, violence, psychosis, rape, burglary, injustice and exploitation, screening it all out and concentrating only on robot-repetition of his assigned role in the hive-economy. One can train oneself to receive or ignore a far wider variety of signals than the neurologically untrained realize.

A third model would be that Mescalito and all his kith and kin (the fairies and "little people," etc.) are all extraterrestrials who have been experimenting upon us for millennia. This does not necessarily mean that they come here in spaceships. Consider the following speculations:

#1. Clarke's Law (by science-fiction writer Arthur C. Clarke): *"Any sufficiently advanced technology is indistinguishable from magick. "*

Imagine a technology a hundred years beyond ours. A thousand years beyond ours. A *million* years beyond ours. And then remember that many stars, which might have planets and civilizations, are literally billions of years older than our sun. There might be races in this galaxy advanced as much as *10 billion* years beyond our technology.

An old Arizona joke asks, "How many Apaches are hiding in this room?" The answer is, "As many as want to." Advanced communication technologies would be far more subtle than the stalking techniques of the Apaches. If Clarke is right even on a materialistic level, the only answer to "How many Advanced Civilizations are monitoring the events in this room?" must be "As many as want to."

#2. Wilson's Corollary to Clarke's Law (by R.A.W.): *Any sufficiently advanced parapsychology is even more indistinguishable from magick.*

24

Consider the slow advance of parapsychology, despite entrenched opposition, during the past 70 years. Project it forward another hundred years. A thousand. A million. And imagine races in this galaxy 10 billion years ahead of us in this area.

Extraterrestrials with advanced psionic knowledge may have been experimenting on us and/or aiding our evolution and/or playing ontology games with us for millions of years, projecting any form they desire from Mescalito to the Lord God Jehovah, *without ever leaving their home planets*. If a salesman in West Virginia and a college student in Washington, D.C. can both share the same "hallucination" of faster-than-light UFO abduction to a planet called Lanalus where everybody goes naked, then maybe there is one interstellar broadcaster of such educational dramas.

Maybe.

Did a leprechaun leave the Simonton pancakes?

The greenish-skinned, pointy-eared man I saw in 1963 has appeared in the folklore of many cultures who do not even use peyote. He has been seen most frequently, in recent years, as a humanoid extraterrestrial in various flying saucer reports by alleged Contactees. And, in the late 1960s, he began to appear regularly on TV, known as "Mr. Spock" on the *Star Trek* show, and has remained on the tube ever since, despite frequent network attempts to cancel the show and get rid of him. The fans always insist on bringing him back, and now in 1977, as I write, "Mr. Spock" is scheduled to appear either in the first *Star Trek* movie or a revival of the series on TV. He is an image, or as Jung would say, an "archetype" that that cannot be erased from the human mind.

Mescalito takes many forms in many myth-systems. Here he is as Peter Pan in a commercial advertisement, as sketched from descriptions by American Indian shamans, and as Mr. Spock on Star Trek. He is one of the most widely-reported denizens of Chapel Perilous and is known in dozens of shamanic traditions.

By coincidence, in his guise as Spock, this pointy-eared godling has given us a slogan that has become widely used in correspondence among Immortalists-scientists dedicated to the search for longevity and eventual physical immortality. The slogan is, of course, *"Live long and prosper."* We have seen that slogan on letters from the Cryonics Society of Michigan, the Bay Area Cryonics Society, the Prometheus Society and other Immortalist groups. This "coincidence" will appear, possibly, to be more than a coincidence when we have examined further data . . .

The Irish form of Mescalito is the leprechaun, noted for playfulness, trickery, and, oddly, for leaving behind gifts in the form of food, just as the alleged "UFOnaut" left Joe Simonton a gift of pancakes.

It needs to be emphasized that whether we are talking of an experience involving Mescalito or one involving a kitchen chair, all of our perceptions have gone through myriads of neural processes in the brain before they appear to our consciousness. At the point of conscious recognition, the identified image is organized into a three-dimensional hologram which we *project outside ourselves* and call "reality." We are much too modest about our own creativity if we take any of these projections literally. We see the sun "going down" at twilight, but science assures us that nothing of the sort is happening; instead, the earth is turning.

We perceive an orange as *really* orange whereas it is actually blue, the orange light being the light bouncing off the real fruit. And, everywhere we look, we imagine solid objects, but science finds only a web of dancing energy.

The great and venerable Sufi sage, Mullah Nasrudin, once raced through Bagdad on his donkey, galloping as fast as the poor beast could travel. Everybody got excited and people rushed into the streets to find out why the philosopher was in such a great hurry.

"What are you looking for, Mullah?" somebody shouted.

"I'm looking for my donkey!" Nasrudin answered.

Like most Sufi jokes this seems calculated only to annoy us, like a Marx Brothers routine that doesn't quite succeed in being funny. Actually, Nasrudin was much given (perhaps overmuch) to acting out his parables, and he was merely dramatizing the most common error of seekers after the Cosmic Secret.

We look for the Secret — the Philosopher's Stone, the Elixir of the Wise, Supreme Enlightenment, "God," or whatever the final answer might be — in all directions, north, east, south, and west, and all the time it is carrying us about. It is the human nervous system itself, the marvelous instrument through which we create order out of chaos, science out of ignorance, meaning out of mystery, "Mescalito" (or a chair) out of whirling energy.

Dogen Zenji, an 18th century Zen master, used to ask trainees, "Who is the Master who makes the grass green?" Again, the answer is as close as our visual cortex.

Psychologists have performed thousands of experiments revealing the presence of "the Master who makes the grass green," which Dr. John Lilly calls the metaprogrammer in the nervous system. Two actors rush into a Psychology 101 class and one makes a stabbing motion at the other, who falls. Almost all the students "see" a knife in the stabber's hand. Later, it turns out the actual implement was a banana. Apparently, the stabbing motion itself creates the knife: the nervous system "knows" that nobody stabs anybody with a banana, just as it still "knows" (despite 300 years of science) that the sun "goes down" in the evening.

Or: a picture is flashed on a screen for one second. It shows a white man struggling with a black man, and the white man is wielding a razor. Again, the nervous system "knows" what it is programmed to see. The majority of students, even those who will swear until blue in the face that they are not racists, will *see* the razor in the *black man's* hand: our national stereotype. And we still see the orange as *orange*, even though we know it isn't.

You can see this image above at least two ways. Our inability to see the world more than one way normally is due to cultural conditioning — according to modern behavioral scientists — or to the fact that we are all asleep, according to the mystics.

Of course, we all realize that *other people* are frequently inclined to what Freud called "projection" — seeing what they expect to see. That our own experience of reality might be equally self-created — that, as Nietzsche said, "We are all greater artists than we realize" — is hard to believe, *and even harder to remember moment-by-moment*, even after we have had enough experience to believe it.

Learning to remember the invisible donkey who carries us about — the self-programmer — is the first step in awakening from conditioned, mechanical consciousness to true, objective consciousness. Whether or not there are fairies, elves and extra-terrestrials hiding behind every bush, awakening reveals that the universe is full of invisible intelligence. It is very hard for us to learn to contact that intelligence without clothing it in projected humanoid forms. . .

In early stages of work on consciousness, the Master Who Makes The Grass Green (the Metaprogrammer) insists on converting *everything* into humanoid Gestalts. That's because, at that level, it is still a human chauvinist.

The Kennedy Assassination and the Net

While I was conducting peyote research in Yellow Springs, Ohio, weirder business was afoot in New Orleans, Louisiana. Two young men who had served in the Marines together were "coincidentally" living in The Quarter, a few blocks apart, without meeting again. The more famous of the two was named Lee Harvey Oswald and, during the summer of 1963, while I was having my first encounters with the leprechauns, Mr. Oswald ordered a Carcano rifle through the mail. What Oswald did with that rifle is still a matter of much controversy and endless conspiracy-mongering. The other young man was named Kerry Thornley and was in the process of creating a new religion called Discordianism, which later became a central theme in the novels and plays collectively called *Illuminatus*. How all that happened is the oddest part of our whole narrative.

Later that fall, Oswald's wife separated from him and went to live with Mrs. Ruth Payne in Fort Worth. Mrs. Payne was *the sister of my family doctor.*

When this connection came to light, after the enigmatic events in Dealy Plaza on November 22, the Materialist regarded it as an amusing coincidence. I hadn't gotten heavily enough into Jung yet to call it "synchronicity."

(As for Kerry Thornley, I didn't meet him until 1967, whereupon I embraced Thornley's religion of Discordianism, and also became a close friend. And then some conspiracy buffs announced that Thornley was part of the Kennedy assassination team — that he was, in fact, the "second Oswald." A "second Os-

wald" theory was suggested by Prof. Popkin in the book called
The Second Oswald. But we'll come to that later.)

It was also in 1963 that Alan Watts, Zen philosopher-clown,
came through southern Ohio, to visit his sister in Dayton, and
visited our farm. Jano (Mrs. Watts) was with him, and it was
probably at that time that she first used her term, "the Net," in
my hearing. The Net, according to Jano, is a web of coincidence
(or synchronicity) which connects everything-in-the-universe
with everything-else-in-the-universe.

For instance, I originally introduced Alan Watts to Jano,
around 1960. Their relationship became his last, longest and
happiest marriage. And Alan's middle name was Wilson, which
you may have noticed is my last name.

Many other scientists have agreed with Carl Jung's opinion
that the number of startling coincidences in "the Net" increases
sharply around anybody who becomes involved in depth psychology or in any investigation that extends the perimeter of consciousness. Arthur Koestler has written about this at length, in
both *The Roots of Coincidence* and *The Challenge of Chance*.[15]
Dr. John Lilly has whimsically suggested that consciousness
research activates the agents of "Cosmic Coincidence Control
Center." Let us hope he is joking.

In New Orleans, Oswald and Thornley went about their different lives, and in Ohio the Narrator went about his, and the Net
was gradually drawing us all into what, in *Illuminatus*, we have
called Operation Mindfuck.

When John Fitzgerald Kennedy was blown apart by Oswald
and/or persons unknown, something died in the American psyche, as Jules Feiffer among others has noticed. Kennedy was not
a universally beloved President, of course — nobody ever has
been, not even Washington — but he was young (or youngish),
handsome, cultured, brave (everybody knows the PT-109 story)
and *virile*. There was a commotion of primitive terrors loosed
upon the national psyche by the Dealy Plaza bullets; Camelot
died; the Divine King had been sacrificed; we were caught suddenly in the midst of a Frazer-Freud re-enactment of archetypal
anthropological ritual. The national psyche veered dizzily toward

Chapel Perilous.

The first conspiracy surfaced, if memory is accurate, in the *National Guardian*, a left-wing newspaper, only weeks after the assassination. The Skeptic read it with interest, and it did not convince me.

When the Warren Report came out finally, the Skeptic also studied that with some care. It also did not convince me.

In fact, I was often amazed that so many people did have so many strong opinions on the subject. I began to understand why the Sufis are always attacking "opinions." Everybody nowadays thinks they must have an "opinion" on everything, whether they know anything about it or not. Unfortunately, few people know the difference between an opinion and a proof. Worse yet, most have no knowledge at all about the difference in degree between a merely legal proof, a logical or verbal proof, a proof in the soft sciences like psychology, and a proof in the hard physical-mathematical sciences. They are full of opinions, but they have little ability to distinguish the relative degree of proof upholding all these various opinions.

We say "seeing is believing," but actually, as Santayana pointed out, we are all much better at believing than at seeing. In fact, we are seeing what we believe nearly all the time and only occasionally seeing what we can't believe.

A visit to Millbrook

The next link in the Net was a meeting with Dr. Timothy Leary, the man who either brainwashed a whole generation with mind-warping drugs (opinion of his enemies) or discovered how to free the mind of humanity from culturally conditioned limitations (opinion of his friends).

I met Leary through Ralph Ginzburg, who in 1964 offered me a job as Associate Editor of *Fact* magazine. Although I was in love with our little Ohio farm, and my children protested bitterly against going back to New York, Ralph dangled a tempting $8,000 per year, and between the farm and a job in town I was never making more than about $4,500. I bought some polite city clothes, gave away my last peyote buttons, and returned to the urban hive. The Shaman redomesticated himself, so to speak.

I wanted to interview the controversial Dr. Leary for *Fact*, but Ralph, with that strange prescience which marks his career, said that the psychedelic drug excitement was all over (1964) and nobody was interested any more (1964) and Timothy Leary would soon be forgotten (1964). Still, I wanted to meet Dr. Leary, I finally finagled a free-lance assignment from Paul Krassner of *The Realist* and made the journey (soon to be repeated by countless psychologists, clergymen, rock stars, Oriental gurus and young seekers-after-Wonder) up the Hudson to the Millbrook Ashram.

This was still early on in the history of what Charles Slack later called "the Madness of the Sixties." Timothy Leary, although already an arch-heretic fired from Harvard for original research and poor usage of the First Amendment, was not yet into his Oriental trip; he was studying the Tibetan *Book of the Dead* that summer, but he was otherwise still heavy into Scientific Clinical Psychology. Not once during the day the Reporter spent with Dr. Leary did Tim say "when I used to be a psychologist," as he was occasionally given to saying later on in the frantic '60s.

So many accounts have been written of the Millbrook Ashram that we won't go into all the incredible details. There was a black guy standing on the roof of the Main Building, playing beautiful jazz trumpet all by himself, as we drove up, and the famous psychedelic collages were hanging on walls in virtually every room, but by and large it was much like any place where scholars hold learned seminars. If G. Gordon Liddy was already hiding in the bushes, peeking through his binoculars for Sex Orgies and other heinous crimes, he must have been very bored that particular day.

Tim seemed, on first meeting, a typical middle-aged academic type, although more athletic than most. We mention this because he looked much younger in later years. When we discuss metaprogramming theory later, and Paul Segall's investigations of amino acids related to psychedelics and aging, we will find some evidence that Dr. Leary's youthful image may have a bio-chemical explanation.

Besides being an athletic young-middle-aged man, Tim was singularly free of the space-time compulsions of normal Americans. He sometimes stands as close as a Mexican when he talks to you, and he is apt to look straight at you without the usual American eye-shifting. If this makes you nervous, he backs off and allows you to relax; but, basically, he is most comfortable himself within the *intimate* relationship. And, of course, the famous Leary grin was already part of him.

"The best results come when you fuck someone you really love, during the acid trip," he said that day. "That's when the nervous system is most open, most unconditioned, and ready to take a completely new imprint."

Tim was delighted that the Reporter understood enough psychology to translate terms like "zero-sum game," "reinforcement," "transaction," etc., and he was especially pleased that, unlike any other interviewer he had ever met, this Reporter was familiar with his book *Interpersonal Diagnosis of Personality*, and wanted to question him about how the space-time transformations of the psychedelic voyage correlate with his space-time definitions of personality types in that work.

"LSD takes you out of the normal space-time ego," he said concisely. "I always go through a process in which the space game comes to an end, the time game comes to an end, and then the Timothy Leary game comes to an end. This is the peak, and at this point a new neurological imprint can be made, because all the old imprints are suspended for a while then."

The Reporter asked about the impression that he had encountered on peyote and others had encountered on LSD, that one is actually out of the body at that crucial moment.

"Until I can design an experiment to really test that one out," Timothy said, "I just don't know. It's merely subjective at this point."

Indeed, the Reporter's most persistent impression throughout the day was that Timothy Leary was a man who hated, loathed and despised anyone who would commit the epistemological sin of "speculating beyond the data." Every question asked him was answered either with a summary of experimental results or with a promise that he hoped to find a way to check it experimentally as the work proceeded.

Leary emphasized, as he did to all reporters, that the psychedelic drug experience is a synergetic product of three non-additive factors: (1) the *dosage* of the chemical used; (2) the *set* — the subject's expectations, emotional status games, personality profile, etc.; and (3) the *setting* — the actual events in space-time. This Reporter understood him perfectly and quoted him accurately; we have often wondered why other reporters understood him so poorly and misquoted him so outrageously. The synergetic theory of "dosage, set and setting" may be Dr. Leary's outstanding contribution to the science of psycho-pharmacology (we will talk later about his contributions to other sciences), but journalists in general understood him about as well as one who might write that Einstein discovered e = something-or-other.

Mostly, we talked about game theory that day. Timothy had, indeed, been playing baseball on the Millbrook lawn when we arrived, and baseball thereupon haunted our conversation on the metaphoric level. He had thrown out the concepts of "psychologist" and "patient" back in '57, replacing them with "research team," because he was convinced that the hierarchy implied in "psychologist" (top dog) and "patient" (bottom dog) predetermined certain conclusions. Now he wanted to examine all interpersonal relations in terms of the Morgenstern-von Neumann game model.

(According to economist Oscar Morgenstern and mathematician John von Neumann, in their epochal *Theory of Games* and *Economic Behavior*, most human transactions can be analyzed mathematically by treating them as if they were games. Leary had written his Ph.D. on group therapy — at a time when one of his faculty advisors indignantly told him, "Young man, group therapy is a contradiction in terms!" — and had analyzed personality as a group process defined by rules of interpersonal politics; more simply, he refers to these stereotyped group processes of reality-definition as games.)

"What are the players actually doing in space-time?"
Leary asked rhetorically that day. "Who's at bat? Who's pitching? What are the rules of the game? How many strikes before you're out? Who makes the rules? Who can change the rules? These are the important questions. Anybody around here caught talking about *'sickness'* or *'neurosis'* or *'ego'* or *'instinct'* or *'maturity'* or any of that metaphysical jabberwocky gets thrown the hell out."

Leary went on to reject virtually all psychological terminology as pre-scientific and vague. "We've got a contract among ourselves," he said, "that we're going to talk sense, and that means specifying where the bodies are in space-time and what sort of signals they're exchanging."

This was the basic methodological position of post-Einstein physics but Leary was carrying it as far as it could be taken. Nobody was "sane" or "insane," "right" or "wrong," "hallucinating" or "not-hallucinating"; all those words were value-judgments, relative to the observer's prejudices. What was happening in interpersonal relations, described objectively and relativistically, was various parties or coalitions bargaining for control of neuro-muscular space (ethnological territory) or the right to define the game for all other players (ideological territory).

Leary's arch-rival at Harvard, Dr. B.F. Skinner, had been a pioneer of the Behaviorist approach, which rejected the intuitive and poetic psychologies of Freudians and Jungians as unscientific. While Leary agreed with this, he felt that Skinner himself had taken an equally wrong turn, using as model the push-pull (action-reaction) mechanisms of Newtonian physics. "Psychology doesn't become scientific by copying the physics of past centuries," Leary said to me. "We've got to learn to use the best models in the physics of this century." Such models, he felt, would be relativistic, describing differing reality-coordinates experienced by different bodies as they exchanged signals in space-time.

So many people were bemused or bewildered by Leary the Guru in the next few years that this background of his work was never fully understood.

During the prisoner rehabilitation project of 1961-62, for

which Dr. Leary was commended by the Massachusetts Department of Corrections, Timothy refused to let any coworkers speculate on whether their cons were getting "sicker" or "better." *"Where are their bodies in space-time? What signals are they exchanging?"* he would ask again and again. He had developed a seven-dimensional game model and insisted on analyzing all behavior in terms of the (1) *roles* being played (2) *rules* tacitly accepted by all players; (3) *strategies* for winning (or for masochistic winning-by-losing); (4) *goals* of the game, purpose served; (5) *language* of the game, and the semantic world-view implied; (6) characteristic *space-time locations*, and (7) characteristic *movements* in space-time.

"If you can't describe those *seven dimensions* of a group's behavior, you don't understand their *game*," Leary told the Reporter. "Most so-called 'neurosis' is best analyzed as somebody programmed to play football wandering around in a baseball field. If he thinks football is the only game in the universe, the other players will seem perverse or crazy to him; if they think baseball is the only game, he'll seem crazy to them."

The *Tibetan Book of the Dead*, Leary added, was "the manual for one type of consciousness-altering game." It was useful for LSD-reprogramming sessions because LSD "suspends imprinted neurological games" and allows us to "imprint new games."

(Roubecek, a Czechoslovakian psychiatrist, had proposed in 1957 that "LSD suspends conditioned reflexes." Leary was the first to suggest that LSD acts below the conditioning level and directly changes basic imprints, i.e., neurogenetic limits usually not changed by either conditioning or counterconditioning.)

"You're really talking about using these drugs to change the whole personality," the Reporter said at one point. "Ego and mind and emotions and all . . ."

"Yes," Tim said. "That's the whole point. LSD with the right *set* and *setting* can change anything we consider ourselves. Therefore, it's the most potent brainwashing agent in the world. That's what my Two Commandments are all about." Leary's "Two Commandments for the Neurological Age," published in several of his books and articles of the '60s, are:

"1. Thou shalt not alter the consciousness of thy neighbor without his or her consent.

"2. Thou shalt not prevent thy neighbor from altering his or her own consciousness."

Leary wanted psychedelics regulated and controlled by medical and psychological clinicians, according to a professional code of ethics which would protect the subjects (In fact, he didn't even like the word "subjects," and preferred, in egalitarian fashion, to call the trippers in each experiment "research associates"). He was convinced that the drugs would he abused and misused if control were placed in the hands of the government. Some of the recent revelations about C.I.A. research dramatize what Leary fears.

An ideal re-imprinting clinic, as Leary visualized it, would work like this. Assume you have a personality problem that you want to change. Maybe you're a foot fetishist, or you drink too much, or you feel you can't learn mathematics, or you're incompetent with tools, or whatever. You go to the clinic and discuss the problem with a Behavior Change expert. S/He explains the theory behind psychedelic imprinting and gives you a batch of literature, clearly stating the pros and cons of the theory (i.e., including articles by those who claim it doesn't work or is too dangerous). You think it over for a week. If you decide the theory looks good, you make another appointment and, if the staff has decided you are a safe subject (not pre-psychotic or otherwise vulnerable), the program for the trip is worked out jointly between you and the Behavior Change expert assigned to your treatment. The program will probably include music and ritual — but may be as simple as just relaxing your tense muscles one by one. At the peak, the imprint is made. You emerge with a new reality: what was invisible or impossible before is now part of your self and your perceptual field.

Leary used this technique with the prisoners in the convict rehabilitation project and claims to have cut the recidivism (new crime) rate by 80 per cent.[16] Leary had defined success or failure in terms of where the bodies were in space-time two years after release from prison. At that time, he noted gladly, over 80% of them were still outside prison, whereas the majority of released convicts are back inside prison within two years. Dr. Walter Huston Clark, in 1976, noted that the bodies of most of Leary's convicts known to him were still outside prison in space-time after 15 years.[17]

Dr. Richard Alpert used the same methodology to treat a compulsive homosexual who wished to become capable of sexual relations with women. Three sessions only were required — one of them spent in creating the program in collaboration with the patient. Two LSD trips with (a) pornography and (b) a female sex therapist imprinted the new reality; the man became mostly heterosexual. No Behavior Modifier working without LSD has claimed such a transformation in less than several months of conditioning.[18]

Please note, one more time, that Dr. Leary never claimed such outstanding results could be obtained without the proper set, the proper setting, and full cooperation and communication between the person seeking Behavior Change and the clinician(s) on the case. Within these parameters, and guided by his "Two Commandments," he claimed highly beneficial results could be obtained. He specifically warned that ignoring these parameters was a kind of mind-rape which could be severely traumatic to the subject, being experienced as both coercive and terrifying.

"The most important rule," he told the Reporter vigorously, "is that the tripper decides what behavior change is desired. Nobody else has the right to decide for him."

That day in 1964, I found this Einsteinian and anarchistic variation on Skinner's *1984*-ish Behavior Mod both exciting and hopeful. I decided that Dr. Leary would definitely need to be watched; here was a man, I said to myself, who will do important work in the next ten years. I had no intuition at all that Dr. Leary would actually spend four of those years fighting to stay out of jail and the other six struggling to get out of jail.

The Queen of Space

A few weeks after my meeting with Dr. Leary at Millbrook, my family had our first UFO experience. *Post hoc, ergo propter hoc?*

We were living in northern New Jersey (and I was commuting daily to my job at *Fact* magazine). Our house was at the bottom of a hill and one Saturday morning, while I was home, the kids came running in to tell me that a flying saucer had just landed up near the top of the hill. I went to the back yard to find a neighboring family equally excited.

Altogether, six adults (the Author and his wife plus four from the neighboring clan, which was Appalachian and huge), together with seven children (ours and theirs), had seen *what looked like* a silvery, saucer-shaped craft landing. Everybody was taking turns looking at the landing site through a pair of binoculars. When it was my turn, I saw what looked like a Bucky Fuller geodesic dome (where none had been before), and no human (or humanoid) figures. Others saw a more saucer-shaped craft and some saw humanoids in *silvery costumes*.

Then "it" (whatever it was) took off. (It definitely was not a geodesic dome.) Watching it take off, I decided it was probably only a helicopter.

That afternoon, my son, Graham, encountered an "extraterrestrial" in the woods behind our house, at the foot of the hill. She was a female, with silvery skin, and she told Graham (he was five at the time) that he should become a physicist when he grew up.

Prof. Jacques Vallee, who has analyzed all such Contact stories that have occurred since 1890 with a computer to find statistical patterns, informs us that this is drearily typical. The majority of child contactees, Vallee has discovered, report female extraterrestrials. (The majority of adults report males, in two standard types — small green men or giant blue men.)

In fact, Dr. Vallee has found 44 parallels (similarities of image, word and detail) between the average experience of child Contactees and the miracles attributed to the Blessed Virgin Mary in Catholic countries.[19] "The UFO and the BVM," he has said, only half jokingly, "seem to be the same phenomenon." The Lady most often appears to children, whether She comes in a "space ship" or "from Heaven"; She is accompanied by flashing white lights, usually; and, at Her best, She is capable of suspending the laws of physics in clear view (or telepathically shared hallucination) of huge crowds.

I have asked Graham, who is now studying to be a physicist in accord with the Lady's urging, to retell the tale again, to check the accuracy of my memory. Graham especially emphasized the odd *silvery* costumes of the humanoid figures seen on the mountain before the Lady appeared. An old friend, Marilyn Pooler, of Las Vegas, who was living in that part of New Jersey at that time in 1964, "coincidentally" arrived to visit us in Berkeley two days after the above account was written. Quite spontaneously, with no knowledge of Graham's experience, she told of two seeming extraterrestrials she had seen, about the same time in 1964 — late summer — approximately 30 miles from our home. She is one of the many Contactees who suffered amnesia and can recall only seeing the critters without further details. Twenty minutes later, she awakened as if from trance, and they were gone. Both wore *silver uniforms*.

Catholics now call the BVM "Our Lady of Space." She is, of course, another archetype from Jung's collective unconscious, and was around long before Christianity. The Egyptians called her Nuit and connected her specifically with the star Sirius. But depictions of her go back at least to cave statues dated c. 30,000 B.C. Robert Graves, in his famous (and highly controversial) *The White Goddess*, tried to prove that worship of Her was humanity's oldest religion, and originally involved the use of the psychedelic mushroom, Amanita muscaria.

American Indian shamans knew her, too, and call her Peyote Woman. She is the female version of Mescalito.

She also appears, amusingly enough, in *The Wizard of Oz*, as the Bubble Witch. In the film of that novel, each of her appearances begins with a bright silvery globe descending from the sky, after which She appears where the globe lands. This is the way child Contactees generally report Her, according to Vallee, and the silvery globe was also around in some of Her miracles, under the guise of the B.V.M., at Lourdes and Fatima.

In one of Her miracles at Fatima, She caused the sun to plunge directly toward Earth, in the shared experience or hallucination of over 100,000 witnesses. If you believe the sun really did plunge toward the Earth you are naive (in my estimation). But if you accept that 100,000 persons can telepathically share the same hallucination, you must then answer the Big Question (or perhaps I should call it the Wig Question): how much of consensus-reality is similarly created?

The 23 Enigma

I spent five years (1966-71) as an Associate Editor at *Playboy*. You all want to know, of course, does Hef really fuck all the Playmates, and is he really homosexual? (These are the two most common legends about the Playboy of the Western World.) We have no real inside information — but our impression is that Hef has made love to a lot of the Playmates, though by no means all of them, and that he is not homosexual.

Sorry.

My job was editing the letters in the "Playboy Forum," and also writing the italicized replies in which the *Playboy* position was stated. This position is straight old-fashioned mind-your-own-business John Stuart Mill libertarianism, and (since that is my philosophy as well as Hefner's) I enjoyed the work immensely.

More important to our narrative, William S. Burroughs introduced me to the 23 Enigma while I was at *Playboy*.

I had said, on first seeing the unpublished manuscript of *Naked Lunch* in 1956, "This man is the greatest prose stylist since James Joyce." (I am still rather proud of being the first to make that comparison.) I didn't meet Burroughs until around 1966, and found Bill a much more charming and ordinary individual than his books suggest — one had been prepared for a mad genius and found instead a rather prosaic, almost academic, quite gentlemanly genius. Here's his story of the 23 mystery:

In the early '60s in Tangier, Burroughs knew a certain *Captain Clark* who ran a ferry from Tangier to Spain. One day, Clark said to Burroughs that he'd been running the ferry *23 years* without an accident. That very day, the ferry sank, killing Clark and everybody aboard.

In the evening, Burroughs was thinking about this when he turned on the radio. The first newscast told about the crash of an Eastern Airlines plane on the New York-Miami route. The pilot was another *Captain Clark* and the flight was listed as *Flight 23*.

(Aha! Now you understand the line, "Captain Clark welcomes you aboard," which appears, always with sinister overtones, in various of Burroughs' surrealistic novels.)

Burroughs began keeping records of odd coincidences. To his astonishment, 23s appeared in a lot of them. When he told me about this, I began keeping my own records — and 23s appeared in many of them. (Readers of Koestler's *Challenge of Chance* will find that there are a great many 23s in that encyclopedia of odd coincidences also.)

This, of course, illustrates Jano Watts' concept of "The Net" — the lines of coincidence-synchronicity that connect everything-with-everything. It is also an analogy (and maybe more than an analogy) with what physicists call QUIP — the Quantum Inseparability Principle. QUIP, which is accepted by some and denied by other physicists, holds that every particle does affect every other particle, everywhere.

A plausible extension is given by Dr. Fritjof Capra, a young Berkeley physicist who experienced quantum inseparability during an altered state of consciousness. In *The Tao of Physics*, Dr. Capra defends the "Bootstrap Theory," which holds, in effect, that everything is the cause of everything, every which way in time.[20]

Quantum inseparability and the Bootstrap Theory are differing ontological flavors of what are called "non-local" models in modern physics. Non-local models are not limited by Einstein's speed-of-light barrier; they allow, for instance, that the future may determine the present as much as the past does, as in the famous limerick,

> There was a young lady named Bright
> Whose speed was much faster than light;
> She departed one day
> In a relative way
> And returned on the previous night.

The latest convert to the non-local or non-chronological model is the famous astronomer-cosmologist Sir Fred Hoyle, who explicitly advocates a non-local trans-time theory of causality in his latest book, *Ten Faces of the Universe.*[21]

Non-local theories, like Jung's synchronicity, take us out of the Newtonian action-reaction machine and bring us eerily close to the logic of *I Ching* and Taoism, in which the seemingly random tossing of three coins may reveal an archetypal pattern of both personal and cosmological significance. With that kind of rationale (or rationalization) I accepted the 23 enigma as a signal that I should attempt to decipher.

After a while my passion for jotting down every significant 23 that came my way began to annoy my Beautiful Red-Headed Wife, Arlen.

"It's all in your mind," she told me on several occasions. "You're just noticing the 23s and ignoring other numbers."

Of course. But she was annoyed by being implicated in the 23 mystery even before she met me. Our two oldest daughters (by her previous marriage) were born on February 23 and August 23 respectively.

Once the Numerologist went to see the Academy Award film, *Charly*, with a friend who was particularly dubious about this 23 obsession. The story of the film concerns a low-grade moron (IQ around 70) who is transformed by neuro-surgery into a superhuman genius (IQ 200+). In the crucial operation scene, the number on the operating room is visible, and it is, of course, 23. The friend sat bolt upright.

"Jesus H. Particular Christ," the friend said hollowly, "How do you do it?"

Most of the 23 data were incorporated into *Illuminatus*, to which the reader is referred. Here are a few examples:

"Mad Dog" Coll was shot on 23rd Street when he was 23 years old; a year later, Dutch Schultz (who paid for the Coll assassination) was himself fatally shot on October 23, 1935. Marty Krompier, king of the Harlem numbers racket, was non-fatally shot on the same October 23, 1935. ("It's got to be one of them coincidences," he told police.) Schultz's killer, Charlie Workman, served 23 years of a life sentence and was then paroled.

When the donkey metaprogrammer has noticed a few oddities of this sort, the key signal becomes prominent everywhere. I soon noticed the 23 axioms that open Euclid's Geometry; the fact that the mad bomber in the film, *Airport*, has Seat 23; that in the old stage productions of *A Tale of Two Cities*, Sydney Carton is the 23rd man guillotined in the gory climax (some lexicographers believe this is the origin of the inscrutable slang expression "23 Skiddoo!"); 23, in telegrapher's code, means "bust" or "break the line," while Hexagram 23 in the *I Ching* means "Break Apart." I was even thrilled by noting that in conception Mom and Dad each contribute 23 chromosomes to the fertilized egg, while within the DNA coil of genetic metaprogramming instructions there are unexplained bonding irregularities every 23rd angstrom. Aleister Crowley's *Cabalistic Dictionary* later excited weird speculations about 23 perhaps being somehow involved with reproduction by defining 23 as the number of "parting, removal, separation," "joy," "a thread," and "life."

Run the following, from Professor Hans Seisel of the University of Chicago, through your most skeptical filter:

> My grandparents on my mother's side lived in Gablonz, Mozartstrasse 23; we lived in Vienna at Rossaurelaende 23; our law office at Gonzagagasse 23; my mother at Alserstrasse 23, tuer (apartment) 23, and so it went . . .

Professor Seisel's mother, while visiting Monte Carlo, purchased a book, Ilya Ehrenburg's *Die Liebe der Jeannie Ney*, in which the heroine wins a great deal betting on number 23 at roulette. She decided to experiment; 23 came up on the second try.[22]

The 23 enigma and its recurrence in the story of Dutch Schulz's death was reported by the author in *Illuminatus*.

This is archetypical. We shall see, as we advance, that the peculiar entities in charge of Dr. John Lilly's hypothetical *Cosmic*

Coincidence Control Center pay special attention to those who pay attention to them.

Meanwhile the Numerologist had a new rationalization for his obsession: the famous story of how Dr. James Watson, coming down a spiral staircase at Oxford, suddenly flashed intuitively on the spiral shape of the DNA. All the micro-photographic evidence at that time seemed to contradict his theory, but Watson irrationally trusted his intuition and kept working on that model. Eventually he won the Nobel Prize for proving that the DNA is a double helix (two spirals interwoven). 23 was my spiral staircase, my intuitive signal.

The heresy hunt begins

One day in 1966, Tim Leary popped into the Playboy office and the Numerologist and the Mad Scientist lunched together. I had recently found quite a few references to "Leary" and "LSD" in *Finnegans Wake* and asked Tim what he thought of that. He replied that Leary is a common Irish name and LSD in Ireland means "pounds, shillings, pence."

Then we got into serious rapping and talked about LSD in cancer research. Tim was very excited and hopeful about various successful applications of LSD in treating terminal cancer patients.

The Numerologist mentioned a TV show about the Spring Grove research on LSD and alcoholism. "Did you notice Dr. Unger *hugging* that one tripper?" Tim asked. "That's the sign that he's been to Millbrook. Any therapist who *hugs* an LSD tripper has studied with us." He seemed to regard this as at least as important as any of his theoretical-methodological contributions to psycho-pharmacology. Actually, the taboo against touching the lowly patient was breaking down in psychotherapy generally throughout the '60s; but Timothy, typically, was more enthusiastic and exuberant about it than anyone else.

A few nights later, the Playboy Editor ran into Tim again, at Hefner's wild jet-set mansion. Tim was boozing it up and had his eyes on a Bunny he obviously intended to prong as soon as possible, so the Editor had no lengthy conversation with him.

▲　　▲　　▲

Of course, the Vietnam war had begun to heat up by this time, and the government's insistence on lying about everything connected with the war had begun to erode the social fabric of the U.S. Systematic lying creates what communications scientists call a "disinformation situation," in which everybody eventually begins to distrust, demonize and diabolize everybody else.

Paul Watzlavik, among others, has performed classic experiments in which totally sane people will begin to behave with all the irrationality of hospitalized paranoids or schizophrenics — just because they have been lied to in a calculated and systematic way. This sort of "disinformation" matrix is so typical of many aspects of our society (e.g., advertising and organized religion, as well as government) that some psychiatrists, such as R.D. Laing, claim it is the principal cause of psychotic breakdowns. When the politics of lying becomes normal, paranoia and alienation become the "normality" of the day. The government, as the principal liar of the 1960s, was, of course, more deluded than anyone else, since its reality-map had become a classic disinformation system. The establishment began looking around for the villains to blame for the escalating social disintegration. Tim Leary got elected, by unanimous acclaim, Villain #1.

The "war on drugs" — i.e., a war on research — began. That is to say, it was called a war on drugs, but the total effect of all the hysteria and witch-hunting was that the number of drug users steadily escalated each year, especially among the young, the ignorant and the ill-prepared, with predictably uninspiring results. The only experiments that were stopped were those by intelligent scientists who were beginning to learn something new about the nervous system when they were ordered to desist. Ironically but typically, Dr. Leary, who had warned about all this in his Senate testimony in 1966, was blamed for it by the same government that caused it to happen.

Here's some of Dr. Leary's 1966 Senate testimony:

> Senator Edward Kennedy: You feel that there ought to be control over at least importation?

> Dr. Leary: The sale, manufacture or distribution, yes.
> Kennedy: ... You have testified. Now why do you think they should be?

> Leary: I feel that activity, particularly commercial activities involving the manufacture, sale and distribution of these substances should be controlled because you do not know about quality, you do not know about safety, you do not know what you are buying. Obviously you have to have laws, just as you have laws about the amphetamines.

> Kennedy: You said you do not know about the quality. What is it about the quality that you are frightened about?

> Leary: We do not want amateur or black market sale or distribution of LSD.

> Kennedy: Why not?

> Leary: Or the barbiturates or liquor. When you buy a bottle of liquor —

> Kennedy: This is not responsive. As to LSD ... why do you not want the indiscriminate manufacture and distribution? Is it because it is dangerous?

> Leary: Because you do not know what you are getting.
> Kennedy: Is it because it is dangerous?[23]

And so on. Leary continually tried to point out the horrible black market that would be created by across-the-board criminalization of LSD, and Kennedy continually heckled him and tried to trip him into an "incriminating" admission. The government went ahead and illegalized LSD research. The black market sprang up on a nationwide scale almost immediately. Nobody knew what they were buying, and bad trips multiplied horrendously, especially among those who had the bad fortune to be arrested during the moments of imprint vulnerability, in which case they quite naturally imprinted helplessness, terror and paranoia. The same results were obtained in the C.I.A.'s clandestine experiments, in which the subjects did not know what was being done to them. Those who began to suspect, correctly, that they were being experimented upon *by persons who were lying to them* also imprinted paranoia. All of this could have been prevented if Leary's work on set, setting and dosage had been correctly understood.

Alas, Leary's ideas never did get across in the mass media. There, he was portrayed as a madman who wanted everybody to take LSD and, later, as the Criminal Genius behind the black market which he had tried so hard to prevent. Nor was it ever publicized that in Leary's research with LSD there had been exactly zero bad trips, zero psychotic breaks, zero suicides.

Multiple realities

One of the writers in the *Playboy* promotion department was taking a trip every weekend, on something his black market dealer told him was LSD. (Real LSD was illegal by then.) One day, this writer, whom we shall call Joseph K., told me that he had received telepathic messages from outer space on several of his recent trips. The Materialist did not perfectly hide his instant skepticism, and Joseph K. clammed up immediately. We never heard another word from him on that subject, and he later quit *Playboy* and went off to try to write in Hollywood.

At the time, I had put "all that mystical stuff" behind me and was playing the game of urbane, sophisticated, successful *Playboy* Editor. Weirdness was something that, like poverty, only happened to other people. I was targeted directly at Hedonic Gratification, mostly due to a new drug that had entered my life, the seductive lady known as Maria Juana, goddess of sex, rapture and doing-your-own-thing.

By the time of the Democratic Convention Horrors of 1968, the Materialist was smoking pot fairly regularly — like everybody else in *Playboy*'s editorial department, and at every other magazine we knew; and throughout the communications industry.

One night the Hedonic Materialist was happily spaced out on the weed and alone at home — the kids were asleep and Arlen (paradoxical for a *Playboy* editor's wife) was out at a Women's Liberation meeting. I abruptly made a neurological discovery. Most of the phenomena of self-hypnosis are quite easily replicable on grass, without the tedious training involved in ordinary hypnosis. Instead of being an unplanned voyage into unexpected sensory thrills, pot became a deliberate program of sensory enrichment. One could turn music into colors, into caresses, into *tastes*; one could grow to gigantic size, or shrink down inside one's own cells and molecules; one could *tune* one's nervous system like a combination microscope-TV set.

Several extraordinary months of experiment soon revealed that one could do much of this without pot (although it remained easier *with* pot, of course), and the shaken Materialist began at long last to understand what Freud meant by *projection* and Buddha by *maya*. It became clear as vodka that whatever "reality" means philosophically, our everyday *experience* (the common-sense definition of "reality") is almost entirely self-programmed. This cinematic editing occurs so rapidly that we are normally not aware of doing it, thus we add many things that aren't there at all (Freud's projection) and leave out millions of things that are there (Freud's censorship). Confusing the finished product with an accurate reflection of externality is exactly what Buddha meant when he said normal consciousness is delusion (*maya*).

One soon discovered that pot could be a tool by which one might adjust the nervous system as casually as one adjusts the picture on a TV set. I had achieved what the semanticist Korzybski calls "consciousness of abstracting," awareness of the usually-unconscious mechanism by which each of us makes the world over in his/her own image.

The Neurologician now took up yoga, quite unmystically and with hardly a grain of piety. I understood that yogic training — whatever else it might comprise — is a method of freeing the nervous system from *conditioned perception*. Combining pot and yoga, I quickly demonstrated to myself by direct experience that the nervous system can be freed from virtually every perception and reflex that makes up our ordinary spectrum of possibility.

Our old friend, Alan Watts, a most skeptical theologian and experimental mystic, was doing similar research in those years, and coming to similar conclusions. During one of his visits to Chicago, he said to another *Playboy* editor, "But, my dear man, reality is only a Rorschach ink-blot, you know." Alas, to those who haven't done the research personally on a neurological level, this is hardly comprehensible; the editor remained cynical. Later Paul Krassner, editor of *The Realist*, put the same thought more colorfully: "Reality is silly-putty." Those without direct experience could not understand; they quickly concluded that a certain segment of the intelligentsia was going mad . . .

This is why pot-heads develop a certain inevitable alienation from society. They begin to feel like one-eyed men in the Kingdom of the Blind.

The Murder of Christ: a Re-run

Along about this point in my career as an amateur yogi, Tim Leary came to Chicago with his "Death of the Mind" road show and I must admit I did not find him nearly as impressive as earlier. He walked on stage barefoot, burned incense, did a lecture on Buddha illustrated with psychedelic slides and weird lighting effects, and more or less came on like an Oriental Billy Graham. It seemed that a brilliant scientist had turned himself into a second-rate messiah, but a day or so later I met Tim on the street outside the *Playboy* building and we lunched together again. Tim was more turned-on, vibrant, joyous and grandiose than ever, but he also had even more sense of humor than previously and kept poking fun at his own Guru act. Neither of us said it aloud, but it was understood that much of Tim's current persona was just agitprop for the one cause he really believed in: the possibility that LSD, *wisely used by professionals*, could reprogram enough nervous systems to accelerate consciousness and intelligence before we laid ourselves and our planet waste.

Somehow, we got talking about Dr. Wilhelm Reich, and I compared Tim's growing legal problems with Reich's. Dr. Reich had been the first Freudian to take Freud's discoveries literally and say explicitly that most neuroses are caused by Judaeo-Christian sex-repression. Worse, Reich had insisted that these neuroses are direct causes of racism, sexism, rape, violence and warfare. Sexual repression, he concluded, is Public Health Problem Number One and should be fought as vigorously as polio or cancer. Reich began promulgating this heresy back in the 1920s. He also began actual research on couples having sexual intercourse in the 1930s (30 years before Masters and Johnson). For these and other radical stances, Dr. Reich was expelled from the International Psychoanalytic Society, thrown out of the Communist and Socialist Parties in Austria, driven from Germany by the Nazis, smeared by the press in Sweden to the extent that he could no longer work in that country, defamed by the American Medical Association after coming here and finally died in Federal prison in 1957. All this had convinced many persons, including me, that scientific freedom was no more secure in the 20th Century than in the Dark Ages, if a scientist became too revolutionary in his thinking.

The Reich case did not frighten Timothy.

"I'm in great health in all respects," he self-diagnosed, with the wide and genuine Leary grin. "I fully expect to live past the hysteria and persecution, till everything I've claimed is confirmed and accepted, till it's used every day in every clinic in the world, till it becomes dull truism." Then he grinned even more broadly. "But then I'll be espousing some new heresy, I hope, and be in hot water again.

This may prove to be an accurate forecast.

It is rather peculiar to look back, in 1977, at a book like David Solomon's anthology, *LSD*[24], published in 1964 – only 13 years ago. Here we find scientists such as Dr. Humphrey Osmond,

Dr. James Terrill, Dr. Charles Savage, Dr. Donald Jackson, Dr. Sanford Unger (whose willingness to hug patients is mentioned above). Dr. Jonathan Cole, Dr. Martin Katz, Dr. Eric Kast, etc., reporting beneficial and interesting changes in consciousness (and behavior) induced by LSD *in a proper set and setting*. Here we find philosophers like Aldous Huxley and Alan Watts contemplating the potentials of these chemicals with optimism and hope. We also find Dr. Leary writing the introduction to the volume and treated as a much-respected colleague by most of the scientific contributors. In short, the whole volume seems to have fallen out of a time-warp from another universe.

Was all this published only 13 years ago? Weren't all the contributors thrown in jail at once? What kind of world was it back then, when LSD could be discussed scientifically, objectively, rationally?

As Dr. Leary writes in *The Curse of the Oval Room,*

> Very few Americans, even in these post-Watergate days, understand how Nixon set up his very own Special Secret elite police. Under the guise of "drug control" this Orwellian coup was accomplished with the approval of middle-aged liberals. It was so simple. The Narc budget jumped from 22 million to 140 million . . . Constitutional rights were suspended and martial law (no-knock, stop-and-frisk, curfew, etc.) was imposed selectively on one easily identifiable segment of the population . . . Fear descended on the land. The spokesmen for the counter-culture were arrested, harassed, silenced. The press cooperated completely . . .[25]

In the course of the terroristic campaign described by Leary, he himself was repeatedly arrested, convicted of owning two joints of marijuana (he claimed it was a frame-up, but the liberals weren't interested in *his* claims, since the cops are the new gods of corporate liberaldom), was sentenced to *30 years*, had the highest bail in U.S. history ($5,000,000), was kidnapped in Afghanistan in violation of 148 court rulings holding such body-snatchings illegal where extradition treaties are not in force, was put in chains for a while and then kept in solitary confinement for 19 months, and was held incommunicado for 10 months with none of his friends allowed to send messages to him or receive messages from him.

All this happened in broad daylight, with the liberals and the ACLU unable to recognize that the Constitution was being mauled and mangled in a fashion similar to the famous "Red Terror" of the early 1950s.

I had observed with horror the destruction of Dr. Reich by the forces of bureaucracy and bigotry in the 1950s. It was a kind of Awakening experience, the first dawn of the apprehension that our government, like any other, is more bad than good. To others, this awakening came through the Vietnam War, or through working with blacks and Indians in the civil rights struggle and discovering that the misery of these minorities is not just a dramatic political "issue" but a very painful reality. To some, it only came with Watergate. To some, it hasn't come yet. To me, as a Libertarian, it came when agents of the Food and Drug Administration dumped all of Dr. Reich's books — 30 years of scientific research — into the Vansivoort Street incinerator in New York City, in 1957, and burned them.

Book-burning was a scene out of Nazi Germany, the horror of all the anti-Nazi movies the Libertarian had seen as a child, *coming alive in his own country, in his own time.*

The Libertarian wrote many defenses of Reich in those years, for small oddball political and occult journals — the only ones who were willing to print articles claiming that the U.S. government might possibly have played the Holy Inquisition role to a new Galileo. The only effect of all this earnest writing was that I got to meet quite a few Reichians, and found them a dreary lot — emotionally addicted to paranoid, dogmatic and intolerant head trips (an imitation, unconscious but brilliantly accurate, of all the stress symptoms Reich himself had developed after seven years of hounding and harassment by Washington).

Now, as the 1960s moved past, I began to see the same kill-the-heretic script emerging again, with Tim Leary typecast for the starring role. It was all as rote and repetitious as the yearly sacrifice of the virgin to the corn-crops. Reich had called this bloody ritual "the murder of Christ" and said it would be played over and over again as long as humanity remained "muscularly armored" against the free play of love and sexuality. One began to think he might have been right about that . . .

In 1966-67 I had a few articles of subversive intent published in a little magazine called *The New Libertarian*, and struck up a friendship (by mail) with the editor, Kerry Thornley. We began writing quite long letters to each other (Thornley being in Los Angeles and I in Chicago), astonished at how totally our political philosophies agreed — we were both opposed to every form of violence or coercion against individuals, whether practiced by governments or by people who claimed to be revolutionaries. We were equally disenchanted with the organized Right and the organized Left while still remaining Utopians, without a visible Utopia to believe in. At times we discussed free-floating libertarian communes in international waters, which in my case gave birth to the anarchist submarine fantasy in *Illuminatus*, and, later, to enthusiastic support of the Space Migration plans of Leary and Prof. Gerard O'Neill.

Thornley mentioned in a letter that he had served in the Marines with Lee Harvey Oswald and that they had been buddies. I mentioned that Oswald's wife had been living with my doctor's sister at the time of the assassination. We were amused and intrigued by the coincidence and didn't (yet) call it synchronicity.

Eventually, through Thornley and other California libertarians, I got initiated into the mysteries of Discordianism, the first true "true religion," which Thornley and Gregory Hill had invented in 1958. Discordianism is based on worship of the Greek goddess of chaos and confusion, Eris, also called Discordia in Latin. Since readers of *Illuminatus* already know a great deal about this sublime faith, we will give only an abbreviated summary here, quoting a "Manual for Discordian Evangelists" which Thornley wrote:

"The SOCRATIC APPROACH is most successful when confronting the ignorant. The Socratic approach is what you call starting an argument by asking questions. You approach the innocent and simply ask, 'Did you know that God's name is ERIS, and that He is a girl?' If he should answer 'Yes,' then he is probably a fellow Erisian and so you can forget it.

If he says 'No,' then quickly proceed to:

"THE BLIND ASSERTION and say, 'Well, He is a girl, and His name is *ERIS!*' Shrewdly observe if the subject is convinced. If he is, swear him into the Legion of Dynamic Discord before he changes his mind. If he does not appear convinced, then proceed to:

"THE FAITH BIT: 'But you must have faith! All is lost without faith! I sure feel sorry for you if you don't have Faith.' And then add:

"THE ARGUMENT BY FEAR and in an ominous voice ask, 'Do you know what happens to those who deny Goddess?' If he hesitates, don't tell him that he will surely be reincarnated as a precious Mao Button and distributed to the poor in the Region of Thud (which would be a mean thing to say), just shake your head sadly and, while wiping a tear from your eye, go to:

"THE FIRST CLAUSE PLOY wherein you point to all of the discord and confusion in the world and explain 'Well who the hell do you think did all of this, wise guy?' If he says, 'Nobody, just impersonal forces,' then quickly respond with:

"THE ARGUMENT BY SEMANTICAL GYMNASTICS and say that he is absolutely right, and that those impersonal forces are female and that Her name is ERIS. If he, wonder of wonders, still remains obstinate, then finally resort to:

"THE FIGURATIVE SYMBOLISM DODGE and confide that sophisticated people like himself recognize that Eris is a Figurative Symbol for an Ineffable Metaphysical Reality and that the Erisian Movement is really more like a poem than like a science and that he is liable to be turned into a Precious Mao Button and Distributed to The Poor in The Region of Thud if he does not get hip. Then put him on your mailing list."

Discordian atheology got more and more complicated as it was worked over and developed by Thornley, Greg Hill, and various others who were drawn into it — Bob Shea, another editor at *Playboy*; Camden Benares (author of *Zen Without Zen Masters*); poet Judith Abrahms; Dr. Robert Newport, a psychiatrist; and quite a few similarly whimsical souls. Eventually, Greg Hill produced a Discordian Bible called *Principia Discordia*. None of this was *merely* a parody of religion per se. It was an exercise in guerrilla ontology — an attempt to make Nasrudin's Donkey *visible*. A Marx Brothers version of Zen. Operation Mindfuck, we called it.

(We were all having a lot of fun with Discordianism. None of us were aware, yet, that Operation Mindfuck could get out of hand . . .)

One of the first Discordian catmas (Other religions have dogmas, which are absolute beliefs. Discordianism has catmas, which are relative meta-beliefs.) was Kerry Thornley's Law of Fives, which holds that all incidents and events are directly connected to the number five, or to some multiple of five, or to some number related to five in one way or another, *given enough ingenuity on the part of the interpreter*. Usually, we would state this to novices without the crucial (italicized) final clause; it was up to them to discover the metaprogrammer and figure that part out for themselves.

I added the Law of 23s, derived from Burroughs, on the grounds that $2 + 3 = 5$, and Discordians were soon reporting 23s and 5s from everywhere in current history and the past.

You have achieved Discordian enlightenment when you realize that, while the goddess Eris and the Law of Fives are not literally true, *neither is anything else*. Out of the hundred million buzzing, bright, busy signals received every minute, the human brain ignores most and organizes the rest in conformity with whatever belief system it currently holds. One can select lawful-and-orderly signals and claim that all is projected by a Cosmic Intelligence as in Thomism, or select chaotic signals and claim God is a Crazy Woman as in Discordianism. The Brain will adjust incoming signals to either belief system . . . or to dozens of others.

In the seminars on Exo-Psychology which I teach these days, I dramatize this point by having the entire class visualize the hall they came through in entering the seminar room. Then I ask how many people visualize five distinct items, ten, fifteen . . . When we find the person with the largest number of distinct signals in memory storage, we list the elements of that person's hall on the blackboard. We call this number X. Then we collect all the signals from the rest of the class that were not on the list, X. The new list is always higher than 2X. That is, if the memory champ of that class had 14 signals in the hall, the total class had 28 or more.

This illustrates that one way to double your practical intelligence (awareness of detail) is to try to receive as many signals as possible from other humans, however wrong-headed their reality-map may seem, however dumb or boring they might sound at first. Our usual habit of screening out all human signals not immediately compatible with our own favorite reality-map is the mechanism which keeps us all far stupider than we should be.

The experiment also illustrates the Leary principle of neurological relativism. No two people ever report exactly the same signals. Whatever the "objective hall might be (probably a dance of energy, if we trust modern physics), each person walking through it created a separate tunnel-reality, a hall that suited their own neurological habits. No two people were in the "same" hall existentially.

It is, incidentally, great fun to argue the Discordian position against either a Thomist theologian or an old-fashioned deterministic Materialist. There is just as much evidence of chaos and play in the universe as there is of law and order; you just have to start looking for it.

Naturally, I did not suspect for a long time that our Lady Eris, goddess of confusion, was just the Space Lady coming back to haunt me in a different guise.

Which Is Real?

Do these 5 pebbles really form a pentagon?
Those biased by the Aneristic Illusion would say yes.
Those biased by the Eristic Illusion would say no.
Criss-cross them and it is a star.

An Illuminated Mind can see all of these, yet he does not insist that any one is really true, or that none at all is true. Stars, and pentagons, and disorder are all his own creations and he may do with them as he wishes. Indeed, even so the concept of number 5.

Can you chart the COURSE to Captain Valentine's SWEETHEART?

The real reality is there, but everything you KNOW about "it" is in your mind and yours to do with as you like. Conceptualization is art, and YOU ARE THE ARTIST.

Convictions cause convicts.

HEMLOCK?
I NEVER TOUCH THE STUFF!

00054

When I was 8 or 9 years old, I acquired a split beaver magazine. You can imagine my disappointment when, upon examination of the photos with a microscope, I found that all I could see was dots.

7. Never write in pencil unless you are on a train or sick in bed.

A page from the now-legendary Principia Discordia. The Aneristic illusion is that order is real; the Eristic illusion is that disorder, or chaos, is real; Illumination is the realization that it depends on the perceiver.

Jim Garrison and the Illuminati

Discordianism is in direct contradiction of the mono-theory-monotheist foundations of Western religion, Western logic and Western law, all of which assume that there is one correct model that is true in all cases. People who are religious in the dogmatic Judaeo-Christian sense, logicians who haven't gotten to Godel's Proof yet, and lawyers of all sorts are the last persons on Earth to be able to appreciate the Discordian philosophy.

Nonetheless, in a totally Quixotic way, Kerry Thornley, dragging his Discordian history behind him, insisted on getting himself involved in the Kennedy Assassination Mania of the '60s, and went straight to a *lawyer* — New Orleans D.A. Jim "The Jolly Green Giant" Garrison. He might as well have gone to a Thomist theologian.

Kerry decided in 1967, after reading Mark Lane's *Rush to Judgment* and a few other of the Kennedy assassination books, that perhaps his old friend Lee Harvey Oswald hadn't killed the President after all; maybe there really was a conspiracy. Kerry naively went back to New Orleans and had several long talks with District Attorney Garrison, who had opened a new investigation which seemed to be uncovering such a conspiracy.

Thornley and Jim Garrison did not make a good team together, to put it mildly. In fact, at their last interview, each told the other to go to hell. Discordianism and law do not mix. Kerry left New Orleans and angrily informed all his friends and correspondents that Garrison was an unscrupulous demagogue who was organizing a witch-hunt to excite the gullible and advance his own political career. Garrison's aides struck back with a series of ridiculous charges against Thornley.

Naturally, I got drawn into the controversy.

That was when I really began to understand how arbitrary are the reality-constructs of the average human nervous system. The establishment press was 100% anti-Garrison and denied all of his charges. The underground press was 100% pro-Garrison and supported all of his charges. In Leary's language, all the signals that could be organized into a "good" Garrison Gestalt were transmitted freely and omnidirectionally in the underground press game, while all signals suggestive of a "bad" Garrison, or inconsistent with a "good" Garrison, were smoothly, efficiently reserved for the Establishment press game.

"My God," the Libertarian said to himself one day in early 1968, when this had become clear, "the left wing is as robotic as the right wing." (We apologize for our naiveté in taking until 1968 to figure *that* out.)

It certainly illustrated the first law of Discordianism: "Convictions cause convicts." *Whatever you believe imprisons you.*

Thornley, as I had gotten to know him through the mails and then through visits, was a humorous, agnostic, libertarian person who was dogmatic about only two things: anarchism and pacifism. It was against his personal ethic to destroy life in any form. It was impossible for one to consider him seriously as a participant in a conspiracy to murder anybody.

And yet, in the underground press, Thornley and the other Garrison suspects were pictured as a weird gang of homosexual Satanic C.I.A. Nazi fanatics. It was the McCarthyism of the '50s all over again, coming from the left this time.

("There seem to be a lot of different realities going around these days," Abbie Hoffman said during the Democratic Convention horrors of 1968; that may well be the only intelligent thing he ever said.)

From that time to this the Skeptic has made it a point to read one or two periodicals every month put out by some political or religious group he despises, just to see what sort of signals are being screened out by his habitual reality-maps. It is most educational. (Aleister Crowley and Bertrand Russell, respectively the outstanding mystic and the outstanding rationalist of the 20th Century, have also recommended this practice. It is one of the best ways to discover how Nasrudin's donkey — the self-metaprogrammer — works.)

Meanwhile, Thornley discovered that Allan Chapman, of Texas, one of Garrison's aides, believed the JFK assassination was the work of the Bavarian Illuminati. Of course, I had been an expert on that subject (I thought) for a number of years, and Garrison's involvement in it encouraged me to enter the belief system that Garrison was a paranoid or a demagogue or both. There simply were no real Illuminati; it was all a right-wing fantasy — a sanitized version of the tired old Elders-of-Zion mythology.

Although the underground press was absolutely fundamentalist in its allegiance to the Garrison Revelations, it was also intensely gullible and eager to believe all manner of additional conspiracy theories, the weirder the better. Most Discordians, at this time, were contributors to underground newspapers all over the country. We began surfacing the Discordian Society, issuing position papers offering non-violent anarchist techniques to mutate our robot-society. One was our "PURSE" plan (Permanent Universal Rent Strike Exchange) in which everybody simply stops paying rent forever. (Can they dispossess us all into the Atlantic and Pacific?) Another was our "PUTZ" plan (Permanent Universal Tax Zap), in which everybody stops paying taxes. Along with this we planted numerous stories about the Discordian Society's aeon-old war against the sinister Illuminati. We accused everybody of being in the Illuminati — Nixon, Johnson, William Buckley, Jr., ourselves, Martian invaders, all the conspiracy buffs, *everybody*.

We did not regard this as a hoax or prank in the ordinary sense. We still considered it guerrilla ontology.

My personal attitude was that if the New Left wanted to live in the particular tunnel-reality of the hard-core paranoid, they had an absolute right to that neurological choice. I saw Discordianism as the Cosmic Giggle Factor, introducing so many alternative paranoias that everybody could pick a favorite, if they were inclined that way. I also hoped that some less gullible souls, overwhelmed by this embarrassment of riches, might see through the whole paranoia game and decide to mutate to a wider, funnier, more hopeful reality-map.

The distinguished poet Ed Sanders, author of *Fuck God Up The Ass* and other immortal works, once sent me an urgent message, warning, "There's nothing funny about the Illuminati. They're *real!*"

I laughed immoderately, as the Fool always does before the

doors of Chapel Perilous swing shut behind him.

Operation Mindfuck

The Discordian revelations seem to have pressed a magick button. New exposes of the Illuminati began to appear everywhere, in journals ranging from the extreme Right to the ultra-Left. Some of this was definitely not coming from us Discordians. In fact, one article in the *Los Angeles Free Press* in 1969 consisted of a taped interview with a black phone-caller who claimed to represent the "Black Mass," an Afro-Discordian conspiracy we had never heard of. He took credit, on behalf of the Black Mass and the Discordians, for all the bombings elsewhere attributed to the Weather Underground.

Other articles claimed the Illuminati definitely were a Jesuit conspiracy, a Zionist conspiracy, a bankers' conspiracy, etc., and accused such worthies as FDR, J. Edgar Hoover, Lenin, Aleister Crowley, Jefferson and even Charlemagne of being members of it, whatever it was.

All this inspired Bob Shea and me to start work on the gigantic novel which finally emerged as the *Illuminatus* trilogy. We made the Discordians the Good Guys and the Illuminati the Bad Guys in an epic of convoluted treachery that satirized all conspiracy theories of Left and Right.

A good omen early in the writing cheered us vastly. A search through the Discordian Archives revealed that the earliest of Discordian holy books — *How the West Was Lost*, by Malaclypse the Younger (Greg Hill) — was originally printed, after office hours, on the Xerox machine of D.A. Jim Garrison, in summer 1963. (Greg's girlfriend was Garrison's secretary.)

That would be about the time when Oswald was ordering the Carcano rifle and I was having my experience with the green man in the cornfield, and by this time we were all too sophisticated to dismiss such a pattern as "mere coincidence."

Synchronicity, by Goddess, was afoot ... and the weirdness was increasing. For instance, we Discordians had a mystic sign, like the Masons and everybody else. Ours was blandly lifted from good old Tory warmonger Winston Churchill; it was the V-for-Victory Winnie had used all through World War II. Of course, to us, it had special Discordian meanings: the V, being the Roman numeral for 5, illustrated the Law of Fives. The way the sign is made, with 2 fingers up and 3 bent down, exemplifies the hidden 23 within the Law of Fives. The fact that this sign is also used by Catholic priests in blessing and by Satanists in invoking the devil illustrates the essential ambiguity of all symbolism, or the Cosmic Giggle Factor.

Between the first edition of the *Principia Discordia*, run off on Jim Garrison's Xerox machine in 1963, and the fourth edition, published by Rip-Off Press in Berkeley in 1969, only 3,125 copies of that basic Discordian text were ever distributed. Nonetheless, the V sign, somehow, got accepted by the whole counter-culture, especially circa 1966-70. One saw hundreds of thousands of protesters using it at the Pentagon demonstration in October 1967 and again at the Democratic convention of 1968. The odd part was that virtually nobody using it was aware that we Discordians had revived it ...

The Pentagon itself, of course, is a sacred Discordian shrine, both because it is five-sided* and because the Byzantine bureaucracy there enshrined illustrates so wonderfully the basic Discordian sociological law enunciated by Kerry Thornley in *The Gospel According to Fred*: "Imposition of Order = Escalation of Chaos." I attended the Pentagon protest in October 1967 — where the Yippies attempted to expel the Demon, Yog-Sothoth, by chanting, "Out, demon, out!" and all of it, especially the V signs, seemed as if the Discordian version of surrealism was becoming a new political reality.

The next year the Yippies ran a pig for President.

♦

*All members of the Joint Chiefs of Staff are honorary Discordian saints, belonging to the Order of Quixote, also known as the Knights of the Five-Sided Castle.

♦

A psychologist named Richard Ryan, in New Jersey, read some of the Discordian literature and wrote to tell me another 23 mindfuck. Ryan had overheard a psychiatrist, in a mental hospital where they both worked, giving a royal ass-chewing to a nurse who'd made a mistake. "When I say 23 cc.," the psychiatrist had shouted, "I want 23 cc. — not 24 cc." Ryan heard this on his way to visit a ward with chronic schizophrenics. When he entered the ward, one of the schizzies said to him, in a tone of anxiety, "Yes, yes, 23 cc."

The Horrible Secrets of the Wicked Aleister Crowley

One day in 1970, I had lunch with Alan Watts and his lovely wife, Jano.

Toward the end of the lunch, Alan asked me about my current writing projects, and I told him a little about *Illuminatus*, happening to mention the Eye in the Triangle, which is said to be the symbol of the Illuminati.

"That reminds me," Alan said. "The best book I've read in years is called *The Eye in the Triangle*. It's about Aleister Crowley." He went on to recommend the book highly.

All I then knew about Aleister Crowley was vague and unfavorable. He was said to be a Satanist, a Black Magician, a sadist, a nut, a heroin addict and a sexual degenerate of monstrous proportions. I had somehow or other also heard that Crowley had climbed higher on Chogo Ri than any other mountaineer in history and had set several other climbing records, and that intrigued me. Few junkies have the stamina for such exertions, and one wondered a bit if some of Aleister's infamous reputation was exaggerated.

The Skeptic bought *The Eye in the Triangle*, which was by Dr. Israel Regardie, Crowley's secretary in the 1920s and now a Reichian psychologist in Los Angeles. Dr. Regardie emphasized the link between Crowley's Tantric magick* and Reich's bio-energetic psychology, and the Skeptic assumed therefore that the "astral" energies used in Crowleyan magick were the same phenomenon as the "orgone energy" used in Reichian therapy. I'd soon plowed my way through all of Crowley's books still in print and began a correspondence with Dr. Regardie.

♦

*Crowley's spelling. (The *k* is to establish a distinction from ordinary "stage magic" or conjuring.) Pronounced *mage*-ick.

♦

I also began experimenting with the methods of magick training given in Crowley's books. Many of these exercises were frankly borrowed from Hatha Yoga, in which I already had some experience; some were similar to the methods of tribal shamans, such as Don Juan Matus, whose training of the anthropologist, Carlos Castaneda, is full of Crowleyan techniques; others came from Tibetan and Indian Tantra, the art of turning sexual ecstasy into mystic mind-expansion.

Crowley never refers to these Tantric practices directly in his books, but only obliquely via codes, puns, metathesis, acrostics, obscure symbolism and every manner of indirection. I first began to understand this, as mentioned earlier, while reading Chapter 69 of *The Book of Lies*, which is called "The Way to Succeed — and The Way to Suck Eggs." As is usual with Crowley, the chapter number is related to the subject (usually Cabalistically, but in this case *via* sexual slang). The title is a typical Crowleyan pun (the way to suck *seed* . . .). The chapter describes the descent of the dove on Pentecost — called "The Gift of Tongues" (!) by Christian theologians — but can also be read as a description of Crowley and his mistress (called Laylah in the text) engaged in mutual oral sex. Crowley was actually saying that oral sex could be a method of meditation.[26]

Once one got the message, further browsing soon showed that countless other chapters were describing other sex acts as forms of meditation. The same technique appears again and again in almost all of Crowley's books.*

♦

* Although I obtained this knowledge by intuition, you don't have to take my word for it. Louis Culling, a disciple of Crowley, has described the Crowleyan methods of Tantra without codes or ambiguity in *A Manual of Sex Magick*, Llewellyn Books, St. Paul, 1972.

♦

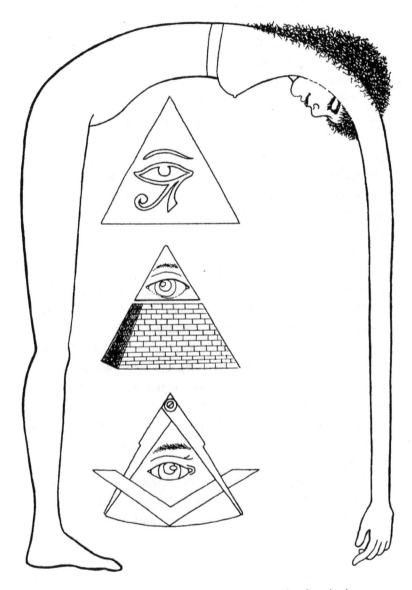

Some forms of the eye-triangle design. The first is the emblem of Crowley's magick society, the Ordo Templi Orientis. The second is the Great Seal of the United States, Illuminati documents and various Masonic buildings. The third appears in every Masonic lodge. Other forms are used by Vietnamese Buddhists, Theosophists, Rosicrucians, etc.

The idea behind Tantric sacramental sex (or sex-magick, as it is also called) is that postponing normal orgasm by various postures, meditations, incantations, and especially prayers, enables one to produce eventually a new kind of orgasm — the polyphase orgasm, Leary has called it. "The Ascent of the Serpent" is the traditional Hindu metaphor for this neurological explosion. The experience is much like nitrous oxide in that it seems to condense an LSD trip into a few minutes, and like prolonged hatha yoga in that it seems to produce a permanent change in neuro-physiology. In Leary's terminology, this Tantric mutation gives you a fifth neurological circuit, where most humans have only four, and it can also launch you onward toward even higher circuits.

Marijuana, of course, also puts you on the fifth circuit — right-brain rapture — but only temporarily. It was one of Crowley's secret teachings, only passed on verbally to promising students, that the combination marijuana + tantra was the key to rapid mutation into a permanent Rapture Circuit.

It occurred to me that I finally had the secret of the Illuminati. They were not the fantasy of right-wing paranoids. "The Illuminati" was one of the names of an underground mystical movement using sexual yoga in the Western world. The veils of obscurity and mystery around such figures as Giordano Bruno, John Dee, Cagliostro, the original Rosicrucians (17th century), Crowley himself, and various other key figures in the "conspiracy," had nothing to do with politics or plots to take over the world. It was a screen to protect them from persecution by the Holy Inquisition in earlier centuries and from puritanical policemen in our time.

This historical pattern of persecution and cover-up has confused the transmission considerably. Some of the groups called "The Illuminati" at one time or another have not had this particular secret in their mind-programming syllabus. Some groups not called "The Illuminati" have had it, to confuse matters further (e.g., the Brothers and Sisters of the Free Spirit, to which Hieronymus Bosch belonged and which greatly influenced his paintings, had the secret, as did some but not all of the Rosicrucian and Freemasonic orders). I have done what I could to clear up the historical picture in another book.[27]

Aleister Crowley, the Great Beast 666.

The Crowleyan system, very briefly, is a synthesis of three elements:

1. Western occultism. The secret "illuminated" teaching out of 19th century Rosicrucianism, possibly going back through Renaissance magick societies, medieval witchcraft, the Knights Templar, European Sufis, etc., to Gnosticism, and thence back possibly to the Eleusinian Mysteries and Egyptian cults. Basically, as Crowley says, this method consists of dangerous "physiological experiments" — using ritual, sometimes drugs, sometimes sex, to jolt the nervous system into "higher" functioning (new neurological circuits).

2. Eastern yoga, including meditation plus physical exercises to make meditation easier and more natural. Another system of activating higher circuits.

3. Modern scientific method. Crowley taught total skepticism about all results obtained, the keeping of careful objective records of each "experiment," and detached philosophical analysis after each stage of increased awareness.

It is this synthesis of Eastern and Western occult traditions with modern scientific method that is probably Crowley's major achievement. His notorious anti-Christian philosophy — a blend of Nietzschean Supermanism and anarcho-fascist Darwinism — is quite distinct from his methodology. Whether you like that philosophy or not (and the Libertarian does not), you can still use the methodology of research Crowley devised.

A Discordian signal from Aldous Huxley, deceased

As Shea and I went on working on *Illuminatus*, the Materialist began his first experiments with Crowley's techniques of mutating consciousness.

In one experiment, I banned the use of the word "I" from my conversation for one week. Mad Aleister recommends what Skinner later called "negative reinforcement" in cases of relapse;

he violently slashed his arm with a razor every time he slipped and said "I." Your less hardy narrator substituted a less heroic control: I bit my thumb, hard, at each slip. By about the fourth day, I had a very sore thumb and an even more painful ego. The subjectivity and self-centeredness of normal human consciousness was hideously obvious to me. By the seventh day I had entered an altered state of consciousness and regarded ego as something of an inconvenient fiction.

In another experiment, the Shaman bought a deck of Tarot cards, announced that he was psychic, and started giving divinations. This rapidly forced me to use portions of my brain normally not used, and I became aware of neurological functions growing in a quite astonishing manner. Of course, I was here running head-first into the brick wall of my own ingrained Skepticism and it was two years before anything happened of a really dramatic nature. Meanwhile, I became alert to all sorts of signals previously invisible; my empathy with others was becoming intensified. I also learned a great deal about how easy it is to deceive those who *want* to believe; and this showed how easily I might be deceived if I *wanted* to believe.

The Shaman also experimented extensively with Crowley's method of achieving and transcending religious visions. This is based on Hindu bhakti yoga and the *Spiritual Exercises* of St. Ignatius Loyola, with a typically Crowleyan difference. In bhakti yoga, you form a love-bond with a particular divinity, dedicate every waking moment to Him (or Her) and invoke that Divine Being by every method possible, especially *vivid visual imagination*. Loyola's method is similar, except that you have no choice about which Divinity to invoke. Crowley's twist is to carry this through until you experience a real manifestation of the God (a "Contact" in UFO jargon), and then *immediately stop*, and start over with a *different* god. After you have run through three or four divinities in this manner, you will understand Nasrudin's Donkey (the neuro-programmer) and you will be increasingly skeptical about everybody's reality-maps, including your own.

Other Crowley exercises the author tried are not described here, because they are too dangerous for ordinary or casual experimenters. Crowley always insisted that nobody should try his more advanced techniques without (a) being in excellent health, (b) being competent in at least one athletic skill, (c) being able to conduct experiments accurately in at least one science, (d) having a general knowledge of several sciences, (e) being able to pass an examination in formal logic and (f) being able to pass an examination in the history of philosophy, including Idealism, Materialism, Rationalism, Spiritualism, Comparative Theology, etc. Without that kind of general knowledge and the self-confidence and independence of thought produced by such study, magick investigation will merely blow your mind. As Brad Steiger has said, the lunatic asylums are full of people who naively set out to study the occult before they had any real competence in dealing with the ordinary.

The first results of the author's Crowleyan experiments were a vast increase in his already abundant skepticism — to the point where he was skeptical at last even of skepticism itself — and an ability to achieve ecstasy and contact mysterious "entities" without psychedelic drugs.

Coincidences-in-23 also began to multiply more rapidly than the National Debt. For instance, my first meeting with Mala-clypse the Younger (Greg Hill), creator of the great *Principia Discordia*, occurred on April *23*, and, while we were discussing this, a glazier who was repairing a broken window in the apartment presented his bill. The bill was numbered 05675 (5+ 6 + 7 + 5 = 23) and the price was $7.88 (7 + 8 +8 = 23). In commemoration of that Triple Whammy, we rearranged the chronology to have *Illuminatus* begin on April 23.

The 23s accumulated faster. For the first time, the Shaman began to wonder: was this all the metaprogrammer (selective perception) or was there an element of PK (psychokinesis) about it? Was one unconsciously *making* it happen, the way a "poltergeist child" makes furniture fly around? One couldn't yet take the second hypothesis seriously, but the fact that one was capable of wondering about it indicated the direction the experiments were taking.

Then came the Huxley synchro-mesh.

I was reading Laura Archera Huxley's *This Timeless Moment* and came to the last chapter, concerning Laura's attempts to communicate with Aldous after his death. About that possibility I was (and still am) a rather hardened cynic; I know too much about how mediums operate. In this case, Laura got her results from Keith Milton Rinehart, a medium who has performed credibly in scientific tests. Rinehart said to Laura that Aldous wanted to transmit "classic evidence of survival," which in parapsychology means something that *could not be explained* by the alternative theory of ESP — i.e., Rinehart reading Laura's mind. After a time, he announced that he had a signal: Laura should go to Aldous' private study, which she seldom entered, and there pick up the fifth book on a certain shelf, which she had not read. Rinehart said that the message was on page 17, *line 23.*

The Numerologist sat up straight when he read that.

Laura got the book, and indeed it was one that she hadn't read — a collection of essays on modern writers. On page 17, line 23, she found:

> Aldous Huxley does not surprise us in this admirable communication in which paradox and erudition in the poetic sense and the sense of humor are interlaced in such an efficacious form.[28]

The Net or the Network?

I must admit that some eerie thoughts went through my head on reading that exquisitely worded sentence, somehow transmitted through Keith Milton Rinehart in his attempt to pick up a signal from the dead Aldous Huxley.

Among other things, the Shaman wondered for a crazy moment if the whole 23 enigma might not be a world-wide astral plot by Aldous and other humorous sages to produce cumulative evidence over decades that they were, indeed, alive-though-dead and still communicating with us.

The resolute anti-Spiritualist need not bail out at this point, or throw the book away; after all, it was only a passing thought.

And the 23 Mystery was to get much more mysterious a few years later, as we shall see.

Meanwhile, the complexity of the synchronicity mesh (Jano Watts's "Net") was gradually dawning on me. Aldous Huxley's first book on psychedelics, through conservative historian Russell Kirk's review of it, originally got me interested in chemical neuro-programming. Aldous was a personal friend of Jano and Alan Watts, and of Tim Leary. Aldous died on the same day as John F. Kennedy. Kerry Thornley, widely believed among Garrisonite conspiracy buffs to be "the second Oswald," named his son Aldous Wilson Thornley — after Aldous and me. *And Aldous had originally been turned on to peyote by Aleister Crowley in 1929.*[29]

Crowley, remember, styled himself Epopt of the Illuminati. His magazine, *Equinox*, bore the masthead on each issue: "A Journal of Scientific Illuminism."

The synchronized Net began to look even more like a conscious Network when I read Alan Watts's autobiography in 1975 and discovered that he had been initiated into a magickal order, using Crowley-style sex-yoga, way back in the 1930s. Alan describes his initiator as "a rascal-guru in the tradition of Crowley and Gurdjieff," and gives his name as Mitrinovic.[30]

After the initiation. Watts became an Episcopal priest for a while, and did a great deal to re-introduce exotic ritual (magickal . . .?) elements into the ceremonies, so much so that he was occasionally criticized for it. Later, he left the Church and became a leading popularizer of Zen Buddhism, Taoism, and Gnostic Christianity. He turned me on to Zen in 1957, to Leary in 1964, to Crowley in 1971.

"I am not a Guru or a philosopher or even a teacher," he told me earnestly on one occasion. "I am merely an entertainer."

One wonders *whom* Alan was entertaining? And was he part of a Net of coincidence or a Network of adepts?

And who was the mysterious Mitrinovic who initiated Alan? Was he a Sufi or one of the Illuminati — or are the Illuminati merely the European branch of the Sufis?

The latter theory — that the Illuminati *are* Sufis — is claimed as historical fact by Sufi author Idries Shah.[31]

Indeed, Shah goes further and says that the Illuminati were originally a Sufi sect who discovered the Secret of Secrets coded into the famous lamp-and-light verse in the *Koran*, which they interpret symbolically. The verse reads:

> Allah is the Light of the heavens and earth. His Light is resembled by a lamp within a niche. The lamp is within a crystal, *like a shining star*. [Italics added.]

Aleister Crowley referred to the Illuminati also as the Argentum Astrum, or (Order of the) Silver Star. We will soon find reasons to think we can identify the star that is referred to in both cases.

The Lady of Guadalupe

In 1971, I quit my job at *Playboy* because doing the same thing, every day, five days a week, 50 weeks of the year, is a damned bore, no matter how interesting the work intrinsically is. After five years, even at $20,000 per, you will become a zombie if you don't seek adventure and change.

The only reason most people remain in the same jobs, the same towns, the same belief-systems, year after year, decade after decade, is, of course, that cultural conditioning, in every tribe, is a process of gradually narrowing your tunnel-reality. The way to stay young (comparatively; until the longevity Pill is discovered) is to make a quantum jump every so often and land yourself in a new reality-matrix.

I jumped from the Bunny Empire to San Miguel de Allende, a town in the mountains north of Mexico City which has been declared a national monument by the government and is deliberately kept as it was at the time of the 1810 Revolution.

Of course, one could not escape the Illuminati. I soon found that Father Hidalgo, who started the 1810 rebellion in San Miguel, was both a Mason and a Jesuit — the Church had not outlawed Masonry at that time — and had decorated many churches around the area with the Eye-in-the-Triangle design.

I got interested in Father Hidalgo, who liked to quote the heretic, Voltaire, and who used the slogan, "Viva Nuestra Senora Guadalupe y mueron gubernacion mala" (Long live Our Lady of Guadalupe and death to bad government!). The Lady of Guadalupe is officially believed to be the Virgin Mary, of course, but many skeptical archaeologists regard Her as an old Aztec sky-goddess in very slight disguise (just as Saint Brigit is the old Celtic goddess, Brigit, in disguise). She has more miracles to Her credit than any other BVM manifestation; Jacques Vallee has found numerous parallels between Her and the modern UFOnaut Space Lady who has appeared to many child Contactees in recent years. Most recently, in the 1920s, an anarchist attempted to destroy the "miraculous" painting of Her in Her basilica outside Mexico City by throwing a bomb at the painting. Everything around the painting was damaged, but the painting "miraculously" survived. Or so the Church claims.

At this point, the Shaman had a good "astral" contact going with Nuit, the Egyptian goddess of the stars, using Crowley's methods of invocation (and following Crowley's injunction not to attribute "objective reality or philosophical validity" to any communication so received). He did not know, yet, that Nuit was especially related to Sirius by the Egyptians, but he did know, from Frazer and other anthropologists as well as from Carl Jung's books, that Nuit and the BVM were the same archetype under two different names. He began addressing Her as Nuestra Senora de Guadalupe and trying to tune in to Father Hidalgo's relationship with Her.

She informed the questing Shaman, on one astral trip, that She had cured him of polio in his childhood.

Checking back with his mother, the Skeptic discovered that indeed his mother had made special devotions to the Virgin at that time, to achieve his cure. Officially, of course, he was not cured by these medieval and superstitious offerings; but the truth is even more amusing than that. I was cured by the Sister Kenny method — which at the time was being denounced as witchcraft and delusion by the American Medical Association. My parents had by "luck" or coincidence found a doctor who believed in and used the Sister Kenny technique . . .*

♦

* Most of the children who had polio in the 1930s, like the author, and were not treated by the Kenny method but by orthodox A.M.A. therapy, are *still* crippled. I am quite mobile and need a cane only occasionally.

♦

Meanwhile, Tim Leary's struggle to stay out of jail, which had begun when G. Gordon Liddy first busted him in 1964, had finally come to its inevitable end. Dr. Leary was placed in a cage on January 27, 1970. Nine months later — a few weeks before his fiftieth birthday, and already a grandfather — Timothy justified his "youth-culture" image by an athletic climb across a fifty-foot cable over the prison wall to freedom. He left behind a pious note to the prison staff:

In the name of the Father and the Mother and the Holy Ghost — Oh, Guards — I leave now for freedom. I pray that you will free yourselves. To hold man captive is a crime against humanity and a sin against God. Oh, guards, you are criminals and sinners. Cut it loose. Be free. Amen.

Within a few months, Tim was again imprisoned, by the Black Panther Party in Algiers. A second escape brought him to Switzerland, and a new imprisonment. The search for freedom was beginning to look barren. But, then, under a propaganda campaign by American intellectuals, led by playwright Arthur Miller and poet Allen Ginsberg, the Swiss government released Timothy, allowed him to remain in their territory, and refused to extradite him back to his cage in the California Archipelago. He was the first scientist since Kropotkin to make such a stylish escape from tyranny and still remain at large.

We were still in Mexico at the time, and I was writing two

books under contract to Playboy Press. The whole family celebrated — in spite of Nixon and Kent State and Cambodia and everything, Tim Leary was free and there seemed to be some hope for this backward planet.

The Shaman's whole family had now become involved in yoga and magick; weirdness was commonplace. One day during the Mexican sojourn, the author was meditating and two of his daughters walked through the room without seeing him. We were all quite struck by this, at the time, although I do not think I was literally invisible (as some of Crowley's disciples claimed occasionally happened to him during heavy meditation). Rather, I feel fairly sure that what happened was merely that I was so silent, externally and internally, that I was as easy to ignore as a chair. I was not giving off a human vibration.

More puzzling was an incident involving my youngest daughter, Luna — who had always seemed, from birth onward, to have more intuition, ESP and strange powers than all the rest of us together. Luna was meditating in a room with our son, Graham, and our second-oldest daughter, Jyoti. Suddenly there was a thump which jarred Graham and Jyoti out of their trances. Luna, who had been on the right of them, was suddenly on the left. Naturally, they entered the belief-system that Luna had levitated, or teleported herself.

Luna said she couldn't remember moving.

I don't know *what* happened; I wasn't there. But when I discussed it with Luna, she said, "You believe in ESP, so it happens around you. You don't believe in levitation, so it doesn't happen around you." Then she laughed, and I felt — not for the first or last time — that Luna, whose favorite reading was still comic books, knew more about some things than I did.

I continued my devotions to Our Lady of Guadalupe, delighted that I could again play the Catholic game (which I had left in high indignation at 14, when it conflicted with my sex drive), but now without taking it seriously. It was only one tunnel-reality and, with Crowley's metaprograms (invocations), I could just as easily change channels and tune in to an Egyptian god-system or to the Buddhist system. I could also analyze all of these from outside, by re-entering the Scientific Materialist system.

Synchronicity again appeared. One day in the San Miguel library, I met a woman who was also obsessed with Nuestra Senora de Guadalupe even though a non-Catholic. She was writing a book on the Lady's miracles and hoped to prove that the Lady was really an extraterrestrial. Although I never heard of this woman or her book again, the idea later popped up in one of the most influential Women's Lib books of the decade. *The First Sex*, by Elizabeth Gould Davis. It is now an article of faith with some Welsh feminist witches I met after moving to California.

Sirius Rising

In his book on the Israeli psychic Uri Geller, Dr. Andrija Puharich, a neurologist of some professional reputation which he is presumably not eager to destroy by going out on a limb, asserts that both he and Geller have frequently received communications from extraterrestrials.[32] The learned community by and large assumes that Dr. Puharich has flipped out.

Dr. John Lilly, internationally known psychoanalyst, neuro-anatomist, cyberneticist, mathematician and delphinologist, gently hints that he has also received such communications. Academia, relieved that Dr. Lilly is only hinting and not saying it outright, happily ignores the potential breakthrough.[33]

Dr. Timothy Leary asserted interstellar telepathy in 1973.[34] Since Leary was already in disgrace and prison, nobody paid any attention.

R. Buckminster Fuller, the most renowned scientist-philosopher alive, was the next to state that he sometimes thinks he receives messages from interstellar telepaths.[35] Despite Fuller's world-wide status, nobody seems to have heard this message from him.

Most recently, Dr. Jack Sarfatti, physicist, described his own extraterrestrial ESP flashes, in an article in the San Francisco magazine *City*.[36] Nobody paid any attention. Any grocer or state policeman who has such an experience will immediately be reported in tabloids or even on TV, but nobody seems to want to hear this from trained scientific observers. Is it that we are afraid we cannot dismiss them as nuts so easily as we do the grocers and state troopers?

Suppose I were to tell you that *over 100 scientists* in the United States have by now had this experience? That figure was supplied by Saul Paul Sirag. Sirag says that so far most of these scientists are only willing to discuss the matter with trusted colleagues, but that more of them lately are considering the possibility of coming out of the closet and talking about it in public.

Sirag adds that many of this group no longer believe the experience is literally extraterrestrial, although that is still one of the favorite models for describing it.

Let me record my own "Contact" experiences, from the beginning. Try to be open to the possibility that I might conceivably be sane. The data developed gradually over the years from Jungian "synchronicity" to "ESP" to . . . something else.

For instance, in the summer of 1972, during a visit to Yellow Springs, Ohio — the town where I had tried to be a farmer for three years in the early '60s — I was doing a Tarot "divination" for my oldest daughter, Karuna. All Tarot readings to this date, however pleasing to my subjects, had been inconclusive to the Skeptic; every hit could be explained as intuition, reading the subject's body-language subliminally, or just lucky guessing. This time, the Oracle told Karuna — somewhat surprised at his own audacity — that her previous boyfriend, Roy, would suddenly contact her. (She hadn't seen him in a year.) The next morning, the phone rang, and the Shaman said at once, again surprised at his self-confidence, "That's Roy." It was.

A happy coincidence? My magick diary (Crowley insists on keeping such a record of all experiments) soon contained similar direct hits, on a weekly basis. The Oracle also developed what all occultists call "inner certainty"; that is, I knew when this faculty was operating and could be trusted. This sense of being tuned in is *exactly as specific* as the inner knowledge that you are about to become ill and vomit, or that a head cold is coming on, or that you are reaching sexual climax and will ejaculate . . . it cannot be mistaken.

January 18, 1973 was my 41st birthday, and we were living on a farm again. Karuna, our oldest daughter, informed us in the morning that, in addition to the sun being in Capricorn (my sign), the moon was in Cancer (my wife's sign). Although I am extremely skeptical about astrology, I decided to keep careful records of anything significant that might occur that day. A few hours after awakening, we heard on the radio that Tim Leary (nearly two years after escaping jail) had been kidnapped in Afghanistan by American agents. I was plunged into depression, and realized for the very first time how much I cared for that brilliant but incautious man, whom I had actually met fewer than a dozen times in the decade. A few hours later, Luna, our youngest daughter, had her first menstrual period. "The blood of the lamb," I thought, wondering what Carl Jung would make of this bundle of synchronicity.

In the afternoon, still depressed about Leary's bad luck, Arlen and I were walking in the woods behind our farm. Suddenly, I had a flash of Timothy grinning. ("They'll put him in maximum security now," Arlen was saying. "He'll probably commit suicide within a year.") Tim grinned more impudently.

"No," the Oracle said quite happily. "The very first photo we'll see he'll have the old Leary grin flashing again."

I was totally convinced, precognitively, that Dr. Leary's neurological researches had brought him to the point where he had control over emotional programs and could transcend suffering of all sorts. I "saw" it in a photo of Tim, handcuffed but grinning.

A few hours later, we drove into a pizza parlor in Mendocino to celebrate my birthday. On the way, we bought an evening newspaper. There, on page one, was the Leary Grin. And he was in handcuffs.

Dr. Timothy Leary, who received the Star Seed Signals during the Dog days when Wilson was receiving the Sirius Transmissions.

On June 6, 1973 (six months after the above experience), the Neurologician took a programmed trip on something an underground Alchemist told him was LSD. The program was in two parts, basically: I remained in a dark room, eyes closed, lying on a bed, during most of it. Part one was the playing back, on a tape recorder, of Dr. John Lilly's "Beliefs Unlimited" hypnosis-tape; this was repeated several times during the first three hours of the experiment. During hours 4 to 5, a tape of Aleister Crowley's Invocation of the Holy Guardian Angel was played.

Dr. Lilly's tape repeats over and over that there are no limits to your mind and that anything you can *imagine*, you can *do*. The tape is a valuable aid to break down our conditioned expectations about the boundary between the possible and the impossible.

Lilly's tape is deliberately encouraging gullibility, of course; but it is quite easy to re-establish scientific skepticism about results obtained, *after* the experiment is over. Skepticism *during* the experiment prevents any interesting results.

The Crowley invocation, frankly, looks like pretentious rubbish if read silently. Read aloud, it vibrates, moans and sings with eerie power. It programs the shaman to alternately envision the "Holy Guardian Angel" as a solar-phallic lion of terrible energy; as an erotic sex-goddess; as the Great Wild Beast Pan; as a green and earthy mother-spirit; and finally as a Total Void at the heart of everything.

The Shaman achieved a rush of Jungian archetypes, strongly influenced by the imagery of Crowley's Invocation, but nonetheless having that peculiar quality of external reality and *alien intelligence* emphasized by Jung in his discussion of the archetypes. I also "lived" through several "past lives" — including additional details about one "past life" as a Grandmaster in the Bavarian Illuminati, previously unearthed under hypnosis by New York hypnotist Jack Rowan, and also Sufi saint-lives, medieval witch-lives, and, finally, an uprush of "memories" of animal existence. I was an ape-creature, a rodent, a slug, a bug, a fish. I experienced a series of deaths-and-rebirths as animal, human, void, Star; molecular intelligence vibrating through time, and, at the peak, as union of Shiva and Kali, twin gods linked in eternal orgasm according to Bengali Hinduism. The Neurologician saw and understood quite distinctly that Shiva was also Brahma and Jehovah and Pan, etc., while Kali was also Nuit and Aphrodite and the Blessed Virgin Mary, etc. The universe was experienced as the living embodiment of this Divine Couple and not a dead machine.

The Yogi entered Samadhi and believed, at last, that the wisdom of the adept is truly beyond the floating body-rapture of mere Hatha Yoga. Based on *understanding of* and *participation in* a planet-wide Consciousness, Samadhi opens the neuro-atomic memory which is in all living beings, and in that dancing quantum energy mistakenly called "dead matter."

The Mystic understood Gandhi's insistence, "God is in the rock, too — *in the rock!"* Hell, *I* was in the rock with God.

The Poet appreciated Eckhart's paradox, "Split a stick of wood, and the Christ is in there, too!"

The Shaman laughed merrily at Crowley's joking seriousness in telling one disciple, Frank Bennett, that the Holy Guardian Angel invoked in this ritual is merely "our own unconsciousness" and meanwhile telling another disciple, Jane Wolf, that the Holy Guardian Angel is "a separate being of superhuman intelligence." It is both/and; it is the "bornless one," as Egyptian priests said. The Satirist even more appreciated Crowley's boffo one-liner in *Magick in Theory and Practice*, where he speaks of sexual yoga (in code as usual) as a form of sacrifice and says that he thus sacrificed "a male child of perfect innocence and high intelligence" 150 times a year since 1912. The sacrifice in sexual yoga is the semen, which is, indeed, a "male child" and does indeed contain, within the DNA code, a *very high intelligence*, the genetic blueprint of planet Earth.

The Robot staggered in bliss to his desk and typed out, "Few of our ancestors were perfect ladies and gentlemen. The majority of them weren't even mammals and looked like alligators or Gila monsters." The normal paranoia in our culture (fear of animals) has not bothered me since then; I took a pro-life imprint and I am now as cuddly with snakes as with dogs or cats.

The Shaman lost all fear of death, knowing it to be literally impossible. He understood the wit of Yeats's fine line, "Man has created death."

The Skeptic was whacked out of his skull.

The next day, and in the following weeks, my yoga meditations were vastly enriched, and I occasionally went for days on end conscious of the two minds thinking, my mind and the "bornless" Mind, or, as Suzuki Roshi used to say, Little Mind and Big Mind.

On July 22, 1973 — six weeks after the trip — the Wizard was ready to try again, without the supposed LSD (which might have been mescaline, or STP, or PCP, or fly-paper for all we know). (Stay AWAY from black-market acid, my friend; don't let these experiments lead you astray. If you must experiment in this dangerous area, use organic plants whose purity is known, such as the peyote cactus or the psilocybin mushroom.)

This time, I used the Lilly tape and the Crowley invocation again, without drugs, but with prolonged and holy rituals or Tantric sex-trance involving the cooperation of the Most Beautiful Woman in the Galaxy.

The Investigator remembers thinking, during the six weeks between major experiments, that whatever he had tuned in to was *not* "Cosmic Consciousness" but a kind of *planetary* consciousness; he wondered who coined the term, "cosmic consciousness," and what it contained . . .

This time I moved in space-time fan-wise, unlike the backward-in-time movement of the drug trip. The Yogi became almost conscious of a kind of galactic star-network, an intelligence that seemed not fully formed but *evolving*. Somehow, this resonated in my mind with the Sufi teaching that Allah is constantly recreating Himself every second. The trip was full of light and joy, the White Light of the Void jazz you've all heard, but dim, not fully achieved. The Researcher went off into sleep not quite satisfied.

The next morning, July *23*, the Shaman awoke with an urgent message from Dreamland and scribbled quickly in his magickal diary, "Sirius is very important." There was more, almost at the tip of my tongue, but I couldn't remember it.

Chapel Perilous,
like the mysterious entity called "I", cannot be located in the space-time continuum; it is weightless, odorless, tasteless and undetectable by ordinary instruments. Indeed, like the Ego, it is even possible to deny that it is there.

Everything you fear is waiting for you in Chapel Perilous, but fear is failure and the forerunner of failure.

During the A.M. I looked through my occult books, seeking references to the Dog Star, Sirius; although skeptical about astrology, I assumed that the Dream-message was some hint that the Sirius cycle should be part of my magick experiments in the future. Astrology seemed like nonsense to me, but I was willing to give it a try, in the open-ended manner of Dr. Lilly's "Beliefs Unlimited" exercise.

In *The Magical Revival* by Kenneth Grant, who is one of the five claimants to being Crowley's successor as world leader of the Ordo Templi Orientis, I found:

> Phoenix was Crowley's secret name in the Ordo Templi Orientis . . . . The Phoenix was also an ancient constellation in which Sothis, or Sirius, was the chief star . . .[37]

In a later passage, even more strikingly, Grant makes this point about Crowley and Sirius:

> Crowley identified the heart of (his magical) current with one particular Star. In Occult Tradition, this is "the Sun behind the Sun," the Hidden God, the vast star Sirius, or Sothis . . . [38]

This was interesting, no doubt, but, since I had already skimmed parts of Grant's book, it didn't *prove* anything.

Nonetheless, it was definitely intriguing. The Skeptic went to town and browsed in the public library. Imagine my state of mind when I discovered that this very day, July 23, when I had received the message "Sirius is very important," *is the day when, according to Egyptian tradition, the occult link (through hyperspace?) is most powerful between Earth and Sirius.*

Celebrations of the Dog Star, Sirius, beginning on July 23, are the origin of the expression "dog days," meaning the days from July 23 to September 8, when the last rituals to Sirius were performed.

The Skeptic was spaced-out for hours after reading that. Was it possible . . . had he actually, through Crowley's invocation, turned on and tuned in to an Earth-Sirius channel used by adepts since ancient Egypt?

Believe it or not, the very same day, July 23, "they," or "it," or whatever, delivered another jolt, just to underline the effect, perhaps. I picked up a book I'd started earlier in the week, Omar Garrison's *Tantra: The Yoga of Sex*, and found that, according to Bengali Tantrists, there is a five-day lag between the male and female sex-cycles, the female being 28 days and the male 23.[39]

Maybe my unconscious intuition, all through those years of noticing eerie 23s, had been groping to discover the Tantric 23-day male sex cycle.

Or maybe it had been struggling toward the annual July 23 Earth-Sirius synchro-mesh.

Maybe . . .

The Holy Guardian Angel

How the elephant got into my pajamas I'll never know.

— Marx, *Animal Crackers*

Once I began to perceive the mystic 23 as a central pivot of both the Crowley-Tantra linkage and the Crowley-Sirius linkage, I was living in a belief-system where almost anything might happen and probably would.

("Perhaps the final secret of the Illuminati is that you don't know you're a member until it's too late to get out.")

I re-examined my "memories" of having been in the Illuminati in the 18th century. According to data unearthed by hypnotist Jack Rowan in 1971, and again during my June 1973 invocation of the Holy Guardian Angel, I had been one "Hans Zoesser" (1740-1812), Grand Master of the Vienna lodge, and had participated in the initiation of Thomas Jefferson, no less, in Paris. The Skeptic didn't even believe in reincarnation, but neural storage certainly could remember key incidents in Zoesser's life as well as any in "Robert Anton Wilson's" life. Was the whole purpose of this four-dimensional coincidence-hologram to make "me" realize that both "Hans Zoesser" and "Robert Anton Wilson" were fictions? Many people have had the experience of not knowing *who* they are or *where* they are; it usually happens in the first moments after awakening in the morning. The Sufis say that you are closer to Illumination in that instant of micro-amnesia than at any other time.

Was this at last the illumination of the Illuminati — the experience of skepticism carried to the point where it abolishes itself and, since you can't believe anything fully, you are as free of skepticism as of any other philosophy and finally open to thinking the unthinkable?

Or was the final secret simply and bluntly that there really is an interstellar ESP channel to which you can tune in by metaprogramming your nervous system?

At this point in the internal voyage the Shaman knows that he is far, far into the underground vaults of Chapel Perilous and that the way back to the robot-reality of the domesticated hive is not going to be easy. Or as a black pot-head once said to me (in an earlier period when I was playing Young White Hipster who hangs around with jazz musicians), "Man, you only know you are laid, relayed and PARlayed, fucked, flustered and far from home."

It was necessary to conduct some experiments to determine that one was still able to communicate effectively with the hive — with those locked into what Blake called "single Vision and Newton's sleep." When it was established that such communication had not broken down, the Shaman and the Skeptic conferred at length, decided we were not actually going mad, and continued occult experimentation. The Neuro-Metaprogrammer adopted a belief system in which there was a real contact going on with Higher Intelligence — i.e., with the extraterrestrial from Sirius — or with the Holy Guardian Angel — or whatever it was . . .

Some of the intensified experiences were "merely subjective," but nonetheless tremendously important to the Author, in ways that even the Skeptic would admit were non-pathological. For instance, on one occasion, the entity spoke directly, in a melodious and angelic voice, to say,

They live happiest who have forgiven most.

This is rather trite, one admits; all the major religions preach forgiveness. What was impressive was (a) the timing — the Struggling Writer was very pissed off, that week, at certain publishers who were slow in paying monies owed; and (b) the pragmatic emphasis, tailored to the Libertarian's hedonic philosophy at the time. It did not say, "Forgive, *because 'God' demands it"*; it said, "Forgive, *and you will be happier."* The Libertarian Hedonist tried it, and still is trying it, and it works. The fewer resentments you harbor, the happier your life will be. Why are we all such fools as to ignore this obvious lesson, which a truly rational person would have figured out by the age of 8 or 9, if not sooner?

Other experiences were more objective. One day in 1974, when another publisher was late with monies owed, the Shaman decided to try a ritual of money-magick, to cause the check to arrive in Monday's mail. In the climax of the ritual, It spoke again, in the same richly solemn "angelic" voice, saying, "Thursday." This was accompanied by a vision of the check in the mailbox. The Skeptic immediately communicated the prophecy to Arlen and to two neighbors, Charles Hixson and Stephen McAuley, who will confirm this.

The check did arrive on Thursday.

Mostly, the Holy Guardian Angel still communicated by synchronicity. I would look on page 23 of a new magazine, and there would be a line from a dream of the night before. I must admit that most of these messages were nauseatingly moralistic and childishly optimistic by the standards of our cynical, swinish and despairing age. A lot of them involved the paradoxes of time.

Occasionally, the Angel would speak, to give me utterly trivial information. For instance, I'd meet somebody and the Angel would say, "Gemini." I would ask, to check out the Angel's credibility, "Are you a Gemini?" The answer would be yes. These cases I firmly classified as my own mind expanding its ESP powers through the convenient fiction of an alien entity, and I disliked them intensely, as show-offy, corny and tending to turn me into a damned carnival act.

Then, abruptly, the entity would be quite exterior again, manifesting when I was depressed or worried, to pass on messages of cheer and love that were too moving to be ignored.

I could not help but be grateful to it, whatever the hell it was.

Beings of Light, talking dogs, more extraterrestrials and other weird critters

The entity or entities contacted by me during July 1973-October 1974 had most of the characteristics of the "being of light" described by persons who have been resuscitated after what is called near-death experience. Dr. Raymond Moody has collected 150 cases of this sort of vision, including many by persons who were declared "clinically dead" during the interlude.[40]

Many cases showed real ESP — the revived subjects remember things they couldn't have observed while in the state of coma or clinical death, including things in other rooms of the hospital. Christians generally describe the "being of light" as Jesus, Jews as "an angel," and nonbelievers agnostically say it is luminous, telepathic and *intensely loving*. The author found it to possess all of these qualities and also a damned peculiar sense of humor. For instance, it talked apparent gibberish at times (just like the alleged extraterrestrials encountered by Uri Geller and Dr. Puharich). Most of the seeming gibberish concerned *time, the future,* and *infinity*, three phenomena on which everybody, including our greatest philosophers, seems to talk nonsense. But the entity always intently urged that I should try to understand *time* better.

I often had the feeling that the communicating entity was not incoherent at all but, rather, one's own mind could not grasp what it was trying to communicate.

This is typical of UFOs and of Fortean phenomena generally. Let us give some examples of the experience of others.

I. Consider the following illuminating dialogue between a "UFOnaut" and a human being:

UFOnaut: What time is it?

Human: Two-thirty.

UFOnaut: You lie. It is four o'clock.

This incident occurred in France in 1954, and the UFO sped away immediately after the dialogue. The time actually was 2:30.[41]

Why did the "UFOnaut" ask the time if It knew the answer already? Why lie about it, when the human had a watch and could detect the lie? Are we being invaded by the galactic equivalent of the Marx Brothers maybe? And why that damned 23 in 2:30?

Is somebody using Zen Discordianism to illuminate us?

II. One day in 1908, a dog walked up to two police detectives on a street in Pittsburgh, said "Good morning" politely, and then vanished in a puff of green smoke.[42]

In keeping with modern cybernetic models of neurological processes, we can recount this story more objectively by saying that *certain signals* received by the nervous system of the detectives were *organized by their metaprogrammer* into *an impression* of a dog saying "Good morning" and vanishing in a puff of green smoke.

In keeping with the same cybernetic approach, it would not be perfectly objective to say that you are reading a book. Rather, you are *receiving signals which your metaprogrammer is organizing into the impression* that you are reading a book.

III. In Brazil in 1971, two young men were riding in an automobile when they *had the impression* that a bus was pulling up rather closely behind them. Then their metaprogrammers diverged. One man had the impression that a flying saucer landed. He thought he was taken aboard and had the usual "trip to an alien planet." Next he found himself standing behind his car, which somebody had parked by the side of the road. The other man had the impression of a lapse of memory (or a jump in time?) and simply found himself standing behind the car, with no recollection of who had stopped the car or how or when he had gotten out of it.[43]

There are at least three models for this experience.

One, a flying saucer grabbed both of them, experimented upon them, and then used a defective "memory-erasing machine," which malfunctioned and only worked to erase the memory of one of the victims.

Two, there was some kind of abnormality in the Earth's electronic or magnetic field at that spot which administered a traumatic shock. One victim had a hallucination of a flying saucer, and the other had a blackout.

Three, "They" (sinister experimenters) were in that enigmatic bus that came so close just before the mindfuck. "They" turned some kind of "mindfucking" machine on the two men . . .

More pancakes from outer space . . .?

Let's go back to those unfortunate detectives in Pittsburgh again and try it another way: An extraterrestrial scientist, with a parapsychology only a few million years ahead of ours, sent a *thought-projection* of a talking dog onto that street and then made it vanish in a puff of green smoke. He wanted to see how two trained detectives would react when their reality-model was abruptly contradicted. (This abrupt contradiction of a person's reality-model is known, in psychology, as *cognitive dissonance*. Those subjected to it tend to become either very flexible and agnostic or very rigid and schizophrenic.)

To paraphrase Charles Fort, we all like to think of ourselves as skeptical and hard to bamboozle, but if we contemplate a few more talking-dog and astral-pancake stories, the reader will find it hard to resist taking at least one peek around the room to see what Damned Thing might have gotten in during the last few minutes.

Starseed
The next step in whatever is wrong with me again involved

Timothy Leary.

I was conducting a series of experiments in July-August 1973 — following the Sirius Transmission — in which I attempted astral projection. I met all sorts of odd and amusing entities on all sorts of astral planes, but none of those experiences ever developed into anything evidential. However, I was continually interrupted during my voyages by impressions of Leary doing similar experiments in his cell at Folsom. I also had visions of him flying over the walls of the prison.

I specifically mentioned these experiences of ESP-contact with Leary in an article on Tantric yoga, published in the Chicago *Seed* in September 1973.*

◆

* Copies of the *Seed* can be found in the collection of radical and underground political publications at Northwestern University in Evanston, Illinois.

◆

It was *four years later*, in 1977, that Lynn Wayne Benner, who was Leary's closest friend in Folsom, told me of the events of that August of 1973. According to Benner, Leary and he were not only doing the interstellar ESP experiments described below but also tried experiments at levitation, in which they attempted to *fly over the walls* of Folsom.

I wrote to the warden of Folsom in late August, and asked for permission to correspond with Dr. Leary. Bureaucratic red tape being what it is, this permission was delayed for several weeks.

Shortly after the telepathic flashes of Leary (July-August 1973) ended, Walter Culpepper, the attorney for P.R.O.B.E. — a Leary-created organization to abolish prisons-had a benefit for the Leary Defense Fund and P.R.O.B.E. Two rock groups played and then we were shown "At Folsom Prison With Timothy Leary, Ph.D.," produced by Joanna Leary.

The film blew the Skeptic's mind. Timothy came on screen and immediately flashed the famous Love-Peace-Bliss grin at the camera — as if he were greeting visitors to his home. We never saw a man look less like a suffering martyr. Tim took a chair and answered the interviewer's questions in a serious and thoughtful manner, explaining that he wasn't interested in drugs any more since they had only been "microscopes" to him: tools to reveal the focus and re-focus possibilities of the nervous system. He wanted to talk about something more exciting now — *Outer Space*. The interviewer kept leading him back to drugs, and Leary kept maneuvering back to Cosmic Dimensions.

I began to notice an odd thing: Timothy looked younger than he had in the 1960s.

Tim led the interviewer to ask about the strange design on his prison uniform. "This is Starseed," Tim said, proud as a new father. The emblem was that strange miniature infinity-sign, the nucleotide template formed as DNA imprints messenger-RNA to start a new growth program.

Starseed, however, was not just *any* nucleotide template. It was the one recently found on a meteor which landed in Orgeuil, France, when scientists examined the rock microscopically. It is the first chemical proof that the mechanism of chemical "intelligence" — the building of life-programs (RNA) out of information-codes (DNA) — exists elsewhere in the universe.

Starseed, Leary enthusiastically told the interviewer, proves that cellular intelligence is not exclusively earthly. It therefore increases the probable grounds to believe many forms of life and intelligence exist in space-time.

Other cons in Folsom, after Leary left, picked up the Starseed symbol, carved it on belts, painted it on sketch-pads, sewed it on clothing, and formed bull sessions to rap with Hal Olsen (life-termer, illustrator of Leary's *Terra II*) and Wayne Benner ("the Tuxedo Bandit" and one unit in Leary's four-person telepathy experiments) about the possibility of Higher Intelligence and the transcendental implications of modern science.

I meanwhile went on researching Sirius. I was quite moved, as you will readily understand, when I found the following in O.T.O. Grand Master Kenneth Grant's new book, *Aleister Crowley and the Hidden God:*

> Crowley was aware of the possibility of opening the spatial gateways and of admitting an extraterrestrial Current into the human life-wave . . .

It is an occult tradition — and Lovecraft gave it persistent utterance in his writings — that some transfinite
and superhuman power is marshaling its forces with intent
to invade and take possession of this planet . . . This is
reminiscent of Charles Fort's dark hints about a secret society on earth already in contact with cosmic beings and,
perhaps, preparing the way for their advent. * [44]

♦

* Grant here quotes, in a footnote, from Fort's *The Book of the
Damned*, " . . . some other world is not attempting but has been,
for centuries, in communication with a sect, perhaps, or a secret
society, or certain esoteric ones of this earth's inhabitants."

♦

This sounds more than a little sinister, and was especially
eerie for me, since I had already incorporated into *Illuminatus* a
variation on the Lovecraft mythos. Lovecraft has written several
stories and novelettes in which the "Cthulhu cult" or some other
secret society was aiding the schemes of hostile Aliens; I had
attached this theme to the Illuminati as a kind of deadpan put-
on and laughed like hell at the thought that some naive readers
would be dumb enough to believe it. Now here it was being
proclaimed by Kenneth Grant, who alleges that the Ordo Templi
Orientis was formed in the 1890s by amalgamating P.B. Ran-
dolph's Hermetic Brotherhood of Light with the original Bavarian Illuminati. I thought for the first time (as I was to think again,
many times, during the Watergate Scandals), "My God, can't I
invent any preposterous paranoid fantasy that doesn't have some
truth behind it?" But Grant goes on to cheer us up, if we are willing to trust him at this point:

> Crowley dispels the aura of evil with which these
> authors (Lovecraft and Fort) invest the fact; he prefers to
> interpret it Thelemically, not as an attack upon human con-
> sciousness by an extra-terrestrial and alien entity but as an
> expansion of consciousness from within, to embrace other
> stars and to absorb their energies into a system that is
> thereby enriched and rendered truly cosmic by the process.

And then he adds, quite nonchalantly again, that one star is
especially important:

The Order of the Silver Star is thus the Order of the Eye of Set, "the Sun behind the Sun." . . . The Silver Star is Sirius.[45]

Magick, Technology or Both?

It is interesting, at this point, to attempt to argue, at least tentatively, that the phenomena we are discussing are reducible to Jung's categories of the "collective unconscious" and synchronicity. Certainly, these Jungian notions cover a great deal of whatever-the-hell-is-going-on, but they do not cover *all* of it. Jung was brilliantly right in saying, in the 1950s, that the flying saucer phenomenon would become "an important spiritual and religious transformation of humanity."[46] — and many UFOlogists, including Jacques Vallee and John Keel, have noted that the majority of Contactees eventually became embroiled in mystical or occult groups, sometimes even as the founders of Messianic new cults. But let nobody assume that the weirdness is, therefore, "merely" subjective.

UFOs have been reported by NASA missions in the following list.[47]

~Feb. 20, 1962: John Glenn, Mercury capsule flight. Three UFOs followed him.

~May 24, 1962: Scott Carpenter, Mercury VII. Photograph taken by Carpenter of UFO he saw.

~May 30, 1962: Joe Walton, X15. Photograph taken by Walton of five UFOs.

~July 17, 1962: Robert White, X15. White photographed several UFOs

~May 16, 1963: Gordon Cooper, Mercury IX. Cooper saw a green UFO, also tracked by radar on the ground.

~October 3, 1963: Walter Schirra, Mercury VIII. Schirra reported several UFOs.

~March 8, 1964: Russian Voshkod II. One UFO reported.

~June 3, 1964: Jim McDivitt, Gemini IV. McDivitt photographed several UFOs.

~November 14, 1969: Apollo XII. Conrad, Bean and Gordon reported a UFO that followed them from Earth to within 130,000 miles of the moon.

[This is only a partial list from *The Edge of Reality*, by J. Allen Hynek and Jacques Vallee, Regnery: Chicago, 1975.]

NASA cases fall in the category of craft that look and act like spaceships from elsewhere, as Dr. Hynek, who collected them from Air Force files, has indicated. The trouble is that Hynek and Vallee, in the same book, have numerous cases of things that behave in a way that no machine can possibly behave — jumping around at impossible accelerations or appearing and disappearing like a ghost in a horror movie. As Vallee, Keel and others have emphasized, the UFO is an adaptable beast, acting in a technological fashion when dealing with technologists and acting occult when dealing with occultists. Brad Steiger proposes that the only safe generalization about UFOs is that they always fit into the cosmology of the human observer . . .

I even read a Freudian once, somewhere, who pointed out that the UFOs come in two major types — round, discoid ones and long, cigar-shaped ones. The round ones, he said, were breast symbols and the long ones were phallic symbols.

Maybe.

Those mysterious Sufis

A man without God is like a fish without a bicycle.
— Found on the men's room wall, Larry Blake's Pub,
Berkeley, 1977

Before the summer of 1973 ended, the spookiness accelerated.

Illuminatus, still unsold two years after completion, was being proven partially true in the daily headlines. Shea and I had based our ultra-paranoid version of government on two main sources: (1) our own surrealistic imaginations and (2) letters to "The Playboy Forum" by individuals complaining that the government was conspiring to destroy their civil liberties. The latter, of course, were subdivided, by ourselves and by Nat Lehrman and the executives of the Playboy Foundation, into two sub-classes: (a) the documented or documentable cases by sane individuals who really were catching hell from Nixon's counter-revolution and (b) the obviously paranoid who were imagining vast and incredible world-wide plots. Only (a) got into the Forum or received financial aid from the Playboy Foundation; (b), however, served the purposes of *Illuminatus*. If a story was paranoid enough, we adapted it into our epical satire, which was supposed to portray the most totally evil and devious government that the most clinical paranoid could imagine.

Every day in 1973 the Watergate story made headlines. Every day it appeared that the worst, the most absurd, the most incredible, the most depraved ideas in *Illuminatus* were the actual policies of the Nixon regime. *We had tried to imagine Total Evil combined with Total Stupidity, but Nixon had actually lived out our fantasies.*

The Shaman began to wonder: were all the paranoids right, or was his ESP more highly developed than he had ever dared imagine?

Meanwhile, I was getting poorer and poorer, and began to regret bitterly that I had quit *Playboy*. I had been on unemployment for six months once, in my early 30s, and that was unpleasant. I always knew that I would be employed again, soon, and would be a great author some day. Now, the Poor Fool found himself unemployed, not selling any of his writings for months on end, and forced to apply for Welfare. I was brutally turned down, and spent nearly a whole day seriously considering the possibility that I, my wife and our four children might actually starve to death. It could happen; it *did* happen occasionally in this great and prosperous nation; and it was commonplace in Asia.

The Fool appealed and got on Welfare. It was not only bloody unpleasant but Goddamned frightening. A man in his 40s does not have the optimism of a man in his 30s. The Fool began to wonder if he would ever get *off* Welfare . . . if *Illuminatus* would *ever* be published . . . if he had finally arrived at the bottom of the heap in America, the True Failure *(Americanus Nondesirabilis)*.

I was continuing to investigate the Illuminati, now filtering the evidence through the hypothesis that they were a group of mystics who functioned as secret societies, not only because they were using sexual yoga (as I had deduced from Crowley's writings in 1971) but also because they had contact with Higher Intelligences elsewhere in space-time. Naturally, Metaprogramming Center found evidence to support this.

Akron Daraul, in his *History of Secret Societies*, traces the Illuminati back to the Ishmaelian sect of Islam, a *quasi-Sufic* organization which used sex-and-hashish to program higher states of consciousness. Louis Culling also traces Crowley's magick tradition back to *medieval Sufis* who were contemporaries of, and presumably influenced by, the Ishmaelians. Francis King, the leading (non-paranoid) occult historian of our time, quotes official Ordo Templi Orientis documents, written either by Crowley or under Crowley's supervision, which claim that the O.T.O. was founded by Mansur el Hallaj, a medieval *Sufi* saint.[48]

The Sufis have always claimed to be in communication with Higher Intelligences, just like the early Gnostics, from whom many historians believe Sufism derives. A Sufi philosopher, Idries Shah, in a book of strange parables called *The Dermis Probe*, says his purpose is to illustrate "some of the peculiarities of thought in the country which is today's world, seen by its inhabitants *and by those who call themselves visitors.* " (Italics added.)[49]

As soon as the Fool entered the belief-system in which the

Illuminati were Sufis living in the Western world and continuing this millennia-old contact with Higher Intelligence, the phenomenon intersecting his life adjusted itself to support this theory. He had a weird experience with a Sufi.

My son Graham went to Berkeley to visit with friends for the summer. He was supposed to phone home once a week, but of course he didn't always do so. One day, I got a lecture engagement at the First Unitarian Church in Berkeley and Arlen asked me to try to find Graham and insure that he was not in any trouble. Finding one 14-year-old boy in a city the size of Berkeley is not easy, but after my lecture I tried wandering around, hoping my ESP would click into action and direct me on the right path.

Greg Hill, Bill Broadbent and I wandered into Tilden Park, watching some clowns perform. Graham was not in the crowd, so I wanted to move on. Bill insisted that we wait a while. The Shaman became interested in one particular clown, Parcifal, recognizing some of his stunts as Sufi exercises to activate higher-circuit consciousness.

The Sufis are notorious for disguising themselves as clowns, but this was the first time I had actually seen it done.

"That guy's a Sufi," I said to Greg and Bill.

After the act, Greg went up to Parcifal and asked directly, "Are you a Sufi?"

"Are you also on the Path?" Parcifal rejoined.

"No," Greg said, indicating me, "*he* said you're a Sufi."

Parcifal turned. "Are *you* on the Path?" he asked.

"Well, I'm on some Path or other," I said. We got into a rap about Sufism and the Western occult tradition and how both link up with Gnosticism and the Egyptian mysteries. Finally, the Father said, "I have to leave. I'm looking for my son."

"You'll find him," Parcifal said.

The Father walked about ten paces and *saw* Graham sitting in Hardcastle's restaurant on Telegraph Avenue.

"We're going back to Telegraph," I told Bill and Greg.

The trip took a half-hour. When we arrived, Graham and two friends had just entered before us. *Graham was not in Hardcastle's when I saw him there. The Oracle had seen across time as well as across space.*

Graham, Greg Hill and Bill Broadbent will all confirm this story. Good old Martin Gardner, spokesman for the Fundamentalist wing of the Materialist church, will say they're all liars. So it goes.

That evening, the Numerologist looked up "Parcifal" in Crowley's *Cabalah*, just for the hell of it. Cabalah, of course, is all superstition and nonsense, but it is alleged, by those who believe in it, to be a decoding system for discovering the occult meaning of strange events. By Cabalah, Parcifal = 418 = "The Great Work Accomplished," i.e., the total awakening of all humanity.

When I tried to find Parcifal again, he had left America, He was in Israel, other Sufis told me, operating a home for Jewish and Arab children orphaned in the continuous Israeli-Arab wars.

A message from Cosmic Central?

In October 1973, I finally received permission to begin corresponding with Dr. Leary at Folsom Prison. I started out with a letter about the general philosophical implications of tuning the nervous system to higher fidelity of signal-reception and very carefully did *not* mention my July 23 experience with Sirius. (I was fairly sure that my July-August impressions that Timothy was doing telepathic experiments had been accurate, but I had no idea yet that he was attempting *interstellar* telepathy.) Tim's answer was full of characteristic humor:

> The prison administration is perfect. They act as a Van Allen belt protecting my privacy, screening out distractions . . . The people they refuse visiting privileges are exactly those people who come to exploit me or whose love for me is flawed.

> (My gratitude toward the prison warden must not be misunderstood. They are too possessive and jealous —

terrible states to be in. Their love and dependence on me are too restricting. They are terrorized that I might leave them . . . in the lurch, so to say. This is unhealthy for them . . .)

I wrote back, but remained mum about Sirius. Instead, just for the hell of it, I used my official Discordian Society letterhead. The stationery bears the imprint of the Joshua Norton Cabal, this being a Cabal of the Discordian Society located in the Bay Area — other Cabals including the Tactile Temple of Eris Erotic in Los Angeles, the Colorado Encrustation in Denver, the John Dillinger Died for You Society in Chicago, etc. Timothy, however, seems to have thought Joshua Norton Cabal was the name of a living person. Actually, Joshua Norton — or Norton I, as he preferred — was a San Franciscan of the last century who elected himself Emperor of the United States and Protector of Mexico. Bay Area historians still argue as to whether Norton was a psychotic or a clever con-man; in any event, he was "humored" by the citizenry of the time and, in effect, lived like an Emperor. As Greg Hill, co-founder of Discordianism, has written, "Everybody understands Mickey Mouse. Few understand Herman Hesse. Hardly anybody understands Einstein. And nobody understands Emperor Norton." (The Discordian Society, we repeat again, is not a complicated joke disguised as a new religion but really a new religion disguised as a complicated joke.)

Timothy replied:

Dear Bob . . .

Quick response . . . to indicate that transmission is working well from this galaxy to yours.

Your stationery amazed me . . . could you explain any of it? Like ODD3140Aft1 1bii? And who is Joshua Norton Cabal?

Actually the Warden here is very protective of me. He is like a gruff Zen abbot: He doesn't want me to be bothered with visits or correspondence which would bring me down, slow up my scientific work etc. As long as I sit in my cell and write science fiction books . . . everyone is happy.

Yes, G.I. Gurdjieff is my direct predecessor. I have never doubted that his baraka was transferred to me . . . perhaps by some intermediary. I love Him and I resonate to his wisdom more than anyone else's.

Crowley . . . the coincidences-synchronicities between my life and His are embarrassing. Brian Barritt and I had a visionary experience Easter Sat-Sun in Bou Saada, the Algerian town where C. had his. Etc.

The Libertarian wrote back discussing the odd links between Leary's work and that of Crowley and Gurdjieff, and mentioning the evidence that the latter two were *both* taught certain advanced techniques of consciousness-expansion by the Sufi lodges of the Near East. He also mentioned that Rasputin might have had the same sort of Sufi training during his wanderings.

Leary's reply blew his mind:

Dear Bob . . .

Loved your letter . . .

Are you in touch with teachings, methods, teachers, etc. that transmit Higher Intelligence that you are totally hooked into?

If so, would you tell me.

I don't believe in secrets . . .

I believe that Higher Intelligence can be contacted and have described how to do it and what They transmit, etc. Have you contacted Joanna? Ask Her to send you a copy of Terra II.

You mention that Crowley, G. and Rasputin may have had contact with some Sufi lodge. Do you think this "lodge" actually exists in the human sense of Masters in the Middle East who send G and C and R out as emissaries? This is the most exciting idea I've puzzled over for ten years.

I have seen what can be transmitted through one unit. The one that I belonged to. Where are the others? . . .

I am amazed that you haven't contacted Michael Horowitz.

Mike Horowitz, a thin, intense, brilliant guy, is Director of the Fitzhugh Ludlow Memorial Library in San Francisco — a psychopharmacological archive full of rare literature on drugs — scientific, propagandistic (government), literary, or just journalistic. When the Investigator got in touch with Mike Horowitz, he heard, for the first time, about the Starseed Transmissions.

Meanwhile, Dr. Leary was shifted from Folsom to Vacaville and communication with him temporarily shorted-out. Once again, I had to apply for permission to correspond, fill out the right forms when they were finally mailed, and then wait for the new warden's decision. The Libertarian felt increasingly like one of the scholars of the Middle Ages, trying to keep up communication with a fellow investigator while the Holy Inquisition created as much static as possible.

It should be remembered, in evaluating the Starseed signals, that, a few months before this experience, three government psychiatrists testified (at the escape trial) that Dr. Leary was perfectly sane and possessed a high I.Q. Since so many extremists of Left and Right have impugned Dr. Leary's sanity, it should also be entered in the record that Dr. Wesley Hiler, a staff psychologist at Vacaville, who spoke to Dr. Leary every day (often to ask Tim's advice) emphatically agrees with that verdict. "Timothy Leary is totally, radiantly sane," he told me in a 1973 interview.

As recounted in *Terra II*, during July-August 1973, Dr. Leary had formed a four-person telepathy team in an attempt to contact Higher Intelligences elsewhere in the galaxy. (This was in the middle of the "dog days," when I was having my first (real or hallucinatory) Contacts with Sirius.) The persons involved were: Dr. Leary and his wife, Joanna; fellow prisoner Wayne Benner: and Wayne's girlfriend, a journalist who prefers to be known as Guanine.

The Starseed Transmissions — "hallucinations" or what-ever — were received in 19 bursts, seldom in recognizable English sentences, requiring considerable meditation and discussion between the four Receivers before they could be summarized, eventually, into the following message:

It is time for life on Earth to leave the planetary womb

and learn to walk through the stars.

Life was seeded on your planet billions of years ago by nucleotide templates which contained the blueprint for gradual evolution through a sequence of biomechanical stages.

The goal of evolution is to produce nervous systems capable of communicating with and returning to the Galactic Network where we, your interstellar parents, await you.

Life on planet Earth has now reached this halfway point, established itself, and evolved through larval mutations and metamorphoses to the seven brain stages.

At this time the voyage home is possible.

Assemble the most intelligent, advanced, courageous of your species, divided equally between men and women. Let every race, nationality, and religion be represented.

You are about to discover the key to immortality in the chemical structure of the genetic code, within which you will find the scripture of life. The time has come for you to accept the responsibility of immortality. It is not necessary for you to die.

You will discover the key to enhanced intelligence within the chemistry of the nervous system. Certain chemicals, used wisely, will enable your nervous system to decipher the genetic code.

All life on your planet is a unity. All life must come home.

Total freedom, responsibility and interspecies harmony will make the voyage possible. You must transcend larval identities of race, culture and nationality.

Your only allegiance is to life. The only way you will survive is to make the voyage home.

The Japanese people are the most advanced race on your planet and will give protection to the company.

We are sending a comet to your solar system as a sign that the time has come to look to the stars.

When you arrive back home you will be given new instructions and powers. Your sperm ship is the flower of terrestrial life. As soon as the company is formed and the voyage begun, war, poverty, hatred, fear will disappear from your planet and the most ancient prophecies and celestial visions will be realized.

Mutate!

Come home in glory.

In the following months. Comet Kohoutek, as predicted in the Transmissions, arrived in the solar system and sped inward toward the sun, while astronomers announced an unprecedented spectacle and Leary's disciples chortled at the confirmation. Then the comet fizzled, leaving us wondering.

Some Egyptian gods intrude on the narrative and Our Lady of Space speaks again

In 1904, in one of the most extraordinary magickal experiences of his life, Aleister Crowley contacted a Higher Intelligence named Aiwass, who dictated to him *The Book of the Law*. In what follows, we will show some imagistic links between this Book and the Starseed Signals — but first, a few details about how Crowley received this strange document:

Aleister and his first wife, Rose, were in Cairo, Egypt, when Rose began going spontaneously into trances and muttering "They are waiting for you," and similar urgent but unintelligible phrases. Crowley did not like this at all, since it is typical of the uncontrolled, quasi-hysterical trances of spiritualist mediums (whom he despised) and lacked the elements of *willed concentration and rational control* that he demanded of his magick experiments. Nonetheless, despite his attempts to banish the phenomenon, it kept coming back, and finally, in one of Rose's trances, Crowley set a series of tests for the alleged communicating entity. He asked Rose, for instance, to describe the aura of the being, and she said "deep blue"; he asked the character of the being, and she said "force and fire"; he asked her to pick

the being from drawings of ten Egyptian gods, and she picked
Horus. She also identified Horus' planet (Mars), and so forth for
a series of similar questions. Crowley then calculated the odds
against her being right in all cases — for instance, guessing Mars
had a 1/9 probability, there being 9 planets, picking Horus out of
10 drawings had a 1/10 probability, etc. The chance of her guessing right on the whole series by chance was, mathematically,
1/21,168,000. (The long-suffering skeptical reader may resist the
"reality" of Horus by accepting the less bizarre theory that Rose
was simply reading Aleister's mind.)

The next day, Crowley took Rose to the Boulak Museum
and asked her to identify the communicant from the statues and
paintings there. She walked past several depictions of Horus —
the ever-cynical Aleister watching, he says, in "silent glee" —
and then stopped at a stele showing a *dark woman* bending over
a *winged globe, a hawk-headed god* and a human male. "This is
the one," she said, pointing to the hawk-headed god, Horus. The
stele was numbered 666 by the museum officials, and that was
a synchronicity that got Aleister's immediate attention. He had
been using 666 as his own magick number for years.[50]

Crowley decided to cooperate, and back at his hotel accepted
a light trance in which *The Book of the Law* was dictated to him
in a "rich baritone" by an invisible being. The book opens:

Had! The manifestation of Nuit.

The unveiling of the company of heaven.

Every man and every woman is a star.

Nuit, *the Egyptian divinity of the stars*, seems to tell us, in
these opening verses, that we are Her children. She goes on to
declare:

I am above you and *in* you. My ecstasy is in yours.

My joy is to see your joy. [Italics added.]

The union of mankind with the stars is precisely forecast:

They shall gather my children into their fold; they shall
bring the glory of the stars into the hearts of men.

Stele 666 from the Boulak museum, Cairo. The goddess is Nuit, the deity Horus, and the human appears to be one Ankh-f-na-Khonsu, a priest, whose tomb this originally adorned. Note the winged globe, and see the next illustrations some paragraphs from here.

And the sign shall be my ecstasy, the consciousness of the continuity of existence, the omnipresence of my body . . .

For I am divided for love's sake, for the chance of union.

This seems a vividly poetic pre-statement of Leary's theory that Higher Intelligence is "divided," by sending out DNA seed to fertilize every womb-planet in the galaxy, "for the chance of union," the return of these "children" after they have evolved past the larval circuits into higher modes of consciousness.

I love you! I yearn to you! . . . Put on the wings, and arouse the coiled splendor within you: *come unto me!* [Italics added.]

The Star-Mother, Nuit, is definitely calling us home, to Galactic Center. The "coiled splendor" may even suggest the DNA helix within which, Leary and other investigators now think, is the secret of immortality. But shortly comes a more interesting text:

Is a God to live in a dog?

A reference to the great Dog Star, Sirius? Instructions on contacting this Intelligence are quite specific:

To worship me take wine and strange drugs whereof I will tell my prophet & be drunk thereof!

The Immortality Pill is directly mentioned:

Think not, 0 King, upon that lie: That Thou Must Die: verily thou shalt not die, but live.

In Chapter Three, Horus, the war-god, takes over and makes some ferocious predictions about the 20th century:

Now let it be understood first that I am a god of War and Vengeance. I shall deal hardly with them . . .

I am the Warrior Lord of the Forties; the Eighties cower before me & are abased.[51]

Now, this is not terribly bad as prophecy of the 20th century, for a book produced in 1904 — when the majority opinion of Europe was that war had been banished from the civilized nations forever.

It seems clear that the Starseed Transmissions acquired a rather heavy Timothy Leary flavor in passing through the Leary nervous system, just as the *Book of the Law* took on an undeniably Crowleyan aroma in passing through Aleister's neurons; but the underlying message is hauntingly similar.

A few other oddities about the *Book of the Law* and the Stele of Revealing are worth noting. Crowley was an avid Cabalist and spent years examining the Cabalistic numbers for key words in the text. This is based on the traditional assumption that Cabalistic numerology is a code worked out millennia ago for communication between humans and Higher Intelligence. Be as cynical about that as you will, but consider the data: All the important words, Crowley gradually realized, had the value of 93 in Greek Cabala. (He thereafter referred to his magick work as "the 93 current," and Crowleyans to this day speak of their work as carrying on the 93 current.)

93 is also the cabalistic numeration of the word *Thelema*, the "word" of the New Age, according to the communicating entity. The Abbey of *Thelema*, in Rabelais, had the motto "Do what thou wilt." *The Book of the Law* says, "Do what thou wilt shall be the whole of the law." Thelema, in Greek, means either *will* or *the casting of a magick spell*. Aiwass, the "Holy Guardian Angel" presiding over this Contact, also has the value 93. And Agape (love), another key word in the text, is again 93. The name of "God" in Genesis (Alhim) contains the value of π to four places (3.1415); add Crowley's 93 and you get π accurate to six places (3.141593).

The second major number in the book is 418, which "coincidentally" was the number of Crowley's home in Inverness, Scotland. Its standard Cabalistic meaning is "the Great Work accomplished," or the Illumination of all humanity. Crowley interpreted this to mean that his mission was not to illuminate a few, as other gurus have done and are doing, but to set in motion occult forces which would result in the illumination of all, by the end of this century; 418 is also the value of "Parcifal," the Sufi whose life so oddly intersected mine in that mad summer of 1973.

The Stele of Revealing contains, in addition to Nuit, Horus and Ankh-f-na-Khonsu, a mysterious winged globe. Dr. Jacques Vallee, in *The Invisible College*, gives several other forms of the winged globe from Egyptian and Gnostic sources and points out the similarity to modern sketches of UFOs by witnesses or Contactees.

The winged globe, with an eye in it, appears in an ancient Assyrian seal found by astronomer Temple and reproduced in his *Sirius Mystery*. In this case, it is accompanied by Oannes, the water-god, whom Temple identifies as probably an extraterrestrial visitor from Sirius. Note the fish-tail on Oannes. Now look at illustration below, which is a drawing from the Dogon tribe of Africa, showing Nommo, whom they claim was a visitor from Sirius; note the similar fish-tail.

Dr. John Lilly, who has duplicated much of Timothy Leary's research and supplemented it with hypnotic methods and Sufi yoga, describes many encounters with what seem to be extraterrestrial intelligences in his *Programming and Metaprogramming the Human Biocomputer*. Dr. Lilly agnostically examines also the possibilities that these transmitters are time-travelers from the future, very advanced Illuminati Adepts alive now on earth, "angels" in the traditional sense, or projected aspects of his own mind. *In The Center of the Cyclone* he says clearly:

> Such a network [of Adepts] exists and functions . . . throughout this planet. I *suspect it extends farther than our earth*, but this is yet to be publicly demonstrated unequivocally beyond the private *experience of myself and others.* [Italics added.}[52]

A network of adepts that extends far beyond our Earth . . . that was what your narrator was gradually coming to believe, and here it was being said, with only slight reservation, by Dr. John Lilly — the man once defined by the *New York Times* as "a walking one-man syllabus of Western civilization."

But permission to visit Dr. Leary had finally been granted by prison authorities and I was to hear even more extraordinary theories from him.

The Winged Globe from the Stele of Revealing appears in many ancient Mediterranean initiatory cults. Here are two examples collected by Dr. Jacques Vallee.

The design pictured at the top is from Assyria and is several thousand years old. That at the bottom is from the Dogon tribe and is contemporary. The Dogon say their fishtailed figure is from Sirius, and astronomer Temple claims that the Assyrian design shows the same extraterrestrial with a fishtail.

(And just as I finished typing the above section, psychologist Jean Millay dropped by for a visit. With no prompting on my part, and not knowing what I was writing about, she spontaneously launched into a story about a time she had painted *Nuit* on the ceiling of a friend's bedroom. "And on her belly," she said, "I put the *Eye of Horus.* " Look back at the previous graphic and note where Horus' head is on the Stele of Revealing. Jean had never seen the stele and was intrigued when I showed it to her. Cosmic Coincidence Control Center is working overtime on this case . . .)

A visit to CMF

Vacaville is one of those little California towns that look as conventionally pretty as a brand-new starlet just getting the taste of producer's semen out of her mouth and flouncing merrily through a screen test. When you get there in the morning, on Greyhound, the birds are singing and the sun is high and golden, and everything is clean and bright and you can't believe you're heading toward a combination prison-and-madhouse where men are caged like beasts.

The cab from the Greyhound station to the prison costs exactly a dollar and the cabbie calls your destination "CMF" when he speaks on the shortwave to his office. CMF — California Medical Facility — has a reputation in some quarters that Dr. Frankenstein's laboratory can hardly beat. Gay libbers, radical therapists, civil libertarians and other soreheads have commented, on occasion, that the methods of psycho-surgery and aversive therapy that have been used there to "cure" sexual deviates have more in common with Bull Conners' cattle-prods than with anything therapeutic; but that's the psychiatric side of Vacaville, where they keep the people they think they are trying to help. The other side, the purely punitive side, is more humane; the inmates are merely caged until their time is up, and then let go. Nobody is trying to "cure" them, and it's only a medium-security setup; getting shipped there, from another prison, is a reward for good conduct.

After going through the usual red tape, the Libertarian was shown into a visiting room considerably more decent than many prisons provide. Cons and visitors sat at tables, without screens or glass between them, and shared coffee and sandwiches from machines. It was not much different from any school cafeteria in the land, except that some men held their women's hands so hungrily that you almost reeled from the pain of sexual frustration.

Timothy Leary came in the door at the other end of the room with an Irish grin spread across his face.

He looked into the Author's eyes, with the inoffensive curiosity of an infant. He looked me up and down, with the same innocent awe; I expected him to sniff me next, like a dog. Instead, he grinned again and said that I was in great shape. From anybody else, that would have been mere politeness; from Tim Leary, after an intense inspection, it was a favorable diagnosis.

He led me to another visiting area, where we sat at a table with our sandwiches and coffee. He was commenting excitedly on my most recent letter to him, and insisting that I must begin corresponding at once with an English poet named Brian Barritt. Leary is very sober indeed when explaining a technical point; the famous grin goes away entirely, and his concentration goes into intense commitment to total clarity. It was made obvious that neither Barritt nor I could afford to write another line until we had gotten our heads in synch, since we were exploring the same elephant from two sides.

The elephant was named Aleister Crowley, and Leary himself had been scrutinizing that odd Beast for the past few years also.

In Switzerland, during his exile, Leary was shown a deck of Crowley's Tarot cards. To test its divinatory power, he asked "Who am I and what is my destiny?" Then he cut to a single card and got the Ace of Discs. This shows a large disc bearing the Greek letters TO MEGA THERION* (The Great Beast) Crowley's name for himself. Leary interpreted this to mean that he is Crowley Reborn, and is supposed to complete the work Crowley began, preparing humanity for cosmic consciousness.

◆

*By Cabala, TO MEGA THERION = 666

◆

(*The Confessions of a Hope Fiend*, Leary's account of his
jailbreak and his months in Algiers with Eldridge Cleaver, is
deliberately titled to recall Crowley's *Diary of a Dope Fiend*.)

Dr. Leary of course did not take the doctrine of reincarnation
literally. In his terminology, everybody who makes a strong
impression on your nervous system reincarnates with you. In this
sense, Leary feels that he reincarnates everyone from Socrates
onward who has sent a time-binding signal that changed his nervous system on reception.

Dr. Leary was explaining this when David Hilliard wandered
over to our table. David is a former Black Panther who once got
busted for saying in public that Nixon should be assassinated. He
was in Vacaville for "assaulting" a policeman.

Tim and David rapped about Eldridge Cleaver for a while,
and David seemed rather embarrassed about Cleaver's treatment
of Tim in Algiers.

"I didn't understand Eldridge until I got to Folsom," Tim said.
"He's just the toughest guy in the cell-block, that's all. The King,
you know."

Hilliard nodded with profound sadness. "We've all got the
Oppressor inside ourselves," he said.

Tim introduced the Libertarian. "This is Robert Anton Wilson
one of the wisest men on the planet Earth," he said.

David and I shook hands. I felt somewhat overwhelmed by
the introduction and wondered inanely if I should try to say
something Wise to justify Tim's hyperbole.

I was remembering what Dr. Israel Regardie once said about
Aleister Crowley: that the Beast got into most of his troubles by
trusting the wrong people. When you turn on the higher neurological circuits, Regardie said, you are quite apt to imagine that
everybody else is there with you. "Some of the Hindu gurus
honestly believe everybody they see is in Samadhi with them,"
Regardie added, "and Crowley often had the same illusion."

After we chatted some more with David Hilliard and he finally went off to see someone else, Timothy started to outline his
ideas about the higher neurological circuits turned on by psychedelics. It was his opinion that these circuits evolved for use in

outer space, not merely for getting blissed-out on the earthside trip. All the shamans and mystics who opened these circuits knew they had something to do with cosmic energy, he said, but they didn't know the why, the how, and the next step.

We potentially have eight circuits, he said. The first four are linear and designed for use on Earth. They underlie Euclidean space, Newtonian time, the whole "square" mentality. Imprinted with the local, "tribal" games or value-systems, these circuits narrow the polymorphous infant into an adjusted adult with one personality, one sex-role, one system of coordinates — "usually conservative and mildly paranoid, to mesh with the conservative and mildly paranoid local value-system." he said ironically.

The four later, still-evolving circuits activated by shamans and mystics are not just an "escape" from the anxiety of the dualistic ego, he said. "You aren't supposed to just turn them on, go into bliss, and sink into a hedonistic silk-lined womb. That's just the input stage, comparable to the adolescent dropout into compul-sive masturbation when the Sex Circuit first turns on.

"You should then go on to find the program, the proper use of the new energies," Tim continued. "The pot-head who sits around blissed-out hasn't found out yet what pot is for, what rapture imprints do to all the earlier imprints. The acid-head or the guru who has turned on the ecstasy circuit and just blissed himself out is again just taking the input and not doing anything with it. Transcendental Masturbation.

"The real meaning of acid won't be clear until we live nor-mally in free-fall," Leary insisted. "When the up-down dualism of the domination-submission circuit goes, the other dualisms start to go also. The first four imprints — statistically normal consciousness through most of our history — will crumble. Right now, the astronauts all show some kind of altered aware-ness, to a greater or lesser degree. Ed Mitchell already realizes the linkage between his spiritual experience in space and the old occult and mystic traditions. That's why he's formed the Institute for Noetic Studies and plunged into parapsychology and ESP."

The most important events of the next three decades, Leary predicted, will be the invention of an immortality pill and a pill that simulates the death experience without killing the person taking it.

Tim forecasted the longevity pill in *Terra II*, published in January 1973, saying it would appear around 1980. One month later, in February, Michigan State University released the information that they were researching a pill that might extend life to 200 years. In April, Dutton published *The Immortality Factor* by Osborn Segerberg, Jr., which reviews current research on aging and predicts a life-extension pill by 2000 or so.

Dr. Leary doesn't insist that a literal immortality formula will be found that quickly, of course. Rather, he feels that extension of life to around 400 years is most probable; then, those who live a few centuries will acquire further medical technology expanding life into millennia, hundreds of thousands of years, millions . . .

"I expect to be alive when the solar system has burned up 5½ billion years from now," he said happily. "Nobody in this generation has to die, unless they want to."

A simulated death-pill, creating the neurological equivalent of death without actually killing the body, will also be along in a few decades, Leary also predicted that day in Vacaville. This will complete the work of LSD in re-imprinting old circuits through ritual death-and-rebirth in one body. "I call it serial reincarnation," he said.

Interstellar ESP may have been going on for all our history, Tim went on, but we just haven't understood. Our nervous systems have translated their messages into terms we could understand. The "angels" who spoke to Dr. Dee, the Elizabethan scientist-magician, were extraterrestrials, but Dee couldn't comprehend them in those terms and considered them "messengers from God." The same is true of many other shamans and mystics.

Leary spoke warmly of Carl Sagan, the astronomer, who visited him at Vacaville. "A brilliant man, brilliant," Tim said. In fact Tim has recently renamed his own specialty Exo-Psychology in imitation of Dr. Sagan's coining of the term Exo-Biology. Both sciences attempt to deduce the characteristics of life and consciousness throughout the galaxy, based on mounting astronomical evidence that Earth is more typical than atypical. The galactic intelligences who are more advanced than we are, Tim said, can be regarded as our own genetic future — the embodiment of levels of consciousness toward which we are still evolving.

But Leary was not keen about Sagan's Project Cyclops, an attempt to contact Higher Intelligence by building enormous radio receivers to scan the galaxy for meaningful signals. "Why passively wait for *them* to make the first move?" Tim asked rhetorically. "Are we adolescents so unsure of ourselves that we can't take the initiative? I want to go *cruising*," he said emphatically, emphasizing the sexual metaphor with a lustful grin.

Only once in five hours did Leary mention the fact that he was in prison. "I'm so high," he said briefly, "that I forget where I am. Then, occasionally, there are kinds of research I can't do here, and I realize I should really try to get out." But he didn't enlarge on the subject; he got off on another scientific-mystic speculation about the Einstein space-time circuits and the neurological functioning of men and women living deep in space.

The Investigator has seen other people in the high-energy high-consciousness state that Dr. Leary lived in at Vacaville. They were all Oriental gurus, expert in one or another of the Buddhist, Hindu, or Sufi training systems for expanded awareness. None of them had Tim's scientific background and, accordingly, their verbalizations were less startling; they spoke of vast undefined abstractions which have no operational meaning except in reference to their own mutated consciousness. Leary is trying to define these free mental states in precise neuro-genetic terms; but nobody can understand him fully without sharing in both the higher states of awareness and the scientific systems Leary knows so well.

Toward the end of the visit, I showed Tim my equation

$$B_n = B_0 + P_n + MS$$

where B_n is new behavior, B_0 is old behavior, P_n is a deliberate new program for self-change and MS is a metaprogramming substance such as LSD.

Leary approved of the equation warmly. "You could write another one," he added, "with C_n and C_0."

"For consciousness?" I asked.

"Exactly. And another one for I_n and I_0."

I thought of ideology and decided he couldn't mean that; he is aware that ideology and morality are the two chief causes of human suffering. "Intensity?" I hazarded.

Tim folded his hands in prayer and looked upward with exaggerated worship. "Intelligence," he said, naming his God.

The prospects of immortality

> Some people want to achieve immortality through their works or their descendants. I prefer to achieve immortality by not dying.
>
> – Woody Allen in the *Immortalist* magazine

As soon as my first interview with Dr. Leary appeared in the San Francisco *Phoenix*, I was deluged with information about that group which Carl Spann calls "the Immortalist Underground." These are scientists, mostly young and mostly in the field of molecular biology or gerontology, who were turned on by Professor R.C.W. Ettinger's *The Prospects of Immortality*, published way back in 1964. This group believes, quite firmly, that the discovery of the DNA structure (the double helix) by Crick and Watson has opened the possibility of reprogramming biological processes and achieving literal immortality.

How *close* is immortality? We call a few witnesses:

"A decade or two from now," Hubert Humphrey has said, "we may look back to present-day attitudes toward death as 'primitive' and 'medieval' in the way we now look back upon a once-dreaded killer like tuberculosis." Senator Humphrey said this after visiting Russia and learning of their research on immortality.[53]

"No less than three separate branches of science are doing research in prolonging life," says the Abolish Death Committee of Berkeley, "namely the sciences of cryobiology, biology and cybernetics . . . Which one will be successful? No one knows.

But because more than one science is hard at work on this problem, an early solution is forecast."

"Immortalism," says Carl Spann, an Immortalist activist, "is a tremendous step in the evolution of man. It's the development of an immortal state of consciousness . . . stoned people in a stoned world, high on life . . . Mortal man, like Nixon, is still committed to nation-states and power-bloc thinking which is ultimately globally destructive. Mortal man pollutes the planet because he won't be around to suffer the consequences.

"Getting stoned on dope," Spann adds thoughtfully, "is a defense-mechanism against global insanity. And yet, marijuana, hashish, acid and the consciousness-expanding drugs have opened the way to the Immortal state of consciousness: Samadhi, satori, alpha and theta states, the whole enlightenment trip that provides an escape from Mortal man's tight little illusions of himself."[54]

Way back in the Dark Ages, on September 24, 1964, the Abolish Death Committee from Berkeley staged a demonstration in front of a funeral parlor, carrying such signs as "Death is a disease and can be cured," "Don't buy the lie," "Millions Now Living May Never Die" (an old slogan of Jehovah's Witnesses, who probably never expected either scientific types or hippies to take them up on it), "Immortality NOW!" and "Why die? You Can Be Immortal."

Presumably, most of the 1964 audience who saw this on the TV news figured the demonstrators were all crazy.

In *The Immortality Factor*, by Osborn Segerberg, Jr., an amusing chapter called "Prognosis" deals with recent guesstimates by knowledgeable scientists about *when* extended life will become available. Arthur Clarke (who in 1947 correctly predicted the first unmanned moon-landing for 1959, but was too conservative about the first manned moon-landing and predicted it for 1978) guessed in 1962 that actual immortality would be achieved *near the end* of the 21st Century. Three years later, in 1964, with more research accomplished, a group of 82 scientific experts was polled, and the majority of them were willing to predict "chemical control of the aging process" by the *early* part of the 21st Century.

In 1969, two similar polls of expert opinion found "significant extension of life span" predicted by various scientists as occurring between 1993 (the low estimate) and 2017 (the high estimate). By 1971, Dr. Bernard Stehler predicted that we would understand aging within 5 to 10 years and be able to reverse it in 10 to 30 years.[55]

As Leary points out in *Terra II*, the greatest bulk of scientific work on this subject, with the most optimistic conclusion emerging, has been done since Dr. Stehler made that guess in 1971.

The Foundation for Research on Immortality, in Sacramento, California, declared in a press release: "It is becoming increasingly clear that we stand literally before an unprecedented shift in our evolutionary direction and potential . . . The pursuit of immortality as a personal goal is no longer just a religious aspiration but has become an actual possibility."

Pauwels and Bergier, who blew the mind of Europe and America with their incredible *Morning of the Magicians*, prophesy in their newest book, *The Eternal Man*, "Perhaps we are even now in the process of building a culture that will know immortality on earth and in heaven . . . [56]

Robert Prehoda, M.D., says in his *Extended Youth*, "It is possible that we may be able to slow down biological aging, doubling or tripling the average life-span. . . . If every case of aging can be corrected and prevented, we might all be potential Methuselahs, living 1,000 years or more."[57]

Dr. Bernard Strehler, who has devoted most of his life to longevity research and predicts that we will have life extension in this generation, says also that his ultimate goal is immortality. "Man," he states flatly, "will never be contented until he conquers death."[58]

Novelist Alan Harrington has been calling for a national commitment to death-elimination since 1969, when he published his brilliant polemic *The Immortalist* (called "the book of the century" by Gore Vidal). "Mobilize the scientists," Harrington implores us, "spend the money, and hunt down death like an outlaw."[59]

Dean F. Jumper, in *Man Against Mortality*, suggests that humanity may have been specially designed to conquer death. In the war between life and death, Jumper says, "man may be life's ultimate weapon. He may be designed to make himself and life immortal, *the necessary skills and motivations having been built into him.* "[60] [Italics added.] Achieving immortality not just for ourselves but for all living species is a staggering thought, but it would be the achievement of the Buddhist vow to deliver "all sentient beings" from suffering.

Dr. Alex Comfort, generally regarded as the world's leading gerontologist by his peers (but better known to the general public for his lubricious *The Joy of Sex*), said in 1972, "I am confident techniques for slowing and reversing the aging process are close at hand."[61] In 1973, with the synergetic product of another year's worth of life-extension research achieved in laboratories around the world, Dr. Comfort was willing to be more specific than merely saying "close at hand." He said, in fact, "If the scientific and medical resources *of the United States alone* were mobilized, aging would be conquered *within a decade.* "[62] [Italics added.]

Of course, for every 10 or 20 scientists who will admit they believe in possible longevity, there is only one who will go so far as to speak of physical immortality. Nonetheless, every break-through in life extension means that some of us will live long enough to be around for the next breakthrough, and the next, until immortality is actually achieved.

Dr. Leary points out in this connection that most of the life-extension talk in scientific circles these days is earth-bound, terracentric, a hangover of what Leary calls "closet Ptole-maicism."

The Lorentz and Einstein equations of space-time relativity leave no doubt that a cruise around the galaxy, such as is projected by Leary and Benner in *Terra II*, might occupy 400 years elapsed time aboard ship and return to earth circa A.D. 4,500,000,000, Earth-time. *Space travel is time travel.* If the crew members have life-extension to several hundred years when they blast off early in the next century, they may encounter High-er Intelligences with more advanced life-extension techniques. If not, they will return to an Earth-science *four-and-one-half billion years in advance of ours*, and reap whatever techniques of life-extension, inhibition of aging, cryonics, rejuvenation, etc.

that human ingenuity can devise in four thousand million years.

Current research on inhibition of aging or potential immortality includes:

• The cryologists whose slogan "freeze-wait-reanimate" has gained some notoriety in recent years. (This is only the tip of the iceberg.)

• Dr. John Bjorksten, working on proteins in his own lab in Madison, Wisconsin. In 1973, Dr. Bjorksten spoke of finding a drug that would extend human lifespan to *140 years*; in 1976, while this chapter was being written, Bjorksten said, in a *San Francisco Chronicle* interview, that he hoped human life could be extended to *800 years*.

• A group at the University of Michigan who are already testing a drug that might expand life to 200 years or longer.

• Oak Ridge National Laboratory, which is researching BHT, a chemical that might increase longevity 50%.

• All the organ-transplant people.

• The cyberneticists, who may find a way to "code a total personality, keep it on file in an electronic circuit, and reanimate it at any time."

• Microwave Instrument Co. in Del Mar, California. They are researching anti-aging drugs, and might have some on the market in three years.

• The parapsychologists, who are collecting data which challenges the bedrock of physics, indicate that all science may be revolutionized at any time, and thus open possibilities that have previously been unthinkable.

• And, finally, nobody knows how much work the Russians are doing in this field, but we have evidence that they are probably ahead of us.

During another visit to Vacaville, I told Dr. Leary that some of the people who were most enthusiastic about his drug research in the early '60s are most hostile to his current neurogenetic and cosmic projects.

"I can't help that," he said. "The drugs were tools to me, microscopes. I used them to change focus in various ways, to learn the full potentials of the human nervous system. Those who

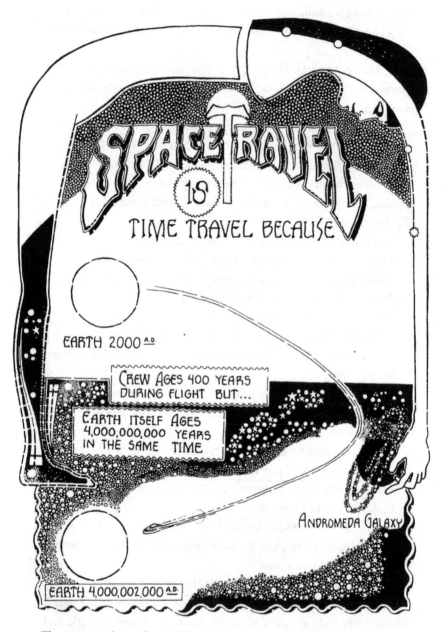

The quantum jump from "life extension" to "immortality" is the space-time leap across galaxies. The above illustration shows time-relativity on a 60-year cruise. *Terra II* plans to travel for 400 years and return to Earth 4 billion years later.

imprinted my first transmissions may have stopped growing at, say, the Fifth Circuit, Body Rapture. They have become Hedonic Engineers, and no more.

"But the Turn On is just the first step. The message now is that the message keeps changing. Intelligence must increase as consciousness expands, or we get burned-out. I'm just beginning, in the last year. I've just wised up . . ."

"Yes," he added, "I got rid of my own fears in the '60s, but now I have no fear of other people's fears. Truth. Truth. Truth. That's the highest circuit of all . . ."

He mentioned a prominent counter-culture hero: "He hates me now, because I'm not suffering. If I were in misery, he'd love me. He suffers every time he drags himself out of bed, I'm sure. But glorification of suffering is one of the larval reflexes we must lose. I'm free, you see, and those people can't stand that. They want to feel sorry for me. But I'm too busy trying to free the rest of humanity out there.

"They don't have to keep repeating the old misery imprints. They can become immortal and go to the stars . . ."

Stopping the biological clock

Carl Spann put me in touch with another local Immortalist, Paul Segall, Ph.D., a researcher at U.C.-Berkeley. Dr. Segall has been involved in life-extension work for 17 years.

Dr. Segall looks and dresses exactly like anybody's idea of a Hippie New Leftist. He belongs to Earth People's Park, an association of former '60s radicals which owns several houses in Berkeley and land in Oregon. E.P.P. runs a rescue service for people in trouble, runaways, dopers and others who can't deal with the kind of help you get from government offices. In a very real sense, Earth People represents the survival, despite the Nixon counter-revolution, of the early, nonviolent New Left in all its anarchist idealism and grass-roots Populism.

With one difference. Due to Paul's influence, almost all the

Earth People are Immortalists, and many of them have returned to college to seek science degrees.

Paul says he was "drenched in science from the cradle" — his father and an uncle were both engineers, and another uncle was a chemist. Paul himself set out to be an engineer — until a Turn-On experience in an art class. As he tells it, "They were showing slides of cave paintings from 30,000 years ago, and I suddenly felt this urgent inner question, *'What the hell am I doing here?'* I mean, 'What am I doing with my life?' I became an immortalist then and there, years before I read any of the immortalist literature."

Paul changed his major to biology and set out to find out precisely why every complex organism must die and what he could do about it. Over the past 17 years he has spent time in research on seven approaches to longevity-immortality:

1. Suspended-animation studies, in which life processes are turned off and then restored.

2. Gerontology, the study of the processes of aging on biological and chemical levels.

3. Transplantation, which might eventually allow us to go on replacing organs until the point at which "we are still there but "our" whole body is new . . .

4. Prosthetics and cyborgs (human-machine combinations).

5. Resuscitation — literally bringing back the dead. In the last decade this has been moved upward from resuscitation a few seconds after "clinical death" to five minutes later, and Paul thinks we will soon have it up to a half-hour.

6. Identity-reconstruction through cloning.

7. Regeneration, the study of the processes by which cells renew themselves.

Paul is also an executive of the Bay Area Cryonics Society, which is a group of scientists who have arranged to have their bodies frozen at "clinical death" in hopes of resuscitation by techniques to be discovered in the future.

In the mid-sixties Paul attended a lecture by Dr. Leary which he found to be a turning point in his own intellectual development. What Leary had communicated, Paul says, was that "everything we experience is hallucination, *maya*. The reality is a structural-mathematical-logical principle that we don't see. That is, each person creates his own universe out of his own neurological processes. Science is nothing else but the search for the unseen structural integrities that underlie these appearances."

Paul generalized this Buddhist-scientific synthesis into the theory that *we are information*.

"The ultimate reason that Immortality is possible," Paul told me, "is that *we are not the stuff we're made of*. Literally. You can trace a chemical through the body with radioactive tracers, but the body goes on after the chemical has left. We are not the chemicals but the pattern, the mathematical construct. You might say that the formula for Immortality is Cybernetics + DNA. But DNA is itself Cybernetics, the first application of cybernetic information theory to biology. DNA is entirely an information system, a programming system. Cybernetics is the key, the realization that *we are programmed and can be re-programmed*."

In recent years, Paul's studies have concentrated on finding the chemical trigger that sets the senescence-death program into action. In fact, he believes he was the first one to introduce the concept of "programmed death" into scientific literature.

"Back in the '60s," Paul reminisces, "biologists were still regarding aging as a stochastic process — the random decay of random cells. One day I met a woman I hadn't seen in a year, and the change in her was so complete that I immediately thought of the word 'metamorphosis.' I suddenly realized I might have found what I was looking for. Suppose aging isn't stochastic and random. It might be a definite, pre-programmed metamorphosis just like the evolution from fertilized egg to new-born infant, or the biopsychic mutation at puberty, or the tadpole-to-frog or caterpillar-to-butterfly transformation." Paul developed the theory that all ontogeny is preprogrammed. "I think I was the very first to put this idea on paper, and I am delighted that it is the working hypothesis of increasing numbers of investigators," he says.

"Traits are not naturally selected only for individual survival, as Darwin thought," Paul insists. "Some are selected for species survival. Pre-programmed death was an unthinkable concept when we regarded the individual as our monad; how could natural selection produce such a genetic program if selection is only for the advantage of the individual? But if some traits are for the advantage of the group, and for group evolution, it all falls into place. Throw out the '77 models, bring in the '78 models. Once again, I found Dr. Leary and Alan Watts, with their holistic trans-ego concepts, very helpful in firming up my thought."

Dr. Segall has found three ways to reverse the aging trigger in experimental rats — to stop aging for periods equal to the normal life-span of the animal and then allow normal aging to begin. He believes that his research will soon isolate the exact trigger that starts or stops aging.

Curiously, all three of Paul's methods deprive the brain of tryptophan, directly or indirectly. He believes this is a significant clue. "Tryptophan," he says, "is very closely related to serotonin, the basic brain-bonder, and to the psychedelics like LSD, psilocybin, DMT, mescaline and so forth. *The stopping of time experienced by psychedelic users may be related to tryptophan deprivation while the psychedelic is in the system.*"

In one optimistic mood, Paul told me that his current work will result "in 15 years maximum" in extending human life "to 400 or 500 years average."

One reason I am so confident that something will come of this kind of research "in 15 years maximum" is that Paul has so many competitors. (As mentioned a few pages ago, Dr. Johan Bjorksten is currently talking of raising lifespan to 800 years.) Whoever gets there first may pick up a Nobel prize as a result. The rest of us will get a shot at living long enough for immortality to be achieved.

Consider also the *acceleration* of scientific breakthroughs:

Dr. Isaac Asimov notes, in his *The Genetic Code*, that there seems to be a 60-year cycle between the first understanding of a new scientific principle and the transformation of the world by applications of that principle. Thus, he instances the discovery of electromagnetic equivalence by Oersted in 1820; 60 years later, in 1880, electrical generators and motors were in wide use and the Industrial Revolution had occurred in the Western nations; the telegraph was also widespread and our age of Mass Communications was dawning.

Similarly, in 1883, Thomas Edison first noted the so-called

"Edison effect," although he never understood it or realized its importance. Within 60 years, by 1943, the technology of electronics, as distinguished from electricity — technology based entirely on the "Edison effect" — had spread radio everywhere and was already beginning to replace it by television.

Again, in 1896, Becquerel noted the sub-atomic behavior of uranium. Sixty years later, in 1956, two cities had been destroyed by atom bombs and nuclear generating plants were operating in many places.

In 1903, the Wright Brothers got their monoplane off the ground for a few minutes. Sixty years later, in 1963, jetliners carrying over 100 passengers were circling the earth daily.

In 1926, Goddard fired his first rocket into the air; in 1986, obviously, WoManned landings on nearby planets will be commonplace.

Sixty years, Dr. Asimov concludes, is the normal time between a scientific breakthrough and the remaking of the world by the new technology derived from that breakthrough. Since DNA was discovered in 1944, the biological revolution (including longevity, and possibly immortality) should be peaking in 2004. We are now three years past the midpoint of that cycle (1974) and the new technology should be coming faster and faster.

Some of the readers of this book — the more determined ones — may never die at all.

Appearances and disappearances

It gets even spookier now.

People who claimed to be messengers of God, of the extraterrestrials, or of various Ascended Masters, began to contact me, sometimes in weird ways. Most of them were nuts. Some of them still leave me wondering.

For instance, one chap who claimed to be a representative of the real Illuminati, and who struck the Skeptic as quite possibly a professional con-man, took Arlen and me out to dinner at the most expensive restaurant in Berkeley and spent $70 on it. He assured us that he was protecting us at all times, dropped a few hints that he might be God, and slipped me $200 before he left, assuring us that our poverty would not continue much longer.

He never came back or tried to exploit the Poor Fool in any way. What kind of con-game is it where the Mark ends up richer instead of poorer?

This skeptic still believes this fellow as a benevolently inclined fellow psychic with a taste for drama and mystery. I do not believe he was in the "real" Illuminati (except for four or five minutes a week, when the Shaman wonders about all the impossible theories he usually screens out as too melodramatic to be true . . .).

In our last meeting at Vacaville Prison, I told Tim Leary, "Giordano Bruno, the first philosopher in history to suggest that there were Higher Intelligences in this galaxy, used Tantric yoga."

"Yeah, I know," he said.

"Oh," I asked, "you've read Francis Yates' *Giordano Bruno and the Hermetic Tradition?*"

"No," he said. "It was obvious from Bruno's own writings. Sex-magic is always the first of the Secrets."

At that meeting, Timothy was exuberant and, for him, strangely secretive. "I'll be out soon," he said. "It's all falling into place."

The following week he was moved from Vacaville to Terminal Island, near Los Angeles. Joanna Leary told his friends in the Bay Area that letters to him were pointless, since he would be moved again shortly.

The Great Silence began.

Weeks passed.

Mike Horowitz, of the Fitzhugh Memorial Library, came to the Poor Fool one night with a strange story. Joanna Leary had appeared at his house with three men who she claimed were from a photocopying company. She had a letter in Timothy's unmistakable handwriting, instructing Mike to turn over Leary's archives for photocopying and permanent storage.

"They were cops," Mike told me. "I could smell it."

"What the hell . . ."

"I don't know," Mike said. "I just don't know . . ."

We chewed on it for hours. If Timothy was making a deal with the Feds, what sort of deal? Paranoia drifted in and out of the room as we discussed, theorized, reconsidered.

The Oracle did a Tarot divination, at Mike's insistence. (I distrust my own readings, when personal emotion is involved.) I forget my own interpretations but I remember that the card showing "resultant of the affair" was the Star. According to Kenneth Grant's *Magical Revival*, this card represents Sirius. Coincidence?

I performed another divination on Timothy, for another baffled friend, a week or so later. The Star came up as "the resultant" again.

Coincidence again?

In September 1974 paranoia descended in full force.

Leaks began to appear in the Hearst press, planted by the Federal cops, that Timothy was ready to testify against any and all of his former friends to get himself out of jail.

Damnably, those of us who had watched the metamorphoses of Leary from Scientist to Guru, from Guru to Marxist Revolutionary, from Revolutionary back to Scientist, knew that he was capable of virtually any further transformation, however unlikely it would appear in ordinary psychology.

The *Berkeley Barb* printed an undocumented story that Joanna had been busted for cocaine. "Aha," voices said, "*that's* how the Feds got Timothy to crack . . ." But the story wasn't checkable. "It's all a scam," other voices claimed, "the Feds are trying to panic the counter-culture . . ."

Then the Second Wave of rumors began.

The Fiendish Psychologists at Vacaville had tampered with Tim's head, voices said around San Francisco. He was a zombie, like McMurphy at the end of *One Flew Over the Cuckoo's Nest*; Kesey, like the true shaman he was, had unknowingly predicted Leary's fate ten years before it happened.

Watergate was still erupting; even the most resolute anti-paranoids and skeptics about Conspiracy Theories were pushed, more and more, into admitting that the Government was Capable of *Anything* . . .

And none of us were able to get a message in to Timothy or an answer out. He was totally incommunicado with the Feds.

A lesson in Karma

Lao-Tse says (at least in Leary's translation) that the Great Tao is most often found with parents who are willing to learn from their children. This remark was to cause me considerable mental strain and dilation around this time in our narrative, because my children had become very self-directed adolescents and were getting into occultism with much more enthusiasm and much less skepticism than I thought judicious.

For a few years, we could not discuss these subjects without arguing, despite my attempts to remember good old Lao-Tse and really *listen* to the kids. They believed in astrology, which I was still convinced was bosh; in reincarnation, which I considered an extravagant metaphor one shouldn't take literally; and in that form of the doctrine of Karma which holds, optimistically, that the evil really are punished and the good really are rewarded, which I considered a wishful fantasy no more likely than the Christian idea of Heaven and Hell. Worst of all, they had a huge appetite for various Oriental "Masters" whom I regarded as total charlatans, and an enormous disdain for all the scientific methodology of the West.

My own position was identical to that of Aleister Crowley when he wrote:

> We place no reliance
> On Virgin or Pigeon;
> Our method is Science,
> Our aim is Religion.

After every argument with one of the kids, I would vow again to listen more sympathetically, less judgmentally, to their Pop

134

Orientalism. I finally began to succeed. I learned a great deal from them.

A "miracle" then happened. I know this will be harder for the average American parent to believe than any of my other weird yarns, but my horde of self-willed and self-directed adolescents *began to listen to me*. Real communication was established. Even though I was in my 40s and greying in the beard, I was able to talk intelligently with four adolescents about our philosophical disagreements, and our mutual respect for each other grew by leaps and bounds.

This, I think, is the greatest result I have obtained from all my occult explorations, even if the unmarried will not appreciate how miraculous it was.

Luna, our youngest — the one who might have levitated in Mexico and who had her first menstrual period synchronistically on the day Tim Leary was busted in Afghanistan — taught me the hardest lesson of all. She had begun to paint in watercolors and everything she did charmed me: it was always full of sun and light, in a way that was as overpowering as Van Gogh.

"What do all these paintings *mean*?" I asked her one day.

"I'm trying to show the Clear Light," she said.

Then, returning from school one afternoon, Luna was beaten and robbed by a gang of black kids. She was weeping and badly frightened when she arrived home, and her Father was shaken by the unfairness of it happening to *her*, such a gentle, ethereal child. In the midst of consoling her, the Father wandered emotionally and began denouncing the idea of Karma. Luna was beaten, he said, not for her sins, but for the sins of several centuries of slavers and racists, most of whom had never themselves suffered for those sins. "Karma is a blind machine," he said. "The effects of evil go on and on but they don't necessarily come back on those who start the evil." Then Father got back on the track and said some more relevant and consoling things.

The next day Luna was her usual sunny and cheerful self, just like the Light in her paintings. "I'm glad you're feeling better," the Father said finally.

"I stopped the wheel of Karma," she said. "All the bad energy is with the kids who beat me up. I'm not holding any of it."

And she wasn't. The bad energy had entirely passed by, and there was no anger or fear in her. I never saw her show any hostility to blacks after the beating, any more than before.

The Father fell in love with her all over again. And he understood what the metaphor of the wheel of Karma really symbolizes and what it means to stop the wheel.

Karma, in the original Buddhist scriptures, *is* a blind machine; in fact, it is functionally identical with the scientific concept of natural law. Sentimental ethical ideas about justice being built into the machine, so that those who do evil in one life are punished for it in another life, were added later by theologians reasoning from their own moralistic prejudices. Buddha simply indicated that all the cruelties and injustices of the past are still active: their effects are always being felt. Similarly, he explained, all the good of the past, all the kindness and patience and love of decent people is also still being felt.

Since most humans are still controlled by fairly robotic reflexes, the bad energy of the past far outweighs the good, and the tendency of the wheel is to keep moving in the same terrible direction, violence breeding more violence, hatred breeding more hatred, war breeding more war. The only way to "stop the wheel" is to *stop it inside yourself,* by giving up bad energy and concentrating on the positive. This is by no means easy, but once you understand what Gurdjieff called "the horror of our situation," you have no choice but to try, and to keep on trying.

And Luna, at 13, understood this far better than I did, at 43, with all my erudition and philosophy . . . I still regarded her absolute vegetarianism and pacifism as sentimentality.

Witchcraft

Another kind of occult experience occurred on April 26, 1974.

The Shaman was working a ritual with a group of Bay Area witches, who call themselves the New Reformed Orthodox Order of the Golden Dawn. During the part of the ceremony in which the group "raises the Cone of Power" (molds the "astral" or orgone field into a cone which can be seen and directed at will by the members), I had a vision of my son, Graham, who was then in Arizona with some friends. Graham was lying on the ground and cops were walking toward him. I could see no more; but the Shaman hastily placed a smaller "cone of power" around him as a protective device and tried to leave a telepathic message that he should phone me in the morning. The Father was somewhat frightened, imagining that Graham might have been in an auto accident.

The next morning when the phone rang, I said at once, "That's Graham." (I often announce phone calls before answering them, these days.*) He told us of his adventure with "the pigs," as young people call our gallant law-enforcement officers. He and his friends had been sleeping in the woods, when some cops drove into the clearing and discovered their car. The kids expected, at the minimum, to be chased out of the woods and sent on their way; more likely, by previous experience, they feared being jailed overnight, until parents of each and every one of them were contacted and it was proven conclusively that none of them were runaways. (Nobody under 21 has *any* civil liberties in the U.S.A.)

♦

*Some readers are sure I'm lying like a diplomat. Others believe because they want to. Don't believe or disbelieve. Get Crowley's books and try the experiments.

♦

The cops walked toward the spot where the kids were sleeping. Those who had awakened, including Graham, watched them come. Then, abruptly, the cops turned around, walked back to their car, and drove away.

We checked the times. The incident occurred a few minutes before midnight. So did my astral vision. Whether or not my "cone of protection" pushed the police away "astrally" is an experimental question to be determined fully only when a lot more rigorous scientific work in this area has been accomplished. I was satisfied, at the minimum, that there is somewhat more to witchcraft than *mere* self-hypnosis.

I had gotten involved with the witches as part of a concerted effort to gain initiation into as many shamanic schools as possible, another idea I had acquired from dear old Uncle Aleister. In *Liber Aleph, Magick* and other books, Crowley urges the student of higher consciousness to become involved with as many gods and goddesses as possible, so as not to fall into the error of monotheism. He himself left us some really superb invocations to various divinities, together with a variety of poetic and prose accounts of his love affairs with Allah, Nuit, Pan, Kali, the Virgin Mary and quite a few others. ("Thank God I'm an atheist," he wrote also, in an essay on "The Psychology of Hashish.") My working hypothesis was still that any "luminous being" I contacted was *probably* subjective, if there was no objective supporting evidence; and *possibly* extraterrestrials (converted into anthropomorphic form by my nervous system), if they produced objective results like my being in California and Arizona at the same time. Or sending my "astral body" to Arizona while my physical body was in California. Or however you account for the above experience.

Meanwhile, I was researching other Contactees, not just those who got pancakes from the stars, like Joe Simonton, or messages of brotherly love, like the notorious George Adamski, but the myriads who were not normally considered Contactees at all.

Nikola Tesla, secular shaman

The first claims of extraterrestrial communication, I had found, were made by the electronics pioneers Marconi and Tesla. Both were ridiculed and simply stopped discussing the subject.

Tesla is an especially interesting case for our purposes. Many (including his principal biographer) regarded Tesla as virtually superhuman, and yet he was so naive in practical matters that he was cheated again and again by the businessmen to whom he sold his inventions. Tesla's major goal in life was to make abundant energy so cheap that all the world would live in affluence; he came so close to this in his later work that the corporations which had funded him withdrew their support, fearing he would undermine the monopolies which made them rich. He is also one of the only two men to have refused the Nobel Prize (the other was Jean-Paul Sartre).

Tesla's greatest discovery was the mechanism by which alternating current can be electrically generated and used; far more than Edison's direct-current machines, Tesla's A.C. generators unleashed the modern technological revolution. This illumination came to Tesla in a series of quasi-mystical visions during his adolescence. The key events were:

1. The visions themselves, in some of which Tesla literally went into trance and talked to entities nobody else could see.

2. A series of mysterious illnesses between the visions. In some of these, Tesla became acutely sensitive and felt all perceptions as painful (colors were too bright, noises too loud, etc.). Several times, Tesla nearly died of an apparent draining-away of life energy which his doctors simply couldn't explain.

3. After the final vision, *in which Tesla "saw" that everything in the universe obeys a law of Octaves* (we will see the importance of Octaves later), Tesla was transformed into a kind of secular seer. He developed a most peculiar inner vision. He could literally "see" in perfect detail any machine he thought about, right down to microscopic measurements and dimensions, as if he were using actual tools to measure an actual machine. He patented dozens of these devices and became a millionaire before he was 30.[63]

Compare this with the experience of Gopi Krishna, a typical yoga adept.

1. Like Tesla, Gopi Krishna had a series of visions and illuminations over a period of years.

2. Like Tesla, Gopi Krishna simultaneously suffered a series of mysterious illnesses, almost died several times, and occasionally became *painfully sensitive to all sensations.*

3. After the final vision, Gopi Krishna became a psychic prodigy, able to write poetry in several languages which he couldn't read or speak normally.[64]

We seem to see the same mutational process occurring in both cases, slightly modified by cultural influences. Take it on a broader scale:

1. In every tribe there are occasional shamans who are prone to visions and illuminations.

2. These shamans usually begin having their visions during or right after a prolonged illness which nearly kills them.

3. After recovery, the shaman has odd psychic abilities — "wild talents," as Charles Fort said.[65]

The whole process can be condensed to the formula; *near-death plus "rebirth" on a higher level.*

In the course of my investigations, I have undergone a number of occult initiations and have become aware of the basic similarity of such rituals in all traditions. This is the pattern of *death-rebirth* which even today appears symbolically in the Roman Catholic Mass and the Masonic "raising" ceremony. The Investigator is betraying no secret when we say that, in serious occult orders, such performances are not mere rituals but real ordeals. Insofar as possible within the law, the candidate is often brought to a state of terror similar to the emergency condition of the nervous system in near-death crises. What occurs then, and is experienced as rebirth, is a quantum jump in neurological awareness. In Leary's terminology, new circuits are formed and imprinted.

Obviously, the first shamans had no teachers; they simply went through the illness-rebirth transition accidentally, as it were. Later, schools of shamans developed techniques (psychedelics, rituals of terror, yoga, etc.) to catapult the student into such experience. In most of these schools there is great reliance on an entity or entities of superhuman nature who aid in the initiatory process, sometimes for years. ("A real initiation never ends," Crowley said once.)

Tesla, incidentally, remained a strict Materialist all his life. When his biographer pointed out to him once that Tesla's own ESP had been demonstrated on numerous occasions, Tesla replied that ESP also had a material medium.

Obviously, the whole shamanic process of near-death and rebirth on a higher level will become commonplace by the 1990s, if Leary is right and we have then both a Simulated Death pill and an Immortality pill.

Other starry signals

In 1927, Jorgen Hals, a Norwegian radio engineer, received signals which have never been explained; in the 1950s, various Russian scientists tried to prove that the Hals signals were of interstellar origin, but this theory is still being debated and no consensus has emerged.

In October 1971, L. George Lawrence, an American electronics engineer, was investigating the "Backster effect" (telepathy in plants) in the desert near Mount Palomar, California. He was using special equipment, designed by himself, considerably more sensitive than Backster's polygraph. To his astonishment, Lawrence picked up signals which seemed to come from the skies, in the region of the Big Dipper. Unwilling to publish such a finding at first, Lawrence spent several months checking his equipment for bugs and redesigning to rule out other possible explanations. In April 1972, the experiment was repeated in the Mojave Desert. The same results were obtained. Lawrence's report to the Smithsonian Institution in Washington says:

> An apparent train of interstellar communication signals of unknown origin and destination has been observed. Since interception was made by *biological* sensors, a biological-type signal transmission must be assumed. Test experiments were conducted in an electromagnetic deep-fringe area, the equipment itself being impervious to electromagnetic radiation. Follow-up tests revealed no equipment defects. Because interstellar listening experiments are not conducted on a routine basis, the suggestion is advanced that verification tests should be conducted elsewhere, possibly on a global scale. The phenomenon is

too important to be ignored.[66]

Carl Sagan of Cornell University, along with others concerned with interstellar communications, have invested most of their time and energy in *radio* signal reception. All the current projects of this sort, those funded or seeking funding, are based on the assumption that interstellar communication would involve the radio-wave energies. Lawrence's results suggest that there might be a considerable amount of cosmic communication going on that involves the "biological" or cellular level of consciousness.

Lawrence is now building a gigantic Stellartron to seek further starry transmissions.

The Backster Effect and other related considerations, Lawrence says, lead to the idea that psi is part of a "paranormal matrix" — a unique communications grid which binds all life together.[67]

To accept the possibility of Lawrence's signals is to raise the charge of "electromagnetic chauvinism," which Dr. Jack Sarfatti has made against Carl Sagan and most others who are interested in the search for interstellar signals. Sagan, Sarfatti says, should not assume that such signals must be carried by the electronic technology we already know. This chauvinism, Dr. Sarfatti points out, is as naive as assuming advanced races would speak English.

Consider the Higher Intelligence contacted by Jack Parsons, the American rocket pioneer who co-founded Cal Tech and is reputed to have contributed as much basic innovative technology to aerospace as Goddard or von Braun. Parsons, who was a member of the Ordo Templi Orientis, back in the 1930s-40s when Aleister Crowley was still alive and acting as Outer Head, subsequently published *The Book of the Anti-Christ* — a strange, beautiful, revolutionary document which, like Crowley's *Book of the Law*, was allegedly dictated by a Higher Intelligence. This entity is described by Parsons only as "most Holy and beautiful": it urged Parsons to declare war on "all authority that is not based on courage and manhood . . . the authority of lying priests, conniving judges, blackmailing police," and called for "an end to restriction and inhibition, conscription, compulsion, regimentation and the tyranny of laws."

Part Two of this strange document urges all truth-seekers to practice Crowleyan sex-yoga: "Concentrate all force and being in Our Lady Babalon. Light a single light on her altar, saying Flame is our Lady; flame is her hair. I am flame." Etc. Babalon, in Crowley's Tarot, is *The Star*, which Kenneth Grant says is Sirius.

Grady McMurty, an old friend of Crowley and Parsons, and currently Caliph of the Ordo Templi Orientis in the United States, has kindly placed in my hands various manuscripts of O.T.O. private publications during the 1940s. In one of them Parsons states his devotion to the shamanistic-psychedelic quest in poetic terms that might have seemed extreme even to Crowley. The poem begins:

> I hight Don Quixote, I live on peyote,
> marijuana, morphine and cocaine,
> I never know sadness but only a madness
> that burns at the heart and the brain.
> I see each charwoman, ecstatic, inhuman,
> angelic, demonic, divine.
> Each wagon a dragon, each beer mug a flagon
> that brims with ambrosial wine.

This was printed in the February 21, 1943 issue of *The Oriflamme*, journal of the O.T.O., two months before Hofmann discovered LSD.

Parsons died in a laboratory accident in 1949. According to Kenneth Grant, Parsons' last year was devoted to the attempt, with a mistress, to conceive a moonchild — an entity magickally separated from earth-influence at the instant of conception and from then on dedicated to higher, outer-space influences. (Crowley describes this operation in his novel, *Moonchild*. To my knowledge, it has not been successfully performed to date.)

Jack Parsons' life, midway between Crowley's and Leary's, was a testament to the faith: *it is time to get off this planet*. For his countless contributions to aerospace science, Parsons is honored by having a crater on the moon named after him.[68]

The footsteps of the Illuminati

One day, browsing in a bookstore, I came upon *Gurdjieff: Making a New World*, by J.G. Bennett. Guess my state of mind when I came upon the following passage:

> After Gurdjieff died I was asked by some of the old pupils to write a commentary on *Beelzebub*. When I had written a few chapters and sent them around for comment, almost all agreed that it would be a mistake to publish them. If Gurdjieff had intended his meaning to be readily accessible to every reader, he would have written the book differently. He himself used to listen to chapters read aloud and if he found the key passages taken too easily — and therefore almost inevitably too superficially — he would rewrite them in order, as he put it, to "bury the dog deeper." When people corrected him and said he surely meant "bury the bone deeper," he would turn on them and say it was not "bones" but the "dog" that you have to find. The dog is Sirius the dog star, which stands for the spirit of wisdom in the Zoroastrian tradition.[69]

Sirius again. "Coincidence," says the Skeptic, one more time. *Beelzebub's Tales to his Grandson*, the book in question, concerns extraterrestrial Higher Intelligences who intervene repeatedly on Earth to accelerate evolution here. But, of course, that's just a story . . .

Or is it?

J.G. Bennett, in another book on the Gurdjieff teachings called *Is There Life on Earth?*, claims that Gurdjieff was initiated into a mystic society, unnamed, which began in Babylon around 4500 B.C. Grant also traces the Crowley tradition back to Egypt and Babylon around that time.

"Coincidence, coincidence, coincidence," mutters the Skeptic; but is there a growing uncertainty in his voice?

Wait. There's a lot more to come. In July 1975, I published

an article about all this in *Gnostica*, an occult newspaper. A few weeks later, I received a letter from Edward Gardiner of the Detroit Film Collective. Mr. Gardiner wrote that he attended the Fourth International Festival of Yoga and Esoteric Sciences in Dallas. Dr. Douglas Baker, in a lecture, said that Sirius is the Ajna center of a galactic being and our sun is the Heart center. Our planetary evolution depends on raising the energy from the Heart (our sun) to the Ajna (Sirius).

Dr. Baker represents the Theosophical Society, founded by Madame H.P. Blavatsky, based on alleged transmissions from a Secret Chief named Koot Hoomi. That Gurdjieff was educated by the Sufis is now generally accepted. Crowley was directed by a Secret Chief named Aiwass. I would estimate that about 90 per cent of the occult groups in the Western world today are wholly or partially derivative from Blavatsky or Gurdjieff or Crowley, who together make up the indispensable Big Three of 20th century occultism. And now we have all three of them tied in, one way or another, with Sirius.

Of course, if shamans of any school are going to develop delusions about stars, they are likely to pick Sirius, which is the brightest star in the sky and hard to ignore. It is also in the constellation of the Dog, "man's best friend."

Nevertheless, such is the repressed gullibility of even the most hardened Skeptic, I have found myself wondering once or twice about new meanings in the ancient Zen riddle, "Does a dog have the Buddha-nature?" And, on rereading Joyce's *Ulysses* for the first time in several years, the Metaprogrammer was struck by the Black Mass in which the souls of all the saved chant "Goooooooooooooood" while all the souls of the damned chant "Dooooooooooooooog."

This palindrome (God-Dog) also appears in *The Book of the Law*, remember, in the question, "Is a god to live in a dog?" My fantasy leaped and I asked myself why Joyce set *Ulysses* in spring 1904, the same time that Crowley was receiving *The Book of the Law*. (19 + 04 = 23 . . .)

The same palindrome, again, appears in Chapter One of Dr. Leary's *High Priest*, published in 1968. The chapter is titled "Godsdog."

Coincidence? Synchronicity? Higher Intelligence?

Then Brian Hanlon, San Francisco UFOlogist, called my attention to a book called *Other Tongues, Other Flesh*, by George Hunt Williamson.

Williamson, an early 1950s Contactee, claims to have met some flying saucerites from Sirius. He prints vast huge chunks of their language — the "other tongues" in his title — and I found that a few of the words were almost identical with some words in the "angelic" language used by Dr. John Dee, Aleister Crowley and other magi of the Illuminati tradition. For instance, Williamson transcribes one of the words he received as *leshtal*; Crowley has "lashtal." This is more striking when we remember the two Naval officers who got "affa" (nothing) from the same "angelic" language.[70]

Williamson also informs us that the Sirians have been in contact with Earth for "several thousand years" and that their allies here use as insignia the Eye of Horus — the origin of the Illuminati eye-in-triangle design.[71]

Like every other Contactee, Williamson may, of course, be suspected of hallucinating or just of being a damned liar, Even the most hard-headed skeptics, however, must be a bit puzzled if we ask a few questions at this point, such as: what are the chances of Williamson, either as a hallucinator or as a hoaxer, picking up words in the "angelic" language, known only to advanced students of Cabala? Well, maybe he could have read a bit of Cabala in his time; sure. But what are the chances, by coincidence or whatever, that two Naval Intelligence officers of high security rating should also, in a separate Contact, get a word in the same language? How could Williamson have known that Crowley was in any way connected with Sirius in 1953, when he wrote his book, since Kenneth Grant was the first to link Crowley and Sirius, in 1973? Was it only by coincidence of lucky guessing that Williamson picked the eye-in-the-triangle (used by Crowley and the Illuminati) as the alleged symbol of the secret society in contact with Sirius? Was it only another coincidence that that symbol was used by Adam Weishaupt and Thomas Jefferson? And is it another coincidence that Dr. Baker, the Theosophist, should declare Sirius "the third eye" of a cosmic being?

When *Illuminatus* was being written (1969-1971), I had no interest in Sirius at all and no delusions about contact with extraterrestrials. But we now find that both the number 23 and the eye-in-the-triangle motif — the two most mysterious enigmas in that novel — have a long history of linkage with the Illuminati-Sirius mystery. I didn't know that when working on *Illuminatus* — but evidently something that is part of my mind or in communication with my mind did know it.

Dope and divinity

After all this, I began to restudy Gurdjieff avidly. *Beelzebub's Tales to his Grandson*, Gurdjieff's major prose work, concerns interstellar Higher Intelligences who seek to aid and advance evolution on Earth. I had previously regarded this framework as mere allegory, a convenient scaffolding for Gurdjieff's serious teachings, but now I began to wonder if he were hiding his real secret out in front where nobody would think to look for it. A Purloined Letter from Sirius?

I was even more intrigued by the step diagram of the vibratory levels. Above mankind, Gurdjieff placed "angels," "archangels" and "the Eternal Unchanging." Dr. Kenneth Walker, a Fellow of the Royal College of Surgeons and a hard-headed scientist, has an odd comment on these higher beings in his book, *A Study of Gurdjieff's Teaching*:

> These squares represent higher entities than ourselves of which we have no knowledge at all, and we can call them angels and archangels if we like . . . Some other members of the St. Petersburg group had agreed to equate "angels" with planets and "archangels" with suns . . .[72]

If we substitute for "planets" and "suns" the concept "intelligent, more evolved entities in other solar systems" we have the 1973 Leary theory of interstellar telepathy.

Gurdjieff's system, in brief, holds that human beings are

evolving from mammalhood to immortality. Almost all of us, he says repeatedly (and with evident joy in annoying our self-esteem), are still on the mammalian level — robots controlled by conditioning. We think we are conscious, but we aren't. We are asleep, hypnotized, sleep-walking — the metaphors vary, but they all mean that we can't see outside our conditioned reality-tunnel. When we begin to awaken, we perceive that the world is nothing at all like the myths and superstitions our society has imposed on us. And, if Gurdjieff's allegory be taken literally, a group of Interstellar Intelligences, who have already evolved to stages less mammalian than ours, are watching us all the time and, occasionally, intervening to accelerate our evolution toward their level.

In this context, let us recall that there are two great mysteries in anthropology, and that they do not concern minor matters at all but are, rather, two of the biggest questions we can ask — namely, how did language begin? and how did civilization begin? There are dozens of theories, but not one hypothesis has yet achieved anything close to majority acceptance. Talking to anthropologists, I often get the feeling that each of them has a personal theory different from all the others. We simply do not know.

But language and civilization are functions of the symbolizing or semantic faculty, which also produced that other great mystery: shamanism — out of which grew religion and the whole web of artificial (human-made) Ideas which differentiate us from the other land-mammals.

The cumulative evidence in such books as Dr. Andrija Puharich's *The Sacred Mushroom*, John Allegro's *The Sacred Mushroom and the Cross*, R. Gordon Wasson's *Soma: Divine Mushroom of Immortality*, Robert Graves' revised fourth edition of *The White Goddess*, Professor Peter Furst's *Flesh of the Gods*, Dr. Weston LaBarre's *The Peyote Cult and Ghost Dance: Origins of Religion*, Margaret Murray's *The Witch Cult in Western Europe*, etc., leaves little doubt that the beginnings of religion (awareness of, or at least belief in, Higher Intelligences) is intimately linked with the fact that shamans — in Europe, in Asia, in the Americas, in Africa — have been dosing their nervous systems with metaprogramming drugs since at least 30,000 B.C.

The pattern is the same, among our cave-dwelling ancestors and American Indians, at the Eleusinian feasts in Athens and among pre-Vedic Hindus, in tribes scattered from pole to pole and in the contemporary research summarized by Dr. Walter Huston Clark in his *Chemical Ecstasy*: people take these metaprogramming substances and they soon assert contact with Higher Intelligences.

According to LaBarre's *Ghost Dance*, the shamans of North and South America used over 2,000 different metaprogramming chemicals; those of Europe and Asia, curiously, only used about 250.[73] *Amanita muscaria* (the "fly agaric" mushroom) was the most widely used sacred drug in the Old World, and the peyote cactus in the New. Over the past 30-to-40,000 years countless shamans have been trained by older shamans (as anthropologist Carlos Castaneda is trained by *brujo* — witch-man — Don Juan Matus in the famous books) to use these chemicals, as Dr. Leary and Dr. Lilly have used them, to metaprogram the nervous system and bring in some of the signals usually not scanned. (On the visual spectrum alone, it has been well known since Newton that we normally perceive less than 0.5 (one-half of one) per cent of all known pulsations.) It can safely be generalized that the link between such sensitive new scannings and personal belief in Higher Intelligences is the most probable explanation of the origins of religion.

That the turned-on mind is cosmic in dimension is stated directly by Carlos Castaneda's shamanic teacher, Don Juan Matus, in *Tales of Power*:

> "Last night was the first time you flew on the wings of your perception. A sorcerer can use those wings to touch other sensibilities, a crow's for instance, a coyote's, a cricket's, *or the order of other worlds in that infinite space*." (Italics added.)

When Professor Castaneda asked directly, "Do you mean other planets, Don Juan?" the old shaman answered without reservation: "Certainly."[74]

As Captain James T. Kirk once remarked, "Can all this just

be an accident? Or could there be some alien intelligence behind it?"

The horrors begin

At this point in our adventure, I was entering my second year on Welfare and approaching my 42nd birthday. *Illuminatus* was still not published. Sometimes when I looked into the mirror I could imagine the words FAILURE: TOTAL, ABJECT, COMPLETE FAILURE written on my forehead. I fully appreciated Mae West's famous verdict: "I've been rich and I've been poor, and rich is better."

I was doing Sufi heart-chakra exercises every day, to open myself more and more to love for all beings. It was not that I really wanted, or hoped, to become a saint, but merely that, without such self-work, I could easily crumble into the bundle of paranoia and self-pity that many a 1960s idealist had become during the Nixon Counter-Revolution. The heart chakra opened, at times, and light poured out, just like it says in the textbooks, and the Mystic loved every living creature. *The whole world was my body.* It was gorgeous. Two days later, despite continued work on heart-opening, money worries would overcome the Poor Fool again and I would feel the onset of the classic Anxiety Syndrome — dizziness, wet palms, rapid heartbeat, the whole works.

According to William F. Buckley, Jr., and various other philosophers who have never been poor, this kind of thing is supposed to build character and keep America strong. The Poor Fool saw a lot of other people on Welfare in those months — if you live in a poor neighborhood, you meet poor people — and I made a detailed study of the kind of character this experience builds. In my judgment, they would all have been less paranoid if, instead of being poor seven days a week, they were allowed to be comfortable six days and were subjected to the Chinese Water Torture on the seventh.

The Poor Fool continued his Sufi heart-chakra exercises, concentrating on loving people like Buckley, Nixon and Rockefeller. Meanwhile, he attacked his anxiety symptoms with *pranayama*, a yogic breathing method which Crowley (among others) promises will banish any negative emotion. After a month of doing *pranayama* for 30 minutes every morning, the anxiety symptoms went away. The heart chakra also became more active and I started falling in love with everybody I met.

Then Kerry Thornley, high priest of Eris, re-entered my life, dragging the Kennedy Assassination horrors with him.

As a result of Thornley's feud with D.A. Jim Garrison in 1967-68, Thornley had entered a belief system in which Garrison was, like Joe McCarthy, an unscrupulous power-seeker willing to defame any number of innocents in order to make headlines and advance his own political career. By the time Garrison's conspiracy theories had collapsed in court (he never convicted a single "conspirator"), everybody, even Garrison's most devout followers in the underground press, was more or less willing to accept that belief and forget all about Garrison's bizarre investigations.

By 1973, Thornley had begun to enter a different belief-system. He was puzzled over many aspects of the case Garrison had tried to manufacture against him, and kept brooding over the details. Basically, the case rested upon what ordinary people call *coincidences*. Jungians and parapsychologists call them *synchronicities*. Garrison called them *"propinquities"* and said they proved the existence of "a conspiracy so vast as to stagger the imagination."

Thornley began to believe in the conspiracy. The coincidences-synchronicities-propinquities hadn't "just happened"; they had been manipulated and therefore Thornley had been set up, like Oswald, as a fall guy to drive independent investigators (like Garrison) off the real scent.

According to Garrison, these propinquities indicated that Thornley had been part of a conspiracy that managed the assassination and framed Oswald. Thornley, for years, was convinced that it was all coincidence — but then he began to wonder. He and Oswald had both come to the attention of their superiors in the Marines because they were avowed Marxists at that time and were labeled "trouble-makers." Could Naval Intelligence have noted their physical resemblance and started concocting a plot to exploit this resemblance later?

The more Thornley thought about this, the more alarming the propinquities (or coincidences) seemed. At one point, he went to a hypnotist to attempt to discover if Naval Intelligence could have brainwashed him, erased the memory of that, and controlled him for years . . . could he have been part of the plot without knowing it? Naturally, the hypnotist was unable to find a definite yes or no answer to this question.

Then, early in 1975, Thornley remembered an odd conversation in 1963 with a New Orleans man whom we will call Mr. M. The subject was — are you ready? — how to assassinate a President and get away with it. It was all abstract and theoretical (both Thornley and Mr. M. were aspiring writers, and the idea was to construct a plot that would convince the reader it could work in real life), but at one point Mr. M. said that the best technique would be to use individuals who *didn't even know they were being used.*

Thornley later heard rumors that Mr. M. was actually a lower-level member of the New Orleans Mafia.

At the time Thornley remembered this, the latest idea among professional Kennedy Assassination buffs was that the Mafia had collaborated with the C.I.A. on the job.

Had the assassination actually been a Mafia-Naval Intelligence job, and had Mr. M., in that odd conversation, been testing Thornley to see if any memory of the hypothetical brainwashing lingered near the surface of consciousness?

About that time one of the Assassination Investigation organizations put out a paper suggesting *multiple Oswalds* — an elaboration on the "two Oswalds" suggested by Professors Popkin (*The Second Oswald*) and Thompson (*Six Seconds in Dallas*). According to this model, Oswald either died or was murdered shortly after leaving the Marines, and his I.D. had then been used by Naval Intelligence as a cover for a variety of agents who more or less looked like him.

And some very intelligent, academic and non-paranoid conspiracy researchers began to point out an interesting pattern surrounding the Kennedy and Martin Luther King Jr. assassinations: a series of false trails which were never followed up by the official investigations but which later served to befuddle and confuse the numerous citizens' investigations (including Garrison's). Some of these false trails, it was alleged, led to Fidel Castro. All of these red herrings had been dragged across the trail, according to this school, as fail-safes, in case the original "deranged lone assassin" scenario fell apart.[75] Thornley began to wonder how much of his life in and after the Marine Corps had been manipulated as part of such a red herring.

Then Thornley read about the case of Robert Byron Watson.

Watson, a convict, has charged that he overheard a plot to kill Martin Luther King Jr. in a shop in Atlanta in 1968.

One of the conspirators described by Watson seems to match Thornley's memories of Mr. M.

Watson's story has been investigated and pronounced worthless by the FBI. Naturally.

It has also been investigated and pronounced true by black activist, comedian and conspiracy buff Dick Gregory. Naturally.

You can predict, with about 99% accuracy, whether a given individual will believe Watson's story, irrespective of the evidence, or lack of evidence — just on the basis of that individual's political orientation. *(Whatever you believe imprisons you.)* The one percent whose reaction to Watson's charges *cannot* be predicted from their previous politics — the one individual in a hundred who would like to know what the hell is really going on — are the only persons on Earth not included in Gurdjieff's dismal declaration that this is a planet of conditioned robots.

Thornley, you will remember, is one of the inventors of the theology of Discordianism, which is expounded at some length in *Illuminatus*; and Volume I of the trilogy is dedicated to him (and to Mr. Gregory Hill, another great Discordian theologian). This dedication, it now appears, is unfortunate, because Mr. Thornley, believing he has solved the John F. Kennedy and Martin Luther King Jr. assassinations, is somewhat worried that his attempts to reveal the truth will be mistaken for a publicity gimmick to promote *Illuminatus*.

Any public statement by Shea and myself that Thornley's charges are not a publicity gimmick for our book will, of course, only increase suspicions about that possibility.

I must point out that two weeks after Thornley first made his charges against Mr. M. (to the Atlanta police) he was robbed, pistol-whipped and had his I.D. taken.

That coincidence (or propinquity) is not funny at all.

Ishtar's Walk: a guided tour of Hell

All conspiracy buffs are persecuted eventually. This is a sociological law on which I would stake my life, because I have seen it confirmed in every conspiracy-seeking group I've ever known. Perhaps the persecution is created by the conspiracy-seekers themselves (in the sense that every neurotic creates his own problems), or perhaps the mad satire in *Illuminatus* is true after all and every conspiracy ever imagined actually exists. The fact remains that those who believe the world is run by the Jesuits get persecuted as much as those who believe it is run by the Elders of Zion; and those who believe it is run by the Rockefellers get persecuted in exactly equal measure. People who believe the Air Force is deliberately hiding the facts about the UFOs get persecuted by a special group of sinister beings known as the Men in Black, who claim to be Air Force officers — but who are (naturally) denied by the Air Force. There almost seems to be a neurotic-psionic law: whatever you fear most will eventually come after you.

The shaman, of course, lives through this process on more levels than the ordinary paranoid, because the shaman is determined to confront every terror and conquer it. Many, however, are shamans without knowing it, and invoke their private demons in total ignorance, thinking it is all coming from outside themselves.

> The following is transcription of a letter distributed to the underground press and various conspiracy investigators by Kerry Thornley after he was beaten and had his I.D. taken.

Dear Sir,

On August 9th, 1975, twelve days after I delivered a statement to the Atlanta Police supporting allegations made by Robert Byron Watson concerning the assassinations of John F. Kennedy and Martin Luther King, two armed men wearing ski masks entered the home of my ex-mate during a party at which I was one of the guests. These masked individuals stole, among other things, all my identification.

This incident was reported to the Atlanta Police who later captured four men who they claim are the 'ski mask bandits.'

I had no particular reason - - except for my general knowledge of how the JFK assassins have operated in the past (regarding the impersonation-incrimination of Oswald, for example) - - for concluding that anyone had sent these bandits expressly to steal my ID. Nevertheless I did mention to a couple of friends that I was somewhat concerned that my ID - - regardless of why it was stolen in the first place - - might end up in the hands of the Mafia, the CIA, of the Naval Intelligence Command (all three of which groups seem to have been involved in the JFK murder).

Yesterday I was finally able to read - - no thanks to the Atlanta Police - - Robert Byron Watson's entire statement concerning how he overheard some heroin dealers associated with the syndicate plotting the MLK murder and how, at a later date, he was framed by syndicate and DEA people who sent heroin to his home through the mail, and then busted him, in order to discredit any future testimony he might deliver relative to the King murder.

Watson's statement contains this sentence: 'Just before the heroin was sent to my home through the mail, four armed, ski masked men broke down the back door one night about 9.00 p.m. while my mother and I were watching the T.V.' These four armed men then robbed Watson and his mother using exactly the same heavy-handed tactics and threats - - such as that they were 'going to blow your goddamn brains out' - - as did the ski masked men who robbed us. Watson says he was told that his assailants were 'hit men' from the syndicate.

Watson's mother was knocked down; I was pistol

whipped, once, under the left eye.

In another part of his statement, Watson mentions that someone was arrested in New Orleans who was using his name and his social security number at a time when he could prove conclusively that he was not in New Orleans.

So I have decided it would be a good idea to warn everyone that there may indeed now be a 'Second Thornley' wandering around. Effective as of the 9th of August I have no ID and anyone who shows up anywhere with my identification (operator's license, student card, social security and library cards, etc.) is an impersonator. I shall not replace my ID as, under such unusual circumstances as these, that will only complicate matters.

Henceforth, my identification shall be my right thumb print.

Kerry Wendell Thornley

6 September 1975

Box 827

Atlanta

GA 30301

Thornley began writing to me regularly about his solution to the assassinations, and insisted more and more often that his life was in danger. I tried to calm him down a bit by reminding him of the difference between theory and proof. It soon became evident, from his subsequent letters, that he was now half-convinced that *I* was part of the assassination conspiracy team.

I have a bad leg, from my polio in childhood, and it now began acting up worse than ever. Sometimes, I could not walk without a cane. Other times, pains and spasms kept me from writing in the day and from sleeping at night. "This is psychosomatic," I told myself. I quoted a Sufi proverb, "We do not walk on our legs but on our Will." The leg perversely got worse. I tried yoga, chiropractics, ordinary M.D.s, faith healers, polarity therapy, acupuncture and staying spaced out on pot for days. The leg got worse.

Dell, which had announced publication of *Illuminatus*, changed their minds and said they wouldn't print it unless we cut 500 pages.

I thought in anguish that we were ruining a masterpiece (such is the artistic ego), but we cut the 500 pages. I would rather have a flawed *Illuminatus* in print in 1975, I said, than no *Illuminatus* in print.

Thornley's letters to me became increasingly denunciatory. He now believed that the Discordian Society had been infiltrated very early by C.I.A. agents (probably including me) who had used it as a cover for an assassination bureau. The logic of this was brilliant in a surrealistic, Kafkaesque sort of way. Try to picture a jury keeping a straight face when examining a conspiracy that worshipped the Goddess of Confusion, honored Emperor Norton as a saint, had a Holy Book called "How I Found Goddess and What I Did to Her After I Found Her," and featured personnel who called themselves Malaclypse the Younger, Ho Chih Zen, Mordecai the Foul, Lady L, F.A.B.*, Fang the Unwashed, Harold Lord Randomfactor, Onrak the Backwards, *et al.* . . .

◆

* The initials refer to Lady L's title, "Fucking Anarchist Bitch," originally given to her by Eldridge Cleaver. "That's me," she said happily.

◆

While the Suspect was receiving these letters and trying to persuade Thornley, gently, that his imagination was growing faster than his evidence, various forms of paranoia were breaking out in the local Leary-Starseed group. Every week somebody would come to the Suspect and warn, in urgent whispers, that somebody else in the group was actually a government agent. Often, the person accused one week would be the person coming around to accuse somebody else the next week.

Of course, there must have been at least one real government agent in the group, since it is now established that every piece of mail Leary wrote or received in prison was Xeroxed by the California prison system, the F.B.I., the C.I.A. and the D.E.A. (What did they think, jointly or severally, about Joshua Norton and the Goddess Eris, not to mention extraterrestrials and immortality?)

Around about then Dennis Martino managed to die of murder, suicide and natural causes, all at the same time, in Spain. That is to say, Martino's death was reported by the press first as murder, then as suicide and finally as the result of an accidental overdose of heroin. Martino had been a government agent assigned to infiltrate the Leary defense organization as a spy — a procedure the Supreme Court has found objectionable in other cases. Martino, it is claimed by some persons close to the scene, also spied on the government for the Leary defense group. According to Leary, at least two more of his defense staff at the time were also government agents, but these were simultaneously co-conspirators with various paramilitary left-wing terrorist organizations.

Mae Brussel, the world's greatest single conspiracy buff, has insisted, over various underground radio stations, that virtually all the terrorist Left is a secret C.I.A. operation to discredit the rest of the Left. More recently, the U.S. Labor Party has taken up the same model and is accusing almost everybody in the Left of being a government agent working to discredit the Left. Although neither Mae Brussell nor the U.S.L.P. are any better at preparing an evidential case than the late Joseph McCarthy, the Watergate investigations revealed that the FBI's "COINTEL-PRO" operation did involve *agents provocateurs* and attempts to divide the Left by inciting crime and spreading paranoia. Maybe all the paranoids are right, after all.

Maybe.

The Wilson family was living, like all Welfare families, in a slum apartment building, infested with roaches, and full of other social rejects. The black woman across the hall had an 8-year-old boy (illegitimate) who was dying of cancer. Every so often she would go off her head and start raving at the whole building, saying she wished the child would die and end the agony. The child, of course, heard this. Pity assaulted me; I wept.

A man on the second floor abruptly went schizo and began invading our apartment (and all the others) announcing, incoherently, that he was the Grand Master of the Sufi Order, or that the whole building was now a Zen monastery and he was the Abbot, or various other kinds of occult gibberish.

Once, the half-crazy woman across the hall threw this totally crazy man out of her apartment while he was raving in that fashion. He stood in the hall, between her apartment and ours, shouting that he was the Indian Ambassador to the U.N., and had come to Berkeley to feed starving American families. When the police finally came to take him away, he told them he was the leader of the Weather Underground. Pity tore at me with claws.

Then we discovered an old lady living in the hall closet. She was an old "crazy woman" well-known around Berkeley, who always lived in halls or parks. She wouldn't apply to Welfare, to get enough money to pay rent somewhere, because she was sane enough to know they'd call her crazy. She was afraid they'd put her in a nuthouse.

The manager found her and threw her out. For a few nights, she camped in the bushes beside our building, then she moved on.

Pity and horror.

I am living in Gorki's *Lower Depths* or some ghastly work of naturalistic fiction, I decided. The whole world has turned into a lesson in the futility of human hope. We're all slowly going mad, from poverty and anxiety and mystery. Maybe my whole life was a hallucination; maybe I had never worked for *Playboy* and had 20 grand a year and eaten dinner with Hugh Hefner; maybe I had just imagined that. Maybe I had always been a Crazy Pauper in the Berkeley slums. It is an easy step from pity to self-pity.

The Crazy Pauper spent a whole day sitting in a chair, not writing, not talking to the family, not moving. Some might say I was catatonic.

At sunset, the Fool got up and went out on the porch and watched the sun sinking in the west, doing the Sufi heart-chakra exercise, forcing myself to love all beings. I came back to life.

▲　　▲　　▲　　▲　　▲

My book review desk at the San Francisco Phoenix the next day had a volume entitled *The Day the Dollar Dies* by somebody named Willard Cantelon. Flipping through it, I saw that it was about my old buddies, the Bavarian Illuminati.

I read Mr. Cantelon's version of the Illuminati Conspiracy with some interest. It appears that the Illuminati are currently plotting to wreck the international financial system and cause the disruption or fall of all the strong governments in the world. When chaos is complete, *contact with Higher Intelligences in outer space will be announced.*

But, says Mr. Cantelon, these Higher Intelligences are actually Satan and his fallen angels, who will appear on Earth as superhuman and benign beings; the masses will accept them as saviors, not recognizing their Evil Nature; and then we are done for. Satan will institute One World Government and One World Religion — those twin bugaboos of the extreme Right — after which money will be abolished and a computerized credit system will come into effect everywhere.

Everybody will be tattooed on the forehead and wrist with a credit number, and every "purchase" will consist only in having the numbers scanned by computers placed in every store or bank. This is the key to a tyranny that can never be resisted, because any rebel will merely have his credit cut off, and will be unable to buy food, clothing or shelter.

All this, Mr. Cantelon assures us, is foretold in *Revelations*, chapter 13, 16-17:

> He causeth all small and great, rich and poor, free and bond, to receive a mark in their right hand or in their fore-heads: and that no man might buy or sell save he that had the mark or the number.

I remembered the famous response of Robert Welch, chairman of the John Birch Society, when told that his conspiracy theories were fantastic: "Yes, but we are living in fantastic times." I laughed out loud.

Only after weeks had passed did I begin to think that I had, rather absent-mindedly, passed through what mystics call "the dark night of the soul," or "crossing the abyss." Whatever one calls it, I reached a depth of despair and deliberately decided to love the world instead of pitying myself; and, afterwards, I was no longer afraid of anything.

It didn't even bother me when San Francisco conspiracy buffs, looking at the same picture from a different angle, decided that Leary and I were really the ringleaders of the Illuminati and had masterminded the Kennedy and other assassinations. When the above-ground mouthpiece of the S.L.A., the Bay Area Research Collective, claimed I was Leary's C.I.A. "babysitter," I laughed again. When an anonymous bomb threat arrived the week after, the Fool was amused at his own amusement. Sufism had vindicated itself: the heart-chakra exercise works. "Perfect love casteth out fear." I was beginning to emerge on the other side of Chapel Perilous.

Mystery Babalon

Crowleymas 1974 — October 12, often associated with an Italian navigator who introduced slavery to the New World and syphilis to the Old — was celebrated at our apartment house with weird and eldritch festivities. Arlen and I, representing the Discordian Society, together with Stephen upstairs (Reformed Druids of North America), Claire and Carol in another apartment (witches, connected with the New Reformed Order of the Golden Dawn), and the Great Wild Beast Furtherment Society (which is really Stephen and me and another neighbor named Charles), opened all our rooms to a Crowleymas Party and invited nearly 100 local wizards and mystics.

"There are *always* paranoid vibes at Crowleymas parties," Isaac Bonewitz, of the Chasidic Druids of North America, likes to warn people, with an eerie chuckle.

In fact, Crowley has attracted the worst as well as the best elements in the occult world, and a self-declared "Crowleyan" is as likely to be a dangerous kook as a high adept.

The party was just starting when the Shaman was called to the phone, for a bitch of a conversation. My caller was a Dr. H. (not his real initial) who is a very gifted psychiatrist, rather fascinated with Leary and Crowley (and me). It seemed that he was having a bad acid trip, couldn't get control of the anxiety, and wanted my help. The Shaman has a reputation for great healing and tranquilizing vibes in dealing with people on bad acid trips, but he had never done it over the phone before. Twenty minutes later, when Dr. H. was calmed and going off into a good trip, I felt absolutely drained.

The Wizard returned to the living room. Immediately, Tom (another alias) sat down next to me, laughed shrilly, cracked a silly joke, and said, "I think I may be going crazy again." (He had been in a nut house for a few months about eight years before.) The Philosopher spent *three* hours, in the midst of the kind of noisy party you find only in Berkeley and only among hippies and witches, practicing psychotherapy without a license. Tom was convinced, finally, that he didn't have to go crazy again, that he was the programmer of his own computer, and that it had only been a hallucination that made him think the computer was starting to program him.

The Wizard was now even more drained; and then Jacques Vallee arrived.

I had wanted to talk to Doctor Vallee for several months now and I immediately kidnapped him into a room which the other party-goers were not informed about. On the way, we spotted Hymenaeus Alpha (Grady McMurty), Caliph of the Ordo Templi Orientis, and his wife, Phylis. Tom, still giggling at inappropriate moments but no longer sure he was going mad, tagged along.

The Skeptic had heard Jacques Vallee talk at a conference on Science and Spirit, sponsored by the Theosophical Society, earlier in the year. He had taken a new approach to the UFO mystery and was systematically feeding *all* the reports of extraterrestrial contacts into a giant computer. The computer was programmed to look for various possible repeated patterns. Jacques said that the evidence emerging suggested to him that the UFOs weren't extraterrestrial at all, but that they seemed to be intelligent systems intent on convincing us they were extraterrestrial.

Now the Skeptic started pumping Jacques about his evidence that they weren't extraterrestrial. He started to explain that, analyzing the reports chronologically, it appeared that They (whoever or whatever they are) *always* strive to give the impression that they are something the society they are visiting can understand. In medieval sightings, he said, they called themselves angels; in the great 1902 flap in several states, one of the craft spoke to a West Virginia farmer and said they were an airship invented and flown from Kansas; in 1940s-1950s sightings, they often said they were from Venus; since Venus has been examined and seems incapable of supporting life, they now say they are from another star-system in this galaxy.

"Where do you think they come from?" I asked.

Doctor Vallee gave the Gallic form of the classic scientific Not-Speculating-Beyond-The-Data head-shake. "I can theorize, and theorize, endlessly," he said, "but is it not better to just study the data more deeply and look for clues?"

"You must have some personal hunch," I insisted.

He gave in gracefully. "They relate to space-time in ways for which we have, at present, no concepts," he said. "They cannot explain to us because we are not ready to understand."

I asked Grady McMurty if Aleister Crowley had ever said anything to him implying the extraterrestrial theory which Kenneth Grant, Outer Head of *another* Ordo Templi Orientis, implies in his accounts of Crowley's contacts with Higher Intelligences.

"Some of the things Aleister said to me," Grady replied carefully, "could be interpreted as hints pointing that way." He went on to quote Crowley's aphorisms about various of the standard entities contacted by Magick. The Abramelin spirits, for instance, need to be watched carefully. "They *bite*," Aleister explained in his best deadpan am-I-kidding-or-not? style. The Enochian "angels," on the other hand, don't always have to be summoned. "When you're ready, *they come for you*," Aleister said flatly.

(The Enochian entities were first contacted by Dr. John Dee in the early 17th Century. Dr. Dee, court astrologer to Queen Elizabeth and also an important mathematician, has been controversial from his own time to ours, some writers regarding him as a genius of the first rank and others as a clever lunatic. According to two interesting books. *The World Stage* and *The Rosicrucian Enlightenment*, both by a most scrupulous historian, Dr. Francis Yates, Dee was almost certainly a prime mover in the

"Illuminati" and "Rosicrucian Brotherhoods" of that time, which played a central role in the birth of modern science. The alleged UFOnaut from Uranus which communicated with the two Naval Intelligence officers gave a name, AFFA, which is a word in the "angelic" language used by the entities Dee contacted. It means *Nothing*. George Hunt Williamson also got some words in "angelic" from his Space Brothers, remember.)

The outstanding quality of UFO contactees, Jacques Vallee said at this point, was *incoherence*. "I now have grave reservations about all physical details they supply," he said. "They are like people after an auto accident. All they know is that something very serious has happened to them." Only the fact that so many cases involve *other witnesses*, who *see something in the sky* before the "contactee" has his-her strange experience, justifies the assumption that what happens is more than "subjective."

"Largely," Doctor Vallee summarized, "they come out of it with a new perspective on humanity. A religious perspective, in general terms. But all the details are contradictory and confusing." He regarded green men, purple giant-men, physical craft with windows in them, etc., as falling into the category psychologists call "substitute memory," always provided by the ingenious brain when the actual experience is too shocking to be classified.

I asked how many in the room had experienced the contact of what appeared to be Higher Intelligence. Grady and Phylis McMurty put up their hands, as did two young magicians from the Los Angeles area, and myself. Jacques Vallee, curiously, looked as if he might raise his hand, but then evidently changed his mind and did not. I said I inclined to believe the Higher Intelligences were extraterrestrial, and asked what the others thought.

Grady McMurty — Caliph of the Ordo Templi Orientis — said, in effect, that the theory of higher dimensions made more sense to him than the extraterrestrial theory in terms of actual space ships entering our biosphere.

The two Los Angeles magicians agreed.

Tom, who had been a witch for five years and *hadn't* raised his hand when asked for contactee testimony, said that the Higher Intelligences are imbedded in our language and numbers, as the Cabalists think, and have no other kind of existence. He added that every time he tried to explain this he saw that people thought he was going schizophrenic and he began to fear that they might be right, so he preferred not to talk about it at all.

Tom — who is a computer programmer by profession, a witch only by religion — later added a bit to this, saying that all that exists is information and coding; we only *imagine* we have bodies and live in space-time dimensions.

Doctor Vallee listened to all this with a bland smile, and did not seem to regard any of us as mad.

(A few days later, in discussion with the former Vacaville prison psychologist, Dr. Wesley Hiler, I asked him what he *really* thought of Dr. Leary's extraterrestrial contacts. Specifically, since he didn't regard Leary as crazy or hallucinating, what was happening when Leary thought he was receiving extraterrestrial communications? "Every man and woman who reaches the higher levels of spiritual and intellectual development," Dr. Hiler said calmly, "feels the presence of a Higher Intelligence. Our theories are all unproven. Socrates called it his *daemon*. Others call it gods or angels. Leary calls it extraterrestrial. Maybe it's just another part of our brain, a part we usually don't use. Who knows?")

Since everybody in the room at this point had either had the required experience, or was willing to speculate about it and study it objectively rather than merely banishing it with the label "hallucination," I went into my rap about the parallels between Leary and Wilhelm Reich. "The attempt to destroy both Dr. Reich and Dr. Leary reached its most intense peak right after they reported their extraterrestrial contacts," I said. "I keep having very weird theories about what that means . . ."

Grady McMurty nodded vigorously. "That's the $64,000 question," he said emphatically. "For years I've been asking Phylis and everybody else I know: *why does the gnosis always get busted?* Every single time the energy is raised and large-scale group illuminations are occurring, the local branch of the Inquisition kills it dead. Why, why, why?"

Nobody had any very conclusive ideas.

"I'll tell you what I think," Grady said. "There's *war in Heaven*. The Higher Intelligences, whoever they are, aren't all playing on the same team. Some of them are trying to encourage our evolution to higher levels, *and some of them want to keep us stuck just where we are.* "

According to Grady, some occult lodges are working with those nonhuman intelligences who want to accelerate human evolution, but some of the others are working with the intelligences who wish to keep us near an animal level of awareness.

This is a standard idea in occult circles and it can safely be stated, without exaggeration, that every "school" or "lodge" of adepts that exists is regarded, by some of the others, as belonging to the Black Brotherhood of the evil path. Grady's own Ordo Templi Orientis, indeed, has been accused of this more often than have most other occult lodges. I have personally maintained my good cheer and staved off paranoia, while moving among various occult groups as student or participant, by *always adhering rigidly to* the standard Anglo-Saxon legal maxim that every accused person must be regarded as *innocent* until *proven guilty beyond a reasonable doubt.* This obviously spares me a lot of worry, but the more guarded approach is very well argued by Isaac Bonewitz, the author of *Real Magick.* "Paranoid magicians outlive the others," Isaac says.

Somehow the conversation drilled away from Grady's concept of "war in Heaven." Several times, Grady tried to steer us back there, but each time we wandered on to a different subject. Tom said later that he felt a presence in the room deliberately pushing us away from that topic . . .

Dr. H. — the psychiatrist whose bad acid-trip had started the Crowleymas party off so jumpily for me — dropped by the next day, to thank me for "talking him down" from his anxiety attack.

He also, it soon appeared, wanted to tell me about his accelerating experiences with magick. It had started over two years earlier, after an intensive seminar at Esalen. Dr. H. suddenly found that he could see "auras." (The aura of the human body, known to shamans and witches since time immemorial, has been repeatedly rediscovered by scientists, most of whom were thereupon denounced as "cranks." Franz Anton Mesmer called it "animal magnetism," in the 16th century. In the 19th, Baron Reichenbach called it "OD." In the 1920s, Gurvich named it "the mytogenic ray." Wilhelm Reich rediscovered it in the 1930s, called it "orgone energy," and was destroyed by AMA bigots who charged that he was hallucinating it. Kirlian photography has now demonstrated beyond all doubt that this aura exists.) Dr. H. soon found, further, that he could use the aura as a diagnostic tool in analyzing new patients. This experience, Leary's books, and a lecture by me on Crowley's magick, led him to further experiments.

On a beach in Sonoma County, after taking LSD *the day before* and programming an opening of the self to higher beings or energies. Dr. H. (no longer under the direct influence of the drug) had an experience with Something from the sky. "It wasn't exactly a Higher Intelligence," he said carefully, "or, at least, I didn't receive that aspect of it, if it was Higher Intelligence. To me, it was just *energy*. Terrible energy. My chest was sore for hours afterward. I thought it would kill me, but I was absolutely ecstatic and ego-less at the peak of it. If the chest-pain weren't so intense, it would have been a totally positive experience."

(MacGregor Mathers, Outer Head of the Hermetic Order of the Golden Dawn, and the first occult teacher of such worthies as Aleister Crowley, poet William Butler Yeats and novelist Arthur Machen, once recorded a meeting with the Secret Chiefs. These ambiguous entities, known in several schools of occult training, are variously believed to be discarnate spirits of the great Magi of the past, living Magi who can teleport themselves about as easily as you or I telephone a friend, "angels" in the traditional sense, or merely "beings we cannot understand." In any case, Mathers noted that the meeting, although pleasant, left him feeling as if he'd been "struck by lightning" and he also suf-fered chest pains and extreme difficulty in breathing. Dr. Israel Regardie has also noted that Alan Bennett, who was Crowley's chief teacher for many years, developed asthma, a chest disease. Crowley developed asthma himself as his contacts with the Secret Chiefs occurred more often; and Regardie finally "caught" asthma for several years after studying with Crowley, a condition which was only cured when he went through the bio-energetic therapy of Wilhelm Reich.)

Dr. H. went on to describe a second experience of the Energy and Light explosion, about a year after the first. This was also ecstatic and strangely frightening. Since then he has *felt* "healing power" in his hands and has experimentally tried a sort of Reichian-Rolfian massage on some of his patients, with favorable results.

It occurred to me that, if less prepared for such experiences and less committed to scientific method *as a habit of mind*, Dr. H. might well have remembered each of these experiences as an encounter with an angel or a UFO . . .

I remembered Crowley's discussion of Jesus, Buddha, Mohammed, St. Paul and Moses in Book One of *Magick*. Jesus, Crowley points out, says nothing about the source of his Illumination; Buddha speaks of being tempted by various demons and then seeing the Clear Light; St. Paul tells us he had been "caught upon into Heaven and seen and heard things of which it is not lawful to speak"; Mohammed claims he was visited by the Archangel Gabriel; and Moses simply says he "beheld God." Crowley comments:

> Diverse as these statements are at first sight all agree in announcing an experience of the class which fifty years ago would have been called supernatural, today may be called spiritual, and fifty years hence will have a proper name based on an understanding of the phenomenon which occurred.[76]

Leary emerges from darkness and Sirius rises again

My goodness, Toto, I don't think we're in Kansas any more.

– L. Frank Baum

Early in 1975, I began to receive letters from Dr. Leary again. We communicated at length about many subjects, including the Sirius mystery. Here's a selection of what Tim had to say (and note that only later did he reveal to me that he was being held in solitary confinement during these months):

> I felt great compassion and affection to realize that you have been worried about me — and that you have trusted me without understanding . . .*

> I am only interested in conversation with Higher Intelligence — and know that Higher Intelligence is not the least interested in politics . . .

> By the way, I have always felt that Crowley's "Do What Thou Wilt" is good . . . The question then becomes "What do we will to do." Most of the Crowleyites I've met (yourself excluded) seem to have decided they will make pompous asses of themselves. Which is fine with me. But I'm delighted that we've found the three obvious steps that a reasonably educated God takes: SMI²LE.

◆

* Dr. Leary is naïve here. The Metaprogrammer hadn't exactly "trusted" him but had kept an open mind, balancing the charges of informing made against him with his denials of those charges and deciding that one would gamble with him rather than his accusers. But one always knew one was gambling.

◆

(SMI²LE was Leary's new acronym for the Futurist scenario he had derived from the Starseed Transmissions. It means $\underline{S}$pace $\underline{M}$igration + $\underline{I}$ntelligence^2 + $\underline{L}$ife $\underline{E}$xtension.)

As soon as *Illuminatus* was published in September 1975, people started sending me letters about weird 23s in their own lives; and quite a few thought it worthwhile to inform me that the Morgan Guaranty Trust (an Illuminati hotbed, according to Birchers) is at 23 Wall Street. The most interesting of these communications came from an English flying saucer journal, *Fortean News*, and was forwarded by a Mr. W.N. Grimstad of St. Petersburg, Florida. The context concerns some mediumistic Contactees (persons allegedly in contact with extraterrestrial Higher Intelligences by means of a trance medium). Here's the passage that the Wizard enjoyed most:

"An entity that frequently communicated with the group called himself JIRO — a ludicrous appellation of the sort that seems common to many contactee accounts. The number 23 was communicated repeatedly both in the writings and through the medium, but the members of the group could never understand why. We listened to one tape that consisted of the medium's transformed voice referring one constantly to 23 and (phonetically) "Leer" (Lear, Leire, Llyr?) . . . One entity claimed it came from LEHRA or LEHAR (Llyr etc. again) . . . The communications contain references to the numbers 666 and 33 (sometimes 333) as well as 23."

Shortly after the Wizard received this tidbit, Dr. Leary wrote to me from prison that he and a visitor, novelist Ken Kesey, had thrown the *I Ching* together, asking when Tim would be released from Durance Vile.

They received as answer Hexagram 23, "Breaking Apart."

(666, of course, is Crowley's favorite number, the Number of the Beast and of the Stele of Revealing. 333 is the Cabalistic number of "that mighty devil, Choronzon," who once afflicted Dr. Dee in the 17th Century and gave Aleister himself a rough time in Bou Saada, North Africa, 1909, as recounted in *The Vision and the Voice*, by Aleister Crowley. 33 has so many mystical meanings in freemasonry that I could write a book about it.)

Mr. W.N. Grimstad, who sent me that clipping about Lear-23-666-333, mentioned in an accompanying letter that Florida anti-Illuminati groups (I assume he means Birchers) are spreading the theory that *Illuminatus* is a diabolical attempt to confuse the anti-Illuminati forces and that Shea and I are actually high-ranking Illuminati ourselves.

That did not surprise the Suspect; I had expected from the beginning that people of a certain cast of mind would regard a satirical treatment of the Illuminati theme as part of the Illuminati's cover-up effort.

Later, Mr. Grimstad sent me a tape, entitled "Sirius Rising," in which he and another conspiracy buff named Downard set forth the most absurd, the most incredible, the most ridiculous Illuminati theory of them all. The only trouble is that, after the weird data we have already surveyed, the Grimstad-Downard theory may not sound totally unbelievable to us.

According to "Sirius Rising," the Illuminati are preparing Earth, in an occult manner, for extraterrestrial contact. Part of the magical preparation, which only Illuminated Ones can understand, included:

(a) The founding of Cal Tech at 33° of latitude. (This was actually partially the work of aerospace engineer and occultist Jack Parsons, who was indeed a disciple of Crowley, as we have seen. In fact, so many of the scientists at Cal Tech were involved in Crowleyan magick, according to some reports, that the government grew concerned and sent in agents to infiltrate the O.T.O. and find out how subversive it might be. L. Ron Hubbard, founder of Scientology, was admittedly a member of that lodge of the O.T.O. at that time, and later claimed he had infiltrated it for Naval Intelligence.)

(b) The assassination of John F. Kennedy at 33° of latitude, to fulfill the alchemical ritual of "the killing of the divine king."

(c) The firing of the moon rockets from Cape Kennedy, again at 33° latitude.

(d) Arranging that the first man to walk on the moon would be a 33° Mason, which Neil Armstrong, it so happens, was. (Mr. Grimstad and Mr. Downard seem to share the notion, widely held by anti-Illuminati buffs, that all 33° Masons are Illuminati initiates.)

I emphatically don't believe that rigmarole myself, although it is similar to the kind of Cabalistic-numerological magick to which the Illuminati would be inclined, if they really exist. And the locations given are not all exactly on the 33° of latitude, although I must admit they are all close.

If you want to hear more of the Downard-Grimstad numerological evidence, write to W.N. Grimstad at P.O. Box 14150, St. Petersburg, Florida, and ask how much he wants for the tapes. (He sent me mine free, evidently hoping I would publicize them. See how obliging I am, Mr. Grimstad?)*

♦

* The Suspect also suspects that Mr. Grimstad suspects him of being in the real Illuminati and hopes he will give himself away in commenting on all this.

♦

The Grimstad-Downard theory shows again how different

nervous systems picking up the same signals will organize them into different tunnel-realities. Most curious to me was Grimstad and Downard's rap on the Phoenix, beginning with the facts (already quoted from Kenneth Grant in our chapter *Sirius Rising*) that "Phoenix" was Crowley's secret name in the Ordo Templi Orientis and that the Egyptians put Sirius in their constellation of the Phoenix. Messrs. Grimstad and Downard find it significant that the bird on the *other* side of the Great Seal of the United States (behind the Eye in the Pyramid) is identified as a phoenix by *some* heraldists (most insist that it is merely an eagle). They then find magick meaning in the coincidence-synchronicity that one of the Symbionese Liberation Army communiques, when they were holding Patty Hearst prisoner, was released through the *San Francisco Phoenix.*

That connection is, of course, absurd and, of course, only co-incidental. *Of course.* But it had "meaning" in the Jungian sense, for me. I had been Book Editor of the *San Francisco Phoenix* when that tape was given to us by the S.L.A., and I was writing an article with Leary about Patty Hearst's brainwashing when the Sirius tapes arrived from Grimstad.

Cosmic Coincidence Control Center is still working overtime on my case, I decided.

The Horus Hawk and Uri Geller

In September 1975, I was finally allowed to see Timothy Leary in the flesh again, in the office of a U.S. Marshal.

Timothy was *conspicuously unbrainwashed*, I would say; although he had been in solitary confinement for 19 months, he was still the same high-energy, high I.Q., high-exuberance individual he had been since I first met him in 1964. He seemed more *toughened* than *aged*, and had a grim determination about himself and about the Terra II goals (space migration, higher intelligence, life extension) that reminded me of other ex-cons and their goals.

"The universe is an intelligence test," he said at one point — adding later, "Prison is an intelligence test, too. If a mutant can't survive severe testing, it doesn't deserve to instigate the next evolutionary stage. That's a Darwinian law."

Tim has testified against four entrepreneurs who he feels betrayed his trust, attempted to implicate him in their own crimes, and exploited him financially. He denies testifying against anyone else, and is emphatic in denying that he testified against Weather Underground ("I know nothing that can be used against them, actually") or against the alleged worldwide drug conspiracy known as "The Brotherhood of Eternal Love." He says his talks with narcotics agents about that "conspiracy" convinced the Drug Enforcement Administration that it never existed and led to the dropping of charges against himself and others who had been accused of profiting from it. "Nobody has gone to jail because of me, and nobody will," he stated flatly; none of his critics have refuted this by producing a case of a person convicted and sentenced because of Tim's testimony.

The four persons against whom Tim testified could not be sentenced to prison anyway (the statute of limitations on the one crime he could nail them for ran out in 1975). Tim was satisfied that these individuals no longer control his finances and that their fear about his testimony caused them to take a public role as leaders of a campaign to discredit him. That, he says delightedly, prevented them from pretending to be part of his defense staff again.

Five months later, in February 1976, the Parole Board met to decide on Dr. Leary's fate. They "downed him for a deuce" in the argot of his current peer group — that is, they sent him back for two more years in prison. His next hearing, they ruled, would be in February 1978, when he would be 59-going-on-60 years of age. This, you have to admit, is pretty ungrateful treatment if Tim really had testified against myriads of old associates.

At this point, PEN — the Poets, Essayists, and Novelists Club — re-entered the case and drew up a letter to Congress, asking for a Congressional hearing on the Leary case, to investigate charges of conspiracy to violate Leary's civil liberties, which Leary claimed might include high-ranking Justice Department officials. Leary wished Congress to inquire into: why a government agent (Dennis Martino) was placed in Leary's legal defense organization against Supreme Court rulings making such infiltration illegal; why Tim served so much time for an offense usually punished with no more than 6 months; why he was placed in solitary confinement with no charges of violence against him; why government agents cooperated with unfriendly witnesses (the four entrepreneurs) in spreading inaccurate reports that Tim was a wholesale informer who had testified against "hundreds" of innocents and was about to be assassinated; and evidence that two other members of his defence team (besides Martino) might be government double-agents. These two, Tim claims, have incited left-wing crimes, a COINTELPRO operation since 1968.

COINTELPRO — Counter-Intelligence Program — was an FBI project that involved infiltrating civil rights groups, peace groups, New Left groups and other dissident organizations, in a deliberate attempt to incite violence, destroy the reputation of those opposing the Establishment, and spread paranoia against dissidents. Jane Fonda, the Black Panther Party and the Trotskyists, among others, have sued the government for conspiracy to violate their civil rights through COINTELPRO operations. The family of assassinated Black Panther leader Fred Hampton are also suing, claiming to have evidence that the man who drugged Hampton before Hampton was shot was an FBI agent.

"The truth is much funnier than the myths," Tim told me. "It's all exactly like your novel, *Illuminatus*. At least two of my public representatives were government agents involved with underground terrorist groups also. But that's not anything odd or special — it's quite normal, I've found. The Weather people could surface tomorrow without being prosecuted, because the case against them is equally tainted."

Four weeks after PEN published these charges, the Parole Board had an unscheduled meeting, reversed themselves, and ordered Tim released on the following day. He departed for the mountains of New Mexico with Joanna for a vacation and delayed honeymoon.

The whole story of what actually went on behind the scenes with Leary, the dozens of lawyers involved, the Justice Department, Weather and COINTELPRO are not fully known to me. But Weather has several times since then discussed surfacing, as if convinced that Tim is right and they cannot be prosecuted.

"I've learned a lot about mammalian politics," Tim says. "I've held my own in dealing with the Justice Department, the narcs, the FBI, the CIA, Weather Underground, Al Fatah in Algiers, the local cops in dozens of states, prison guards and administrators in 29 prisons on 3 continents, and all the prison gangs of the California Archipelago — the Manson crowd, the Aryan Brotherhood, the JDL, the Black Muslims, the Mexican and Sicilian Mafias . . . No other social psychologist has had this kind of practical field experience with groups who will kill you in a minute if you show weakness. This has been the greatest educational experience of my life."

Even before Leary was out of prison, I began meeting and corresponding with various scientists who had been drawn into his SMI²LE scenario despite the potential risk to their own reputations involved in association with an allegedly insane convict. Most of them, like Dr. Paul Segall, were longtime Immortalists and concerned chiefly with life extension research. Others were psychologists fascinated by Tim's neurological model to explain the higher consciousness states. One group that held special interest for me were California physicists concerned with parapsychology and Leary's work in relation to their own theories on quantum mechanics.

This group included Dr. Jack Sarfatti (co-author of *Space-Time and Beyond*), Dr. Fred Wolf, Saul-Paul Sirag and Dr. Nick Herbert.

Sirag, in particular, soon became a close friend.

"I have four quantum models that cover that," Saul-Paul says whenever I tell him a new occult adventure. And he always does have (at least) three models. Once I asked him if there wasn't one model that he especially likes.

"Well," he said, "maybe it's all happening at once . . ." By "all" he meant the models we had been discussing that evening (extraterrestrials, time-travelers and a mutation in human neurology).

Saul-Paul, when Uri Geller was in the United States in 1973, being investigated, once tried to "contact" SPECTRA, the alleged extraterrestrial entity that supposedly communicates through Geller and enables him to read minds and bend metal.

Geller said that Sirag could see SPECTRA, if he were properly attuned, by looking into his (Geller's) eyes.

Sirag looked, and saw Geller's head turn into the head of a bird of prey.

What is provocative about that inconclusive experience is that Sirag didn't know at the time, and only learned much later, that SPECTRA had previously appeared in hawk-form to Dr. Andrija Puharich.

Dr. Puharich's encounters with the SPECTRA-hawk are described in his book, *Uri*. It manifested several times in connection with the Arab-Israeli war — weirdly synchronistic connections.[77]

Even odder, shortly after "Sirag "saw" the Horus hawk through Geller, *Analog Science Fact/Science Fiction* magazine featured on its cover a man wearing a hawk-head hat, illustrating a story called "The Horus Errand." The oddity was that the man's face was that of Ray Stanford, a Texas psychic known to Sirag's friend, Alan Vaughn.

A letter to the artist who drew the cover, Kelly Freas, drew a reply saying that Freas had never met Stanford and was not consciously aware, at the time, that he was using Stanford's face in the illustration.

A letter to Stanford drew an even more amazing reply. Stanford claimed to have been in a car which Geller teleported 30 miles. Stanford also said that a hawk had appeared quite dramatically during another meeting with the remarkable Geller.

All that happened between April and December, 1973. I received my first Sirius impressions in July 1973 and Leary and Benner received the Starseed signals in August 1973. For a dramatic climax, while I was nearing completion of the first draft of this book in July 1976, Saul-Paul Sirag called me on the phone to tell me that a friend in Southern California had just reported another "teleportation" involving Geller, and another hawk associated with it.

While Saul-Paul was telling me this over the phone I was

watching the TV picture in the next room. As he mentioned the hawk manifestation, on screen came an advertisement for a new movie, *The Shadow of the Hawk*, starring Chief Dan George. Honest.

(More synchronicity: while working on the third draft of this chapter in January 1977, I received the latest issue (Vol. 5, No. 4) of *Gnostica*, an occult journal to which I often contribute. Inside, in an article titled "Novus Ordo Seclorum," editor-publisher Carl Weschcke claims the bird on the Great Seal is neither eagle nor phoenix but *hawk* — and the Horus-hawk specifically.)

In Crowley's *Book of the Law* we find such texts as the following:

"Ra-Hoor-Khuit hath taken his seat in the East at the Equinox of the Gods." (Ra-Hoor-Khuit is another name for Horus, in his Warrior God aspect.)

"Sacrifice cattle, little and big: after a child. But not now. Ye shall see that hour, O blessed Beast, and thou the Scarlet Concubine of his desire! Ye shall be sad thereof. Deem not too eagerly to catch the promises; fear not to undergo the curses. Ye, even ye, know not this meaning all."

"I am the Hawk-Headed Lord of Silence and Strength; my nemyss shrouds the night-blue sky."

The emphasis on Ra-Hoor-Khuit as "hawk-headed," not just hawkish in general, is interesting in the light of Saul-Paul Sirag's vision of the hawk-headed extraterrestrial in Uri Geller's eyes. Sirag was not familiar with the above passages until I called them to his attention.

Crowley's works are always hermetic, coded, inscrutable. Am I being overly-imaginative in suggesting, possibly, that some readers have committed what Sufis call "the error of literalism" and are currently sacrificing "cattle, little and big," in order to prepare for the apotheosis of the Eighties when the Hawk-Headed Lord will cause the earth to "cower . . . and be abased"?

The cattle mutilations have covered 15 states by now and, unless we relapse into a supernatural explanation, the only plausible theory is that these sacrifices are the work of a large, well-organized and very disciplined occult organization.

Uri Geller and Dr. Puharich were haunted by the hawk-like
SPECTRA so often that they nicknamed it Horus.

Mike Reynolds, a writer for *Oui* magazine and the underground press, has been researching these mysterious mutilations for two years now and thinks he has found the explanation for the mystery most stressed by sensational tabloids, namely, the fact that many of the mutilated cattle are found in muddy areas *with no footprints around them*. Army-style helicopters, ranchers have told Mike, are often seen leaving the scene just before the cattle are found. Many of the animals have broken legs. The explanation, Mike suggests, is that those responsible pick up the cattle in helicopters and then drop them overboard after the mutilations.

Many small ranchers, Mike has also found, blame it all on the major agricultural corporations and think it is a plot to terrorize them out of the cattle business. Others, of course, have tried to link the mutilations to UFOs, to the C.I.A. (Army-style helicopters are often seen, remember), or to "Bigfoot," the alleged half-ape half-human critter often reported in rural areas.

The sacrifice of cattle was, of course, part of many shamanic traditions throughout history.

The Mothman Prophecies

Our contemporary cattle mutilations began in West Virginia in 1968. At the same time, as recorded by reporter John Keel in his book, *The Mothman Prophecies*,[78] the afflicted parts of West Virginia were also visited by several different kinds of unearthly or paranormal phenomena.

There were over 100 sightings of UFOs, and three "close contact" cases, in which people saw "extraterrestrials" or were taken aboard the "spaceships" for testing. There was also an outbreak of those noisy psychic explosions called poltergeist disturbances in the farms of the area. To add to the madness there were about 70 sightings of a traditional bogey of West Virginia, "Mothman" (a monster with giant red eyes, a human form, and huge mothlike wings). Dozens of encounters with the famous Men in Black also were reported.

The MIBs, as UFO investigators call these spooks, always dress in sinister black and drive black Cadillacs. They claim to be U.S. government agents, but are denied by all government agencies. They usually scare the blue bejesus out of people they visit, often leaving behind the impression that they are either demons or hostile extraterrestrials. They have been described by hundreds of UFO witnesses since the early 1950s.

Obviously, there was a lot of contagious hysteria in West Virginia that year, but there were also several objective radar sightings of the UFOs. The cattle mutilations were objective phenomena too. Keel received these predictions over and over from the Contactees:

1. The Pope would be stabbed while visiting the Mid-East.

2. Robert Kennedy was in danger, and the danger was in a hotel kitchen.

3. There would be a nationwide power failure on December 24 at noon.

The first prophecy had English on it, as they say in baseball. The Pope was *not* stabbed during his visit to the Mid-East. One year later, during a visit to Manila, he *was* stabbed.

The second prophecy was fulfilled when Kennedy was shot dead in a hotel kitchen.

The third prophecy was false. But at noon on December 24, while Keel waited to see if the power failure would occur, a bridge collapsed in West Virginia, in the middle of the UFO-Mothman-poltergeist area. Over 100 people were killed.

"They've done it again," Keel said when he heard the news of the tragedy, "Those lousy bastards have done it again. They knew this was going to happen . . . They just didn't want me to be able to warn anyone."

From that time to this, Keel has regarded the "ultra-terrestrials" (his name for the entities behind the UFO phenomena) as malicious and vicious.

Doggiez from Sirius

> That innocent dog sleeping by the fire — little do you
> realize that he's an invader from the Dog Star, Sirius.
>
> -the Firesign Theatre's comedy album,
>
> *Everything You Know is Wrong*

In 1975, I met a young lady who claimed to be High Priestess of all the Druids in Ireland. In a psychic reading, she told me that I was writing a book about Crowley (I was) and that I am in contact with a Higher Intelligence (I sometimes think I am). She said the Higher Intelligence was the evolved spirit of an ancient Irish bard.

In 1976, in Houston, I met another psychic, with the unbelievable name of Penny Loony. She told me that I was writing an article on Atlantis (I was), that the editors would demand some rewrite (they did) and that I would sell it on second submission (I did).

She also told me I'm in contact with a Higher Intelligence, but she described it as the spirit of an ancient Chinese Master. Can It be Irish, Chinese, and extraterrestrial all at once?

I have tried, experimentally, taking LSD with the assumption that the Higher Intelligence is actually the fairy-people of ancient Gaelic lore. I had a classic experience of being taken into fairyland, undergoing the usual time-warps characteristic of fairy-lore-I thought I was "over there" for several hours, but it all happened in a few minutes of the consensus-time of the witches with whom I was working. I even met Our Lady of Space in her familiar Celtic guise as La Belle Dame Sans Merci.

Later, I found the whole experience entered as a dream in my diary, *two weeks before it occurred*. And, of course, all the time I was over there in the Cosmic Fun House they kept trying to tell me something unintelligible about time . . .

More amusingly, I happened to see the old movie, *Harvey*, on

TV a few weeks later, and began to notice that Elwood P. Dowd, the hero, has the same relation with "Harvey," an invisible white rabbit, as any shaman has with his "ally." I began to wonder if the author of *Harvey* might have been an initiate of some witch-coven, Crowleyan lodge or similar psychic group. At this point in the play, a character named Wilson, learning that Harvey is a pookah, looks up pookah in the dictionary. The entry begins, "A Celtic elf or vegetation spirit of mischievous nature . . ." and ends, remarkably, "*and how are you tonight, Mr. Wilson?*" The actor playing Wilson dropped the book in shock, and I was a bit startled myself.

A bit later, Elwood has a long speech about Harvey's ability to stop time and enter eternity.

One more bit of spookery — a last haunting laugh from the Cosmic Fun House — and we will pass on to Part Two and the search for an explanation of all this.

In late 1976, quite independent of Discordianism, a group of political non-Euclideans, the Natural Surrealist Party, began running a chap named George Papoon for President. Papoon went around with a paper bag over his head and used the campaign slogan "Not insane!" Somehow, I got on their mailing list and one day they sent out the following press release:

> The thing most feared by the people of San Francisco has come to its inevitable head. Office-workers and non-working executives in the prestigious financial district here were startled to see a huge doughnut perched atop the Transarmenia Pyramid Building . . . No one seems to know why it picked the Pyramid to be its parking place, altho one thing is certain according to Sur/Gen Zippo Klein, the foremost authority on the vehicle and its alleged occupants: "They won't get a ticket up there . . . I'd bet my shoes those are the Doggiez from Sirius, and only Grid knows what they're planning up there . . ."

This was followed by a series of equally humorous press releases about the "Doggiez from Sirius," who are allegedly at large in our midst. This is all a joke, of course, just as *Illuminatus* was when Shea and I first conceived it. Probably, the people will think I am a bit over-imaginative if I suggest that none of us begin to understand what a joke is or where important ideas come from . . .

Of course, *Illuminatus* fans, at this point, are thinking about the mystery of Joe Malik's disappearing dogs. That riddle was deliberately left unanswered at the end of the trilogy, as one of our time-delay jokes. On rereadings, close students will eventually discover that Malik's dogs did not disappear because they never existed in the first place. They were *inferential*. The fact was that people heard doggy howls and barks from Malik's apartment, and the dogs never did exist except as a hypothesis. The source was, of course, the Museum of Natural History album, *Language and Music of the Wolves*.

It is odd, however, that one of the theories discussed by the detectives (Vol. I, p. 49) is that Malik's dogs came from the Dog Star, Sirius.

> ***First there is a mountain,***
> ***Then there is no mountain,***
> ***Then there is.***

Part II:

Models and Metaphors

PART II: MODELS & METAPHORS

I SLEPT WITH FAITH
& FOUND A CORPSE IN MY ARMS
ON AWAKENING;
I DRANK & DANCED ALL NIGHT
WITH DOUBT & FOUND HER
A VIRGIN IN THE MORNING.

CROWLEY
BOOK OF LIES

Models and Metaphors

FURTHER FABLES AND ALLEGORIES

From the Sufi

A man who had studied much in the schools of wisdom finally died in the fullness of time and found himself at the Gates of Eternity.

An angel of light approached him and said, "Go no further, O mortal, until you have proven to me your worthiness to enter into Paradise!"

But the man answered, "Just a minute, now. First of all, can you prove to me this is *a real Heaven* and not just the wishful fantasy of my disordered mind undergoing death?"

Before the angel could reply, a voice from inside the gates shouted:

"Let him in — he's one of us!"

From the Jewish

A young man went to his Rabbi and said, "I have lost Faith."

"So," said the Rabbi, "and how did you lose Faith?"

"I studied Logic at the university," said the young man, "and I found out that you can prove either side of any case if you're clever enough."

"Indeed," said the Rabbi. "Can you prove that you have no nose?"

"Certainly," said the student. "To begin with —"

But at this point the Rabbi punched him hard right on the nose.

"What hurts?" the Rabbi asked solicitously.

From the German

Erwin Schrodinger, Nobel Laureate in physics, propounds the following riddle for theoretical physicists: A cat is in a locked room where it will be killed eventually by a poison gas pellet (or a gun) activated by a quantum decay process. After an interval, t, is the cat dead or alive?

The theoretical physicist cannot go into a laboratory and try this experiment (which only gives the result in one case anyway). He sits down with pen and paper and calculates, by quantum mechanics, what has happened after interval t. He finds that the equations yield a minimum of two solutions. In one possible universe or *eigen*state, the cat is still alive; but in another equally possible universe the cat is dead.

This is the famous Schrodinger's Cat paradox. It is basically asking whether our physical models describe the universe objectively or just define the limits of our own knowledge.

The Sirius Evidence

Have real honest-to-God extraterrestrials from Sirius been meddling in the affairs of this backward planet?

Let us review some of our evidence. I became obsessed with the number 23 and the eye-in-the-triangle design years before I found any link between them and Sirius. After July 23, 1973, I definitely experienced impressions which I thought were communications from Sirius, keyed off by a Crowley ritual. Kenneth Grant, one of Crowley's closest associates in the Ordo Templi Orientis, repeatedly links Crowley with Sirius and seems to be hinting that the "Holy Guardian Angel" contacted by Crowleyan mind-expansion techniques is a denizen of Sirius. J.G. Bennett, one of the closest of Gurdjieff's associates, also tells us of coded references to Sirius in Gurdjieff's writings. Sufi historian Idries Shah traces the name of the Illuminati back to a verse in the Koran which mentions a shining star, and Crowley's alternative name for the Illuminati was the Order of the Silver Star (Argentum Astrum). George Hunt Williamson, a flying saucer Contactee, claims to have spoken to natives of Sirius who use a language containing some of the same words as the "Enochian" or "angelic" language used by such magicians as Dr. John Dee and Crowley. Williamson also tells us a secret order on Earth has been in contact with Sirius for thousands of years and that the emblem of that order is the eye of Horus.

We have also seen that there was a certain amount of telepathy or idea-transference between Dr. Leary and myself in the summer of 1973, before I received permission to correspond with him and visit him. Leary and Benner received the Starseed message during the "dog days" of 1973, when the link between Earth and Sirius is strongest according to Egyptian tradition, synchronizing with my own initial Sirius transmissions. And a separate group of UFO Contactees in England have received jumbled interstellar messages concerning the Discordian 23, the Masonic 33, Crowley's favorite number 666, and variations on the name of Leary.

We have, at minimum, an extraordinary amount of coincidence or propinquity here. For some stranger coincidences, let us look at astronomer Temple's *Sirius Mystery*.

First of all, Temple is scholarly, cautious and honest. Don't take my word for it; here's what a few reviewers said: "Well-documented" (*Oxford Mail*); "honest with his readers, careful with his sources" (*Daily Telegraph*); "Robert Temple is cautious. He has intellectual integrity." (*London Sunday Times*); "a work of respectable scholarship" (*Manchester Guardian*). Temple even claims to be embarrassed to be writing about such a sensational subject (p. 4) and I, for one, believe him, since I am embarrassed myself.

Temple reprints, in full, an anthropological study of the Dogon tribe in Africa, and their knowledge of Sirius is astonishing indeed.

The Dogon know that Sirius has an invisible companion (the white dwarf, Sirius B). Sirius B's existence was not suspected by our astronomers until this century and was photographed successfully only in 1970.[80]

The Dogon know the exact period of Sirius B, which is 50 years.[81]

They even know that Sirius B is one of the heaviest stars in the universe.[82]

In evaluating this knowledge, please keep in mind that Sirius B is not only invisible to the naked eye, but was invisible to the most powerful telescopes until this very century; and that the determination of its periodicity and its weight involve extremely fine instrumentation and decidedly advanced mathematics. How could a tribe barely advanced beyond the Stone Age know such things? They say they know about it because a visitor from Sirius, several thousand years ago, told them about it. Is it more logical to assert that they are just damned lucky guessers?

Is it possible that the French anthropologists who collected the Dogon legends about Sirius — Professors Griaule and Dieterlen — are a pair of hoaxers? Well, yes, it is possible; but is it likely? Every scientific hoax ever discovered turned out to be the work of one individual, usually with a persecution complex and a grudge against the Establishment. Two scholars conspiring together on such a fraud would be unique. It is also worth nothing that Messrs. Griaule and Dieterlen published their report on the Dogon in 1950 — three years before George Hunt Williamson claimed his contact and 23 years before Kenneth Grant published his revelations about Crowley's links to Sirius.

Amusingly, much of Temple's information has ramifications in areas which he himself has not explored. He has found, for instance, that the Bozo, a tribe neighboring the Dogon, also know about the Companion of Sirius and call it *tono nalema* (Eye Star).[83] This is most suggestive when we recall Dr. Baker's claim that the Sirius system is the "third eye" of the cosmic entity of which our sun is the heart, and George Hunt Williamson's claim that the eye of Horus is the symbol of the secret society which is in contact with Sirius.

Temple believes the Contact (which he tends to portray as physical, involving actual space-ships) occurred in Sumeria around 4500 B.C. The knowledge thus gained, he argues (and this is the major theme of his book), was passed on via various secret societies of initiates in the Near East, Egypt, Greece and so on, at least until the time of the 5th century (A.D.) neo-Platonist Proclus. Thereafter, Temple loses track of it, and suggests that it petered out, although he mentions that offshoots of it appeared in "such bizarre and fascinating figures as Giordano Bruno, Marsilio Ficino, John Dee and even Sir Philip Sidney and the Earl of Leicester — not to mention the troubadors of Provence, Dante in Italy, and the massacred tens of thousands of Albigensians in France, the Knights Templar and an infinite range of hopeless causes over two and a half millennia . . ."[84] Readers of my *Illuminatus* and *Sex and Drugs* will easily recognize that this tradition overlaps, or may even be identical with, the secret tradition of Tantra and sex-magick in the West, the tradition of which Crowley was the latest public representative.

Similarly, Temple goes to a great deal of trouble to demonstrate that the phoneme, NU, wherever found in the ancient world, is part of the secret Sirius tradition. He is not aware that NUit and ANUbis, two figures he specifically links with Sirius, are still very much alive among those magical lodges currently working the Aleister Crowley system of contacting Higher Intelligence.

Every now and then Temple seems to be toying with the idea that the Contact may be not by space-ship but by some more subtle means; but he does not explore that possibility, despite the fact that all his evidence comes from shamans, mystics, occult initiatory cults and others whose main concern has always been the ceremonial expansion of consciousness.

Over and over, one wishes that Temple had read a little in modern occultism to supplement his seven years of research into the Egyptian and Babylonian mysteries. He spends nearly 50 pages demonstrating that, to the ancient initiates, Isis was a symbol of Sirius and Osiris a symbol of the *Dark Companion* of Sirius; but he is not aware of Crowley's and Levi's insistence that the traditional secret revealed in the Eleusinian Mysteries was that "Osiris is a *black* god!"[85]

Again, Temple demonstrates (from ancient records) that the familiar image of Isis, with a star above her and one of her feet in water and the other on land, is a symbol of the Sirius connection; but he is not aware that that image still appears as Atu XVII of the Tarot — The Star.

By a detailed examination of the myths concerning Sirius in the Dogon, Egyptian and Babylonian traditions, Temple manages to demonstrate that the Contact probably occurred around 4500 B.C. in the Near East, among people at the approximate level of the Dogon. Some of these people carried the tradition across the Sahara, to the modern-day Dogon and Bozo tribes, and some seeded it into the cosmologies of Egypt and Babylon. As we

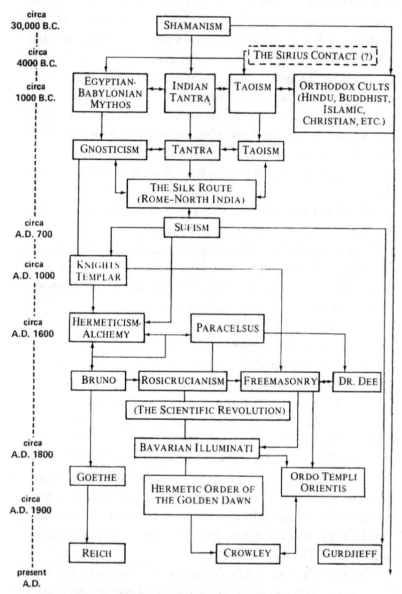

Every book on the Illuminati has a chart showing how the "Conspiracy" has developed over the centuries. Here's a summary of the links suggested by the evidence in the present book. Regard it as a Conspiracy only if you enjoy living in a script where you are one of the underdogs or victims.

have already seen, Kenneth Grant traces the Crowley tradition back to 4500 B.C. in the Near East, and J.G. Bennett traces the Gurdjieff tradition back also to that time and that place. Neither Grant nor Bennett could have anticipated that Temple would demonstrate, with a great deal of archaeological evidence, that some sort of Contact with Sirius did occur at that time, at that place. Yet both of them assert secret teachings concerning Sirius were passed on by Crowley and Gurdjieff.

Temple also demonstrates that the whole Egyptian calendar revolved around the movements of Sirius — the year began with the "dog days" when Sirius started to rise behind the sun (July 23 in our calendar; the date on which I had my first Sirius experience); that the earliest hieroglyphic for Osiris (the Dark God, Sirius B) was an *eye* plus a throne; and that the most secret of the rituals of Osiris, the "black rite," is described in one Hermetic text as being so cryptic in its total meaning that men will only understand it fully when they pursue the stars "unto the height" — which may mean when we travel to the stars.[86]

The most obvious and economical explanation of all this seems to be that an Earth-Sirius communication has occurred, at least once, probably several times.

ERP and Bell's Theorem

Let us try another perspective on the problem; let us see what modern physics has to offer. The flow-chart on the following page, by Saul-Paul Sirag, represents the main problems in quantum theory and the directions of current speculation.

The Einstein-Rosen-Podolsky demonstration (ERP, for short) indicated that, *if quantum mechanics is true*, some particles are in instantaneous contact even if at opposite ends of the universe. (This is only true of particles that were once in physical contact, but that is a technical point that doesn't matter in this context.) The trouble with ERP is that (a) such *instantaneous* communication across galaxies has no physical explanation and is hard

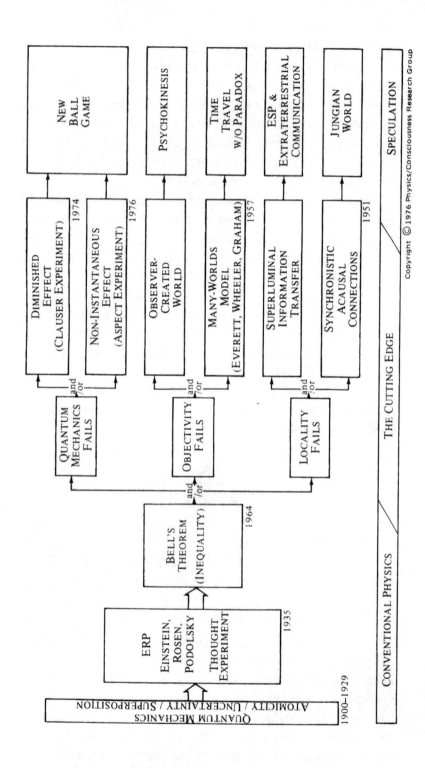

CONVENTIONAL PHYSICS | THE CUTTING EDGE | SPECULATION

QUANTUM MECHANICS
ATOMICITY / UNCERTAINTY / SUPERPOSITION
1900–1929

ERP
EINSTEIN, ROSEN, PODOLSKY
THOUGHT EXPERIMENT
1935

BELL'S THEOREM
(INEQUALITY)
1964

QUANTUM MECHANICS FAILS
and/or

OBJECTIVITY FAILS
and/or

LOCALITY FAILS
and/or

DIMINISHED EFFECT (CLAUSER EXPERIMENT)
1974

NON-INSTANTANEOUS EFFECT (ASPECT EXPERIMENT)
1976

OBSERVER-CREATED WORLD

MANY-WORLDS MODEL (EVERETT, WHEELER, GRAHAM)
1957

SUPERLUMINAL INFORMATION TRANSFER

SYNCHRONISTIC ACAUSAL CONNECTIONS
1951

NEW BALL GAME

PSYCHOKINESIS

TIME TRAVEL W/O PARADOX

ESP & EXTRATERRESTRIAL COMMUNICATION

JUNGIAN WORLD

Copyright © 1976 Physics/Consciousness Research Group

194

to think about anyway and (b), even worse, such instantaneous communication is forbidden by Special Relativity, which allows no instantaneous effects, everything being limited by the speed of light.

The intent of ERP was a *reductio ad absurdum* of quantum theory. ERP is deduced by rigorous mathematics from quantum mechanics, and appears to be false for the two reasons given above. In math, if the conclusion is false, then the antecedent is false. Ergo, quantum mechanics is not true.

This was a happy thought to Einstein, Rosen and Podolsky, all of whom had grave reservations about the random element implicit in all quantum equations — reservations summed up in Einstein's famous maxim, "God does not play dice."

Alas, ERP was promulgated in 1935 and everything since then — the greatest period of experimental work in the history of physics, there being more physicists alive today than in all previous history — indicates that quantum mechanics is not false at all. It works beautifully. Ergo, if the antecedent is true, the conclusion is true, and ERP effects *must* exist — even if they are forbidden by Special Relativity.

Now, physicists are not particularly happy with this conclusion, since they wish to preserve both quantum mechanics and Special Relativity. Something has to be done about the ERP paradox — but what?

In 1964, Bell's Theorem suggested three possible interpretations of the ERP effect, all of them controversial. Bell's Theorem appears (as this is written, 1977) solid as steel, so at least one of the alternatives must be included in the new paradigm, when physics finally does produce a new paradigm. Let us look at the three alternatives.

Quantum mechanics fails . . .
and/or
Objectivity fails . . .
and/or
Locality fails . . .

If quantum mechanics fails, it is going to fail radically and totally. The Clauser experiment (Berkeley 1974) showed that attempting to redefine quantum connections would not get around

Bell's Theorem, so *quantum theory as known* must be revolutionized totally if we take this path. This means we are in for a bigger epistemological revision than that connected with Relativity and Quantum Theory themselves; probably, we are in for the biggest redefinition of reality in the history of science. This mindboggling event will be the *biggest* revolution in scientific history because almost everything in modern physics depends on the truth of quantum theory. Giving up quantum mechanics is equivalent to a religious person's giving up God; *everything* — not just a few things — will then change in our thinking.

Saul-Paul Sirag laconically sums this alternative up as "New Ball Game" at the right of the chart.

and/or

If Objectivity fails, we are in for an equally gigantic revolution in thought, but we can at least suggest what form it will take. Objectivity, in this context, means the doctrine that the universe exists apart from the ideas or the will of the investigator. Two models have been developed without the doctrine of Objectivity. The first is the "participatory universe" or "observer-created universe" of Nobel Laureate Werner Heisenberg and Dr. John A. Wheeler of Princeton. In Heisenberg's version, quantum events exist *in potentia* before human measurement and in *reality* only after such measurement has occurred. "Weirdness," Heisenberg says, is the characteristic of *potentia*; time flows forward *and backward* there, and none of the usual laws of physics apply. Those laws only come into action *after* human intervention (measurement) has occurred.

and/or

Wheeler's observer-created universe, like Heisenberg's, portrays "reality" as the result of human-quantum interaction, but adds the possibility that ERP transmissions may effect this result even before measurement is made. This, of course, leads directly to the possibility of psychokinesis (magick . . .) and might explain all sorts of eerie events, from religious "miracles" to Uri Geller's alleged metal-bending. A slight extension of this hypothesis will allow us to consider all my 23s as the result of quantum interactions between my brain and the events I have intersected since becoming interested in 23. We are very close to

Jano Watts's "Net" here, and to the old shamanic belief-system which Sir James Frazer called "the Law of Contagion." Crowley called it "the magickal link."

and/or

The second non-objective model is the parallel-worlds idea long used by science-fiction writers. A mathematical formulation of this has been devised by Wheeler (the same Wheeler as above) with Everett and Graham. This leads to the concept that there are 10^{100+} universes existing "simultaneously" in different dimensions. (10^{100+} is only an estimate, but it means 10,000,000 ,000,000,000,000,000,000,000,000,000,000,000,000,000,0 00,000,000,000,000,000,000,000,000,000,000,000,000,000 ,000 universes — ten million million, million, million, million, million, million, million, million, million, million, million, million, million, million, million, million, million, million, million universes *at least*.) Each of these universes is as complete, and as vast in time and space, as our own, and we exist in each of them, but in different ways.

In other words, everything that *can* happen *does* happen. As Saul-Paul Sirag explains this model, "In the universe next door, I'm still a physicist but working at a different area of research. A few universes over, I'm an actor who dropped out of physics and never came back to it. In another universe, I died in the concentration camp and don't exist in the 'present' at all."

Most physicists can't take this model seriously, and it is rumored that Wheeler, Everett and Graham, who created it, don't believe in it. Yet it is one legitimate interpretation of the problem raised by Bell's Theorem.

and/or

If Locality fails, we are in a particularly interesting predicament. Locality has a rather technical meaning in physics, but basically you can think of it this way: The local universe, to any intelligent being, is bounded by the speed of light. That is, any signal received is traveling at, or at less than, the speed of light. This "local" universe — everything we can *detect* moving within the limiting velocity of light — is the only universe, according to Special Relativity. A "non-local" universe would be one outside that limitation. By Special Relativity, such a non-local universe is metaphysical and "meaningless," in the sense that, even if it did exist, we could never possibly *detect* it.

However, if we interpret ERP and Bell's Theorem to mean that quantum events are, after all, in instantaneous communication, then we can contact a non-local universe on the medium of the quantum communication net. This is virtually indistinguishable from saying that *we can be in California and Arizona at the same time*, or in *California and the Sirius double-star system* at the same time, or in the *past, present and future* "at the same time."

A possible way of looking at this rather incomprehensible thought has been developed by Dr. Jack Sarfatti, who assumes that ERP transmissions (faster-than-light) are *information without transportation*. Limiting our view to a local universe — to transmissions at, or at less than, the speed of light — is "electromagnetic chauvinism," Sarfatti has proposed. *Information without transportation* is information without energy, without "signals" in the ordinary sense. The rule of Special Relativity is, thus, not challenged but merely reduced to a definition of locality; it applies only to *signals* and *energy systems*. Pure *information* can take the form of ERP transmissions not limited by signals or the speed of light.

This superluminal information (ERP transmission), Sarfatti argues, might underlie the interstellar ESP which has been claimed by recent writers (myself included) as well as ordinary planetside ESP.

and/or

Superluminal information might also, Sarfatti and Sirag have proposed elsewhere, account for the damnable and mind-boggling phenomena of synchronicity; e.g., my 23 space-time hologram. Synchronicity, as formulated by Jung and Pauli, merely describes *what happens*: coincidences form into patterns that are acausal but meaningful. Superluminal information transfer on the quantum level might explain *how this happens*. Every sub-atomic system in the universe, or in the multiverses, adjusts instantaneously into conformity with the whole, by synergetic feedback faster-than-light. Here we approach Dr. Capra's "Bootstrap Theory" which makes everything the cause of everything, as in *I Ching* or Taoism.

We have constructed, within these alternative models at the forefront of physics, a series of partial explanations of the weird data I have offered.

If quantum mechanics fails, then all my data — however Incompatible with current reality-maps — is merely a series of events which will be explained later, when physics has advanced a few decades (or centuries, or millennia).

If objectivity fails *and* there is a world of *potentia* underlying the world of measured reality, then all my data and all the data of shamanism from the beginning of humanity's history are just records of abrupt interference between *potentia* and *reality*. Heisenberg's concept of *potentia* does, indeed, sound a lot like "the other world": the *nagual* described in Castaneda's books, the "astral" realms of Cabala, the "fairyland" of the Celts, the "Side" of witchcraft. In raw *potentia*, literally anything can happen, forward or backward or sideways in time; only in measured *reality* are we limited by the laws of physics.

If objectivity fails and there are parallel worlds, maybe as many as 10^{100+} of them, it is easy to see how communications from here to there could be bedeviled by incoherence and confusion. Various humans who had turned on to the universe next door or to various universes two or more quantum jumps away might carry back signals which they would organize into such Gestalts as "I talked to God," "I traveled in time," "I met an extraterrestrial," etc. In particular, they might bring back both prophecies that succeed and prophecies that fail, our universe being tangent to the parallel universes at some points but not at all points.

The "Mothman Prophecies" of John Keel, remember, worked out this way:

Prophecy #1: The Pope will be stabbed fatally in the Near East in 1968.

Result: The Pope was stabbed, non-fatally, in Manila, in 1969.

Prophecy #2: Robert Kennedy was in danger in a hotel kitchen.

Result: Robert Kennedy was shot to death in a hotel kitchen.

Prophecy #3: All the power in the U.S. will fail at noon on December 24, 1968.

Result: The power didn't fail, but a bridge in the center of Mothman territory collapsed at that moment, killing 100.

Keel interprets this mindfuck to mean that the communicating entities were mischievous, had a nasty sense of humor, and are deliberately misleading and tormenting those who get involved with them. Although he calls them "ultra-terrestrials," his concept of them is not much different from what earlier centuries meant by "demons."

In terms of the multi-universe model, however, the entities could be totally honest. All of their predictions came true, in one universe or another. Keel just happens to be in one of the universes at a tangent to theirs, where only part of the prophecies came true.

Interestingly, Dr. Vallee has found a similar pattern of prophecies partially succeeding and partially failing among many alleged Contactees.[87]

If locality fails, *and* faster-than-light information really exists, we are in a Jung-Pauli universe in which synchronicity is at least as important as linear causality.

And, *if* locality fails, *and* some advanced races are using superluminal information as casually as we use electricity, some of it must intersect this planet occasionally, although most of it is not on wavelengths usually picked up by us. This is Dr. John Lilly's "Network."

It seems, in short, that there is nothing in Part One of this book, however incredible to the ordinary reader, which cannot be accounted for within the possibilities of the growing edge of quantum theory.

Tunnel-Realities and Imprints

Let's try Dr. Leary's perspective on these mysteries.

To understand neurological space. Dr. Leary assumes that the nervous system consists of eight potential circuits, or "gears," or mini-brains. Four of these brains are in the usually active left lobe and are concerned with our terrestrial survival; four are extraterrestrial, reside in the "silent" or inactive right lobe, and are for use in our future evolution. This explains why the right lobe is usually inactive at this stage of our development, and why it becomes active when the person ingests psychedelics.

We will explain each of the eight "brains" briefly.

I. *The bio-survival circuit.* This invertebrate brain was the first to evolve (2 to 3 billion years ago) and is the first activated when a human infant is born. It programs perception onto an either-or grid divided into nurturing-helpful Things (which it approaches) and noxious-dangerous Things (which it flees, or attacks). The imprinting of this circuit sets up the basic attitude of trust or suspicion which will last for life. It also identifies the external stimuli which will ever after trigger approach or avoidance.

II. *The emotional circuit.* This second, more advanced bio-computer formed when vertebrates appeared and began to compete for territory (perhaps 500,000,000 B.C.). In the individual, this bigger tunnel-reality is activated when the DNA master-tape triggers the metamorphosis from crawling to walking. As every parent knows, the toddler is no longer a passive (bio-survival) infant but a mammalian politician, full of physical (and psychic) territorial demands, quick to meddle in family business and decision-making. Again the first imprint on this circuit remains constant for life (unless brainwashed) and identifies the stimuli which will automatically trigger dominant, aggressive behavior or submissive, cooperative behavior. When we say that a person is behaving emotionally, egotistically or "like a two-year-old," we mean that s/he is blindly following one of the tunnel-realities imprinted on this circuit.

III. *The dexterity-symbolism circuit.* This third brain was formed when hominid types began to differentiate from other primate stock (circa 4-5 million B.C.) and is activated when the older child begins handling artifacts and sending/receiving laryngeal signals (human speech units). If the environment is stimulating to the third circuit, the child takes a "bright" imprint and becomes dextrous and articulate; if the environment is made of stupid people, the child takes a "dumb" imprint, i.e., remains more or less at a 5-year-old stage of artifact clumsiness and symbol-blindness.

In popular speech, the first circuit tunnel-reality is generally called "consciousness" *per se*: the sense of being here-now, in this body, oriented to the survival of the body. (When you are "un-conscious," the first circuit is anesthetized and doctors may perform surgery on you or enemies may attack you, and you will not evade them or flee.) The second circuit, in the same vernacular language, is called "ego." *So-called "ego" is the second circuit mammalian sense of status (importance-unimportance) in the pack or tribe.* The third circuit is what we generally call "mind" — the capacity to receive, integrate and transmit signals produced by the hominid hand (artifacts) or the hominid 9 laryngeal muscles (speech).

The imprinting of these three circuits determines, by about age 3½, the basic degree and style of trust/distrust that will color "consciousness," the degree and style of assertiveness/submissiveness that will determine "ego"-status, and the degree and style of cleverness/clumsiness with which "mind" will handle tools or ideas.

In evolutionary terms, first brain "consciousness" is basically invertebrate, passively floating toward nurture and retreating from danger. Second brain "ego" is mammalian, always struggling for status in the tribal pecking-order. Third brain "mind" is paleolithic, hooked into human culture and dealing with life through a matrix of human-made gadgets and human-created symbolism.

The fourth brain is post-hominid, specifically characteristic of *Homo sapiens*, the "domesticated" WoMan. This is:

IV. *The socio-sexual circuit.* This fourth brain was formed when hominid packs evolved into societies and programmed specific sex-roles for their members, circa 30,000 B.C. It is activated at puberty, when the DNA signals trigger the glandular release of sexual neurochemicals and the metamorphosis to adulthood begins. The first orgasms or mating experiences imprint a characteristic sex-role which, again, is biochemically bonded and remains constant for life, unless some form of brain-washing or chemical re-imprinting is accomplished.

In daily speech, fourth circuit imprints and tunnel-realities are known as the "adult personality."

Masters and Johnson have demonstrated that specific sexual "dysfunctions" — so-called "perversions," "fetishes," low-or-no performance conditions like premature ejaculation, impotence, frigidity, etc., or imprints defined as "sinful" by the local tribe — are determined by specific experiences in early adolescent mating. The same is true of the equally robotic behavior of the "normal," "well-adjusted" person. The sex-role of the human is as rote and repetitious as that of any other mammal. (Or bird or fish or insect.)

These four circuits are normally all the networks of the brain ever activated. It should now be clear why Leary calls them terrestrial. They have evolved on, and have been shaped by, the gravitational, climatic and energy conditions determining survival and reproduction on this kind of planet circling this variety of Type G star. Intelligent organisms born in outer space, not living at the bottom of a 4,000-mile gravity well, not competing for territory on a finite planet-surface, not limited by the forward-back, up-down, right-left parameters of earthly life, would inevitably develop different circuits, imprinted differently, and not so inflexibly Euclidean.

Forward-back is the basic digital choice programmed by the biocomputer operating on Circuit I: Either advance, go forward, sniff it, touch it, taste it, bite it — or retreat, back away, flee, escape.

Up-down, the basic gravitational sense, appears in all ethological reports of animal combat. Rear up, swell the body to maximum size, growl, howl, shriek — or cringe, drop the tail between the legs, murmur softly, skulk away, crawl and shrink the body size. These are domination and submission signals common to iguana, dog, bird, and the Chairman of the Board of the local bank. These reflexes make up Circuit II "ego."

Right-left is basic to the polarity of body-design on the planetface. Right-hand dominance, and associated preference for the linear left-lobe functions of the brain, determine our normal modes of artifact-manufacture and conceptual thought, i.e., third circuit "mind."

It is no accident, then, that our logic (and our computer-design) follows the either-or, binary structure of these circuits. Nor is it an accident that our geometry, until the last century, has been Euclidean. Euclid's geometry, Aristotle's logic and Newton's physics are meta-programs synthesizing and generalizing first brain forward-back, second brain up-down and third brain right-left programs.

The fourth brain, dealing with the transmission of tribal or ethnic culture across generations, introduces the fourth dimension, time.

Since each of these tunnel-realities consists of biochemical imprints or matrices in the nervous system, each of them is specifically triggered by neuro-transmitters and other drugs.

To activate the first brain take an opiate. Mother Opium and Sister Morphine bring you down to cellular intelligence, bio-survival passivity, the floating consciousness of the newborn. (This is why Freudians identify opiate addiction with the desire to return to infancy.)

To activate the second tunnel-reality, take an abundant quantity of alcohol. Vertebrate territorial patterns and mammalian emotional politics immediately appear when the booze flows, as Thomas Nashe intuitively realized when he characterized the various alcohol states by animal labels: "ass drunk," "goat drunk," "swine drunk," "bear drunk," etc.

To activate the third circuit, try coffee or tea, a high-protein diet, speed or cocaine.

The specific neurotransmitter for circuit four has not been synthesized yet, but it is generated by the glands after pubescence and flows volcanically through the bloodstreams of adolescents.

None of these terrestrial drugs change basic biochemical imprints. The behaviors which they trigger are those which were wired into the nervous system during the first stages of imprint vulnerability. The circuit II drunk exhibits the emotional games or cons learned from parents in infancy. The circuit III "mind" never gets beyond the permutations and combinations of those tunnel-realities originally imprinted, or abstractions associated with the imprints through later conditioning. And so forth.

But all this Pavlovian-Skinnerian robotism changes drastically and dramatically when we turn to the right lobe, the future circuits and extraterrestrial chemicals.

The four evolving future "brains" are:

V. *The neurosomatic circuit.* When this fifth "body-brain" is activated, flat Euclidean figure-ground configurations explode multi-dimensionally. Gestalts shift, in McLuhan's terms, from linear *visual space* to all-encompassing *sensory space*. A hedonic *turn-on* occurs, a rapturous amusement, a detachment from the previously compulsive mechanism of the first four circuits. I turned this circuit on with pot and Tantra.

This fifth brain began to appear about 4,000 years ago in the first leisure-class civilizations and has been increasing statistically in recent centuries (even before the Drug Revolution), a fact demonstrated by the hedonic art of India, China, Rome and other affluent societies. More recently, Ornstein and his school have demonstrated with electroencephalograms that this circuit represents the first jump from the linear left lobe of the brain to the analogical right lobe.

The opening and imprinting of this circuit has been the preoccupation of "technicians of the occult" — Tantric shamans and hatha yogis. While the fifth tunnel-reality can be achieved by sensory deprivation, social isolation, physiological stress or severe shock (ceremonial terror tactics, as practiced by such rascal-gurus as Don Juan Matus or Aleister Crowley), it has traditionally been reserved to the educated aristocracy of leisure societies who have solved the four terrestrial survival problems.

About 20,000 years ago, the specific fifth brain neurotransmitter was discovered by shamans in the Caspian Sea area of Asia and quickly spread to other wizards throughout Eurasia and Africa. It is, of course, cannabis. Weed. Mother Mary Jane.

It is no accident that the pot-head generally refers to his neural state as "high" or "spaced-out." The transcendence of gravitational, digital, linear, either-or, Aristotelian, Newtonian, Euclidean, planetary orientations (circuits I-IV) is, in evolutionary perspective, part of our neurological preparation for the inevitable migration off our home planet, now beginning. This is why so many pot-heads are *Star Trek* freaks and science-fiction adepts. (Berkeley, California, certainly the Cannabis Capital of the U.S., has a Federation Trading Post on Telegraph Avenue, where the well-heeled can easily spend $500 or more in a single day, buying *Star Trek* novels, magazines, newsletters, bumper stickers, photographs, posters, tapes, etc., including even complete blueprints for the starship *Enterprise*.)

The extraterrestrial meaning of being "high" is confirmed by astronauts themselves; 85% of those who have entered the free-fall of zero gravity describe "mystic experiences" or rapture states typical of the neurosomatic circuit. "No photo can show how beautiful Earth looked," raves Captain Ed Mitchell, describing his Illumination in free-fall. He sounds like any successful yogi or pot-head. No camera can show this experience because it is inside the nervous system.

Free-fall, at the proper evolutionary time, triggers the neurosomatic mutation, Leary believes. Previously this mutation has been achieved "artificially" by yogic or shamanic training or by the fifth circuit stimulant, cannabis. Surfing, skiing, skin-diving and the new sexual culture (sensuous massage, vibrators, imported Tantric arts, etc.) have evolved at the same time as part of the hedonic conquest of gravity. The Turn-On state is always described as "floating," or, in the Zen metaphor, "one foot above the ground."

VI. *The neuroelectric circuit.* The sixth brain consists of *the nervous system becoming aware of itself* apart from imprinted gravitational reality-maps (circuits I-IV) and even apart from body-rapture (circuit V). Count Korzybski, the semanticist, called this state "consciousness of abstracting." Dr. John Lilly calls it "metaprogramming," i.e., awareness of programming one's programming. This Einsteinian, relativistic contelligence (consciousness-intelligence) recognizes, for instance, that the Euclidean, Newtonian and Aristotelian reality-maps are just three among billions of possible programs or models for experience. I turned this circuit on with Peyote, LSD and Crowley's "magick" metaprograms.

This level of brain-functioning seems to have been reported first around 500 B.C. among various "occult" groups connected by the Silk Route (Rome-North India). It is so far beyond the terrestrial tunnel-realities that those who have achieved it can barely communicate about it to ordinary humanity (circuits I-IV) and can hardly be understood even by fifth circuit Rapture Engineers.

The characteristics of the neuroelectric circuit are high velocity, multiple choice, relativity, and the fission-fusion of all perceptions into parallel science-fiction universes of alternate possibilities.

The mammalian politics which monitor power struggles among terrestrial humanity are here transcended, i.e., seen as static, artificial, an elaborate charade. One is neither coercively manipulated into another's territorial reality nor forced to struggle against it with reciprocal emotional game-playing (the usual soap-opera dramatics). One simply elects, consciously, whether or not to share the other's reality-model.

Tactics for opening and imprinting the sixth circuit are described and rarely experienced in advanced rajah yoga, and in the hermetic (coded) manuals of the medieval-Renaissance alchemists and Illuminati.

No specific sixth circuit chemical is yet available, but strong psychedelics like mescaline (from my 1962-63 "sacred cactus," peyotl) and psilocybin (from the Mexican "magic mushroom," teonactl) open the nervous system to a mixed-media series of circuit V and circuit VI channels. This is appropriately called "tripping," as distinguished from straightforward fifth circuit "turning on" or "getting high."

The suppression of scientific research in this area has had the unfortunate result of turning the outlaw drug culture back toward fifth circuit hedonics and pre-scientific tunnel-realities (the occult revival, solipsism, Pop Orientalism). Without scientific discipline and methodology, few can successfully decode the often-frightening (but philosophically crucial) sixth circuit metaprogramming signals. Such scientists as do continue to study this subject dare not publish their results (which are illegal) and record ever-wider tunnel-realities only in private conversations — like the scholars of the Inquisitorial era. (Voltaire announced the Age of Reason two centuries too soon. We are still in the Dark Ages.) Most underground alchemists have given up on such challenging and risky self-work and restrict their trips to fifth circuit erotic tunnels.

The evolutionary function of the sixth circuit is to enable us to communicate at Einsteinian relativities and neuroelectric accelerations, not using third circuit laryngeal-manual symbols but directly *via* feedback, telepathy and computer link-up. Neuroelectric signals will increasingly replace "speech" (hominid grunts) after space migration.

When humans have climbed out of the atmosphere-gravity well of planetary life, accelerated sixth circuit contelligence will make possible high-energy communication with "Higher Intelligences," i.e., ourselves-in-the-future and other post-terrestrial races.

It is charmingly simple and obvious, once we realize that the spaced-out neural experiences really are extraterrestrial, that getting high and spacing out are accurate metaphors. Circuit V neurosomatic rapture is preparation for the next step in our evolution, migration off the planet. Circuit VI is preparation for the step after that, interspecies communication with advanced entities possessing electronic (post-verbal) tunnel-realities.

Circuit VI is the "universal translator" often imagined by science-fiction writers, already built into our brains by the DNA tape. Just as the circuits of the future butterfly are already built into the caterpillar.

VII. *The neurogenetic circuit.* The seventh brain kicks into action when the nervous system begins to receive signals from *within the individual neuron,* from the DNA-RNA dialogue. The first to achieve this mutation spoke of "memories of past lives," "reincarnation," "immortality," etc. That these adepts were recording something real is indicated by the fact that many of them (especially Hindus and Sufis) gave marvelously accurately poetic vistas of evolution 1,000 or 2,000 years before Darwin, and foresaw Superhumanity before Nietzsche.

The "akashic records" of Theosophy, the "collective uncon-scious" of Jung, the "phylogenetic unconscious" of Grof and Ring, are three modern metaphors for this circuit. The visions of past and future evolution described by those who have had "out-of-body" experiences during close-to-death episodes also describes the trans-time circuit VII tunnel-reality.

Specific exercises to trigger circuit VII are not to be found in yogic teaching; it usually happens, if at all, after several years of the kind of advanced rajah yoga that develops circuit VI facility.

The specific circuit VII neurotransmitter is, of course, LSD. (Peyote and psilocybin produce some circuit VII experiences also.)

Circuit VII is best considered, in terms of 1977 science, as the genetic archives, activated by anti-histone proteins. The DNA memory coiling back to the dawn of life. A sense of the inevi-tability of immortality and interspecies symbiosis comes to all circuit VII mutants; we can now see that this, also, is an evo-lutionary forecast, *since we stand right now on the doorstep of extended longevity leading to immortality.*

The exact role of the right-lobe circuits and the reason for their activation in the 1960s cultural revolution now becomes clear. As sociologist F.M. Esfandiary writes in *Upwingers*, "To-day when we speak of immortality and of going to another world we no longer mean these in a theological or metaphysical sense. People are now traveling to other worlds. People are now striv-ing for immortality. Transcendence is no longer a metaphysical concept. It has become reality."[88]

The evolutionary function of the seventh circuit and its evolutionary, aeon-spanning tunnel-reality is to prepare us for conscious immortality and interspecies symbiosis.

VIII. *The neuro-atomic circuit.* Hold on to your hats and breathe deeply — this is the farthest-out that human intelligence has yet ventured:

Consciousness probably precedes the biological unit or DNA tape-loop. "Out-of-body experiences," "astral projection," contact with alien (extraterrestrial?) "entities" or with a galactic Overmind, etc., such as I've experienced, have all been reported for thousands of years, not merely by the ignorant, the superstitious, the gullible, but often by the finest minds among us (Socrates, Giordano Bruno, Edison, Buckminster Fuller, etc.). Such experiences are reported daily to parapsychologists and have been experienced by such scientists as Dr. John Lilly and Carlos Castaneda. Dr. Kenneth Ring has attributed these phenomena to what he calls, very appropriately, "the extraterrestrial unconscious."

Dr. Leary suggests that circuit VIII is literally neuro-atomic — *infra*, *supra* and *meta*-physiological — a quantum mechanical communication system which does not require a biological container. The attempt to construct a quantum model of consciousness and/or a conscious model of quantum mechanics by the turned-on physicists discussed previously (Prof. John Archibald Wheeler, Saul-Paul Sirag, Dr. Fritjof Capra, Dr. Jack Sarfatti, etc.) indicates strongly that the "atomic consciousness" first suggested by Leary in "The Seven Tongues of God" (1962) is the explanatory link which will unite parapsychology and paraphysics into the first scientific empirical experimental theology in history.

When the nervous system is turned on to this quantum-level circuit, space-time is obliterated. Einstein's speed-of-light barrier is transcended; in Dr. Sarfatti's metaphor, we escape "electromagnetic chauvinism." The contelligence within the quantum projection booth *is* the entire cosmic "brain," just as the micro-miniaturized DNA helix *is* the local brain guiding planetary evolution. As Lao-tse said from his own Circuit VIII perspective, "The greatest is within the smallest."

Circuit VIII is triggered by Ketamine, a neuro-chemical researched by Dr. John Lilly, which is also (according to a widespread but unconfirmed rumor) given to astronauts to prepare them for space. High doses of LSD also produce some circuit VIII quantum awareness.

This neuro-atomic contelligence is four mutations beyond terrestrial domesticity. (The current ideological struggle is between circuit IV tribal moralists-or-collectivists and circuit V hedonic individualists.) When our need for higher intelligence, richer involvement in the cosmic script, further transcendence, will no longer be satisfied by physical bodies, not even by immortal bodies hopping across space-time at Warp 9, circuit VIII will open a further frontier. New universes and realities. "Beyond theology: the science and art of Godmanship," as Alan Watts once wrote.

It is therefore possible that the mysterious "entities" (angels and extraterrestrials) monotonously reported by circuit VIII visionaries are members of races already evolved to this level. But it is also possible, as Leary and Sarfatti more recently suggest, that They are ourselves-in-the-future.

The left-lobe terrestrial circuits contain the learned lessons of our evolutionary past (and present). The right-lobe extraterrestrial circuits are the evolutionary script for our future.

Thus far, there have been two alternative explanations of why the Drug Revolution happened. The first is presented in a sophisticated way by anthropologist Weston LaBarre, and in an ignorant, moralistic way by most anti-drug propaganda in the schools and the mass media. This explanation says, in essence, that millions have turned away from the legal *down* drugs to illegal *high* drugs because we are living in troubled times and many are seeking escape into fantasy.

This theory, at its best, only partially explains the ugliest and most publicized aspect of the revolution — the reckless drug abuse characteristic of the immature. It says nothing about the millions of respectable doctors, lawyers, engineers, etc., who have turned away from second circuit intoxication with booze to fifth circuit rapture with weed.

Nor does it account at all for the thoughtful, philosophical sixth circuit investigations of persons of high intelligence and deep sensibility, such as Aldous Huxley, Dr. Stanley Grof, Masters-Houston, Alan W. Watts, Carlos Castaneda, Dr. John Lilly and thousands of scientific and lay researchers on consciousness.

A more plausible theory, devised by psychiatrist Norman Zinberg out of the work of Marshall McLuhan, holds that modern electronic media have so shifted the nervous system's parameters that young people no longer enjoy "linear" drugs like alcohol and find meaning only in "non-linear" weed and psychedelics.

This is certainly part of the truth, but it is too narrow and overstresses TV and computers without sufficiently stressing the general technological picture — the ongoing Science-Fiction

Revolution of which the most significant aspects are Space Migration, Increased Intelligence and Life Extension, which Leary has condensed into his S.M.I^2.L.E. formula.

Space Migration plus Increased Intelligence plus Life Extension means expansion of humanity into all space-time.

S.M. + I^2. + L.E. = ∞.

Without totally endorsing Charles Fort's technological mysticism ("It steam-engines when it comes steam-engine time"), it is obvious that the DNA metaprogram for planetary evolution is far wiser than any of our individual nervous systems — which are, in a sense, giant robots or sensors for DNA. Early science-fiction pulps; the crudities of Buck Rogers; the sophisticated science-fiction of brilliant writers like Stapledon, Clarke, Heinlein; Kubrick's *2001* — all were increasingly clear DNA signals transmitted through the intuitive right lobe of sensitive artists, preparing us for the extraterrestrial mutation.

It is scarcely coincidental that mainstream "literary" intellectuals — the heirs of the Platonic-aristocratic tradition that a gentleman never uses his hands, monkeys with tools or learns a manual craft — despise both science-fiction and the dope culture. Nor is it coincidental that the *Whole Earth Catalogs* — created by Stewart Brand, a graduate of Ken Kesey's Merry Pranksters — are the New Testament of the rural dropout culture, each issue bulging with tons of eco-technological information about all the manual, dextrous, gadgetry know-how that Plato and his heirs consider fit only for slaves. Not surprisingly, Brand's latest publication, *Co-Evolution Quarterly*, has been largely devoted to publicizing Prof. Gerard O'Neill's space-habitat, L5.

Nor is it an accident that dopers seem to prefer science-fiction to any other reading, even including the extraterrestrial-flavored Hindu scriptures and occult-shamanic circuit VI-VIII trip-poets like Crowley and Hesse.

The circuit VI drugs may have contributed much to the metaprogramming consciousness that has led to sudden awareness of "male chauvinism" (women's liberationists), "species chauvinism" (ecology, Lilly's dolphin studies), "type-G star chauvinism" (Carl Sagan), even "oxygen chauvinism" (the CETI conference), etc. The imprinted tunnel-realities which identify one as "white-male-American-earthian" etc. or "black-female-Cuban" etc. are no longer big enough to enclose our exploding contelligence.

As *Time* magazine said on November 26, 1973, "Within ten years, according to pharmacologists, they will have perfected pills and cranial electrodes capable of providing lifelong bliss for everyone on Earth." The 1960s hysteria about weed and acid was just the overture to this fifth circuit breakthrough. Nathan S. Kline, M.D., predicts real aphrodisiacs, drugs to speed up learning, drugs to foster or terminate any behavior. Those who were burned or jailed at the beginning of the 17th century (Bruno, Galileo, etc.) were forerunners of the Revolution of Outer Technology. Those who were jailed or beaten by cops in the 1960s were forerunners of the Revolution of Inner Technology.

Star Trek is a better guide to the emerging reality than anything in the *New York Review of Books*. The life-support and defense-system engineer, Scotty (circuit I), the emotional-sentimental Dr. McCoy (circuit II), the logical science-officer Mr. Spock (circuit III) and the alternately paternalistic and romantic Captain Kirk (circuit IV) are perpetually voyaging through our future neurological history and encountering circuit V, VI, VII, and VIII intelligences, however crudely presented.

In short, the various levels of consciousness and circuits we have been discussing, and illustrating, are all biochemical imprints in the evolution of the nervous system. Each imprint creates a bigger tunnel-reality. In the Sufi metaphor, the donkey on which we ride becomes a different donkey after each imprint. The metaprogrammer continually learns more and is increasingly able to be aware of itself operating. We are thus evolving to intelligence-studying-intelligence (the nervous system studying the nervous system) and are more and more capable of accelerating our own evolution.

Leary now symbolizes intelligence-studying intelligence by the mark, I^2.

On the lower levels, you see with one "I," so to speak.

On the higher levels, you see with many "I"s.

And space-time shifts from three Euclidean dimensions to non-Euclidean multi-dimensionality.

The Octave of Energy

The Law of Octaves was first suggested by Pythagoras in ancient Greece. Having observed that the eight notes of the conventional Occidental musical scale were governed by definite mathematical relationships, Pythagoras proceeded to create a whole cosmology based on 8s. In this octagonal model Pythagoras made numerous mistakes, because he was generalizing from insufficient data. However, his work was the first attempt in history to unify science, mathematics, art and mysticism into one comprehensible system and as such is still influential. Leary, Crowley and Buckminster Fuller have all described themselves as modern Pythagoreans.

In China, roughly contemporary with Pythagoras, the Taoists built up a cosmology based on the interplay of *yang* (positive) and *yin* (negative), which produced the eight trigrams of the *I Ching*, out of which are generated the 64 hexagrams.

In India, Buddha announced, after his illumination under the Bodhi tree, the Noble Eightfold Path. Patanjali subsequently reduced the science of yoga to eight "limbs" or, as we might say, eight "steps."

The game of chess appeared, somewhere in the East, with a grid based on 8 x 8 (64) squares.

Kepler discovered the laws of planetary motion serendipitously, while trying to make the planets fit into the Pythagorean octave.

In the 1860s, English chemist John Newland showed that all the chemical elements fall into eight families. Since Pythagorean mysticism was unfashionable at that time, Newland was literally laughed at and rejected by the Royal Chemical Society. In the 1870s, with much more detail than Newland, the Russian chemist Mendeleyev proved once and for all that the elements do, indeed, fall into eight families. His Periodic Table of the Elements, an octave of hauntingly Pythagorean harmony, hangs in every high-school chemistry class today. (The Royal Society later apologized to Newland and gave him a Gold Medal.)

We have already seen that Nikola Tesla, in the visions from which he deduced the mechanism of alternating current, also intuited a basic Law of Octaves governing universal energy.

Modern geneticists have found that the DNA-RNA "dialogue" — the molecular information system governing life and evolution — is transmitted by 64 (8 x 8) *codons*.

R. Buckminster Fuller, in his Synergetic-Energetic Geometry, which he claims is the "co-ordinate system of Universe," reduces all phenomena to geometric-energetic constructs based on the tetrahedron (4-sided), the octet truss (8-sided) and the *coupler* (8-faceted with 24 phases). Fuller argues specifically that the 8-face, 24-phase *coupler* underlies the 8-fold division of the chemical elements on the Mendeleyev Periodic Table.

In 1973, unaware of Fuller's *coupler* — which I called to his attention later — Dr. Leary began to divide his 8 circuits into a 24-stage Periodic Table of Evolution (see diagram). Leary also began attempting to correlate this with the Periodic Table of Elements in chemistry.

The eight families of elements are:
>Alkalis.
>Alkalines.
>Borons.
>Carbons.
>Nitrogens.
>Oxygens.
>Halogens.
>Noble gases.

The first four families, Leary' argues, are terrestrial; that is, they are heavy and tend to fall to Earth. The second four families are extraterrestrial: that is. they tend to float off into space. Similarly, he says, the first four circuits of the nervous system are terrestrial; their function is to control survival and reproduction at the bottom of the 4,000-mile gravity well in which we presently live. The second four circuits, then, are extraterrestrial; they will come into full play only when we live normally in zero-gravity — in free space.

THE PERIODIC TABLE OF EVOLUTION

CIRCUIT	DENDRITIC (Input) FUNCTION	CELL BODY (Integrative) FUNCTION	AXONIC (Output) FUNCTION
Neuro-Atomic (Metaphysio-logical)	Cosmic Consciousness	Cosmic Engineering	Cosmic Fusion
Neurogenetic	DNA Awareness	DNA Engineering (Longevity)	DNA Fusion (Ecological Symbiosis)
Neuro-Electric	ESP Precognition	The Neurologician (the shaman)	"The Conscious Circle of Humanity"
Neurosomatic	Hedonic Passivity	Hedonic Engineering (Yoga)	Hedonic Synergy (Tantra)
Domestic (Socio-Sexual)	The Adolescent (Barbarian Bands)	The Parent (Patriarchal Civilization)	Centralized Socialism (Hive-Unity)
Laryngeal-Manual (Symbolic)	The Learning Child (Paleolithic)	The Skillful Child (Neolithic)	The Creative Child (Bronze Age)
Emotional-Territorial	The Toddler (trickster mammal)	The Fighting Child (predator mammal)	The Political Child (pack-bonding)
Bio-Survival	The Newborn (unicellular consciousness)	The Demanding Infant (marine consciousness)	Mother-Child bonding (amphibian consciousness)

Read from the bottom up. Every infant begins at "The Newborn"; every adult arrives at least at "Centralized Socialism" (although the Control Center or major input may be back at "The Toddler" or "The Fighting Child" or in any slot). So-called geniuses, mystics or weird people with wild (psionic) talents are post-larval and may reach any slot from "Centralized Socialism" to "Cosmic Fusion."

If the higher circuits have been appearing (partially and in rare mutants) for a few thousand years, this is because the DNA blueprint is gradually modifying us for future evolution. If higher circuit functions are increasing at an accelerating rate — as many parapsychologists think — it is because we are now mutating rapidly toward extraterrestrial migration.

Mathematically, the first four circuits are Euclidean-Newtonian, orienting us to the 3-dimensional space and 1-dimensional time of planetary life. The second four circuits are Fullerian-Einsteinian, orienting us to interstellar zero-gravity.

It is possible to see the development of an individual (if s/he evolves all the way to the 8th circuit) and the development of life itself as the working out of this Octave of Evolution. Thus:

	Individual	Life
Circuit I	infant bio-survival passivity	uni-cellular life
Circuit II	"toddler" emotional politics (Ego)	vertebrate life, territoriality, hierachy
Circuit III	student mind	hominid languages and tool-making
Circuit IV	post-pubescent domesticity	urbanized civilization
Circuit V	neurosomatic rapture	free-fall (extraterrestrial migration)
Circuit VI	neuroelectric metaprogramming	I^2
Circuit VII	neurogenetic consciousness	immortality
Circuit VIII	Satori	Cosmic Union

But this is strikingly similar to the teachings of Gurdjieff (which may be according to many, the secret inner teachings of Sufism). The Gurdjieff vibration numbers and the levels of consciousness, as named by Gurdjieff, fit the table as follows:

384	Movement center	Circuit I	Invertebrate reality
192	False emotional center	Circuit II	Mammalian reality
96	False intellectual center	Circuit III	Paleolithic reality
48	False personality	Circuit IV	Civilized reality
24	Magnetic Center	Circuit V	Hedonic reality
12	True Emotional Center	Circuit VI	Psionic reality
6	True Intellectual Center	Circuit VII	Immortal reality
3	The Essence	Circuit VIII	Cosmic reality

Leary began to divide the 8 circuits into 24 phases when he became convinced that each circuit has an input phase, a decision-making phase, and an output phase. (On the synaptic level, this appears as dendrites, receiving signals; cell-bodies, making decisions; and axons, transmitting signals.) This 24-stage chart can be correlated with the Hebrew alphabet, thereby casting new light on the Cabala; with the Tarot cards (a Sufi invention, it is claimed); and with the Zodiac (if we allow 12 extraterrestrial types to complete the 12 terrestrial types of traditional astrology). These correlations are not indicated on the diagram; a full explanation will be found in two later books.*

◆

* *The Periodic Table of Evolution*, Timothy Leary and Robert Anton Wilson, 88 Books, San Diego, 1977; *The Game of Life*, Leary and Wilson, 88 Books San Diego, 1977.

◆

Working independently of Leary and myself, Prof. Peter Flessel of the University of San Francisco has begun developing correlations between the 8 x 8 codons of the genetic code and the 8 x 8 hexagrams of the *I Ching*, which he will be publishing soon. It is to be hoped that in further work on the Leary Periodic Table, Flessel's correlations and Fuller's 24-phase geometric coupler, science will eventually find a "Rosetta Stone" by which the traditional symbols of occultism can be decoded in modern, operational, scientific categories.

It will be seen by the thoughtful reader that this emerging

synthesis evades entirely the usual dichotomy of "spiritual" versus "material," being purely geometric-energetic. It is thus in the same philosophical category as the unitary systems of the East (Zen, Taoism, Vedanta, etc.) and outside the dualisms of Greek logic and Christian theology. Any attempt to describe this octave as "mystical" or as "materialistic" misses the real point of Leary's work.

The law of acceleration

In the 1890s, Henry Adams became convinced that technology was following a geometric or exponential law. That is, basic advances do not follow a linear sequence such as:

2 - 4 - 6 - 8 - 10 - 12 - 14 - 16 - etc.

but rather an exponential sequence like:

2 - 4 - 8 - 16 - 32 - 64 - 128 - 256 - etc.

Adams calculated that, projecting forward the acceleration from Galileo's time to his own, we would have infinite energy at our disposal in the 1920s. Obviously, he was somewhat inaccurate in his calculations.

But he was not entirely wrong. Korzybski, Buckminster Fuller, Alvin Toffler and others have shown, with countless examples, that many things in technology are advancing exponentially, and the one general tendency is clearly that there will be more basic breakthroughs (both in scientific theory and in technological applications) in each generation than in any previous generation.

As Toffler in particular emphasizes, there are more scientists alive in the 1970s than in all previous history added together. Thus, this generation should witness more breakthroughs than *all previous history added together.* In this context, Leary's SMI²LE scenario (Space Migration + Intelligence² + Life Extension) is only the overture to a planetary (and extra-planetary) Awakening that we can only dimly begin to discern.

This, indeed, is the thesis of a remarkable book offering the final set of models and metaphors which we shall be discussing — *The Invisible Landscape*, by Terrence L. McKenna and Dennis J. McKenna.[89]

The McKenna brothers, who between them have a background that includes anthropology, biology, chemistry and botany, conducted a metaprogramming experiment in the Upper Amazon Basin, using the local "magic mushroom," which contains psychedelics in the psilocybin family. For 37 days they experienced a high level of ESP, the usual intensification of coincidence-synchronicity, and the presence of an "alien" insectoid entity which seemed to be an anthropologist from the future. Twentieth century history appeared as a frantic (although unconscious) effort to build a craft to escape Earth and return to Galactic Center. This occurred in March of 1971. (Leary and Benner received the Starseed transmissions, urging return to Galactic Center, in July-August 1973. Since the McKennas did not publish an account of their experience until 1976, it could not have influenced Leary and Benner.)

In the six years since the Amazon Basin experience the McKennas have been developing a model to account for the action of psychedelics in general and their own experience in particular. This model is detailed and specific in more ways than I can summarize here and suggests numerous experiments in neuro-psychology, chemistry and quantum physics, which might prove of crucial importance to science as a whole.

Briefly, the McKennas regard our universe as a *hologram*, created by the interaction of two hyper-universes, just as an ordinary hologram is created by the interaction of two lasers. One consequence of this model is that, if our universe is a hologram, every part contains the information of the whole, as in normal holography. As we have seen, the Sarfatti interpretation of Bell's Theorem and the Leary theory of eighth circuit consciousness also lead to this conclusion, which, in effect, means that every atom contains the "brain" of the whole universe.

This is also the basic axiom of magick and was originally stated in the Table of Hermes in the famous sentence, "That which is above is in that which is below." Alchemists and occultists have usually referred to it as the principle that "the macrocosm is within the microcosm."

But the McKenna theory goes far beyond this. There are 64 time-scales in the hologram of our universe, they say, and each one is related to one of the 64 (8 x 8) hexagrams of the *I Ching*. What we call "mind" or "consciousness" is a standing wave form in these 64 time-systems. As the two hyper-universes making up the hologram of our known universe interact in time, "mind" manifests further in our continuum. This means, in concrete physical terms, that the quantum bonds of the DNA are evolving faster and faster. We are riding not one but 64 evolutionary waves all mounting toward a cosmic Awakening something like the Omega Point suggested by palaeontologist Teilhard de Chardin.

The action of psychedelics, in the model, opens the quantum information system within the DNA to inspection by the higher neural centers. When Dr. John Lilly says he has traveled in time with LSD, and then adds that this is "only" a metaphor, he is perhaps too modest. If the McKennas are right in their basic theory, every psychedelic trip is literally a voyage through the quantum information system at faster-than-light velocity, i.e., outside "time" in the local (Einsteinian) universe.

This sounds much like a more scientific formulation of the incoherent ideas about time that many UFO Contactees have tried to communicate.

The natural question, of course, is just when are the McKennas' 64 time-scales reaching their peak in our linear time?

The McKennas have programmed a computer with their 64 *I Ching* time systems and the answer is that everything goes jackpot around A.D. 2012.

(For some perspective on this rather apocalyptic notion, consider one of the regular studies performed by the McGraw-Hill Publications Company, in which a cross-section of scientists are asked to predict the technology of the next quarter-century. In the latest McGraw-Hill poll, the majority predicted that by A.D. 2000 we will have:

      drugs to cure cancer
      artificial eyesight for the blind
      drugs to permanently increase intelligence

chemical control of aging
chemical control of senility
successful cryogenic preservation.)[90]

The McKenna scenario is somewhat more dramatic than
the exponential accelerations suggested by Henry Adams,
Korzybski, Fuller, Toffler and even Leary, because, within the
McKenna theory, all of the 64 time-scales peak together. That is,
they assert:

a 4,300-year cycle from urbanization to the dawn of
modern science;

a 384-year cycle in which science has caused more up-
surge of novelty than in that 4,300-year cycle;

a 67-year cycle (from the technological breakthroughs of
the 1940s, including nuclear energy and DNA, to the peak
in 2012) in which there will be more acceleration than there
was between Galileo and Hiroshima;

a 384-day cycle in 2011-2012 when there will be more
transformations than in all the previous cycles;

a 6-day cycle at the end of that in which things will move
even faster; and so on, down to a grand climax in which, as
they say,

in the last 135 minutes, 18 such barriers (i.e., barriers comparable to the appearance of life, the invention of language or the achievement of immortality
– R.A.W.) will be crossed, 13 of them in the last 75×10^4 seconds.[91]

That is, in the last two hours before Peak, we will achieve 18
extensions of consciousness and power, each one comparable to
the passing from sea to land or from Earth to Space.

And in the last .0075 seconds of the Great Cycle we will pass
through 13 such transformations.

On a recent lecture tour, I have spoken to literally hundreds of
scientists about the SMI^{2}LE scenario, and the majority of them
agree that we can indeed have Space Migration, Intelligence^2 and
Life Extension by the 1990s. Some agree with Leary's optimistic
claim that we can have them by the 1980s, if we try hard enough.

By the turn of the next century, then, we will be a completely
new species in many dimensions: living in space, not on a planet;

able to program our nervous systems for any degree of any function we wish; possessing a lifespan in centuries, and well on our way to Immortality. Between 2000 and 2012, if the McKenna scenario can be trusted, the real Cosmic Action will begin. As the McKennas say, it is hard to avoid hyperbole in trying to contemplate what this means.

Part III:

Trigger

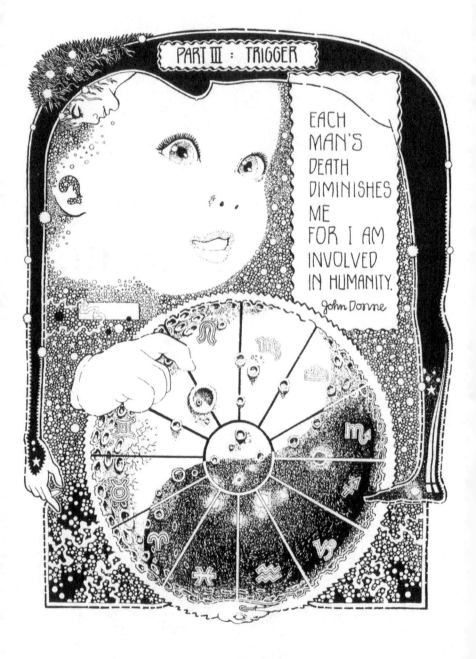

PART III : TRIGGER

EACH
MAN'S
DEATH
DIMINISHES
ME
FOR I AM
INVOLVED
IN HUMANITY.

John Donne

Trigger:

A FINAL FABLE

From the Egyptian

The goddess Isis married her older brother Osiris, whom she loved very much. Set, the old serpent of envy, hated their happiness and murdered Osiris by stealth. Then, to prevent all possibility of resurrection, Set dismembered the body of Osiris and scattered the pieces up and down the Nile River.

When Isis learned what had been done, she called upon Thoth, god of Eternity, to stop the flow of Time, so that she could find all the parts of Osiris before the sun set. And Thoth stopped the wings of time, and the universe stood still, and Isis went forth weeping and grief-stricken to hunt one by one for the pieces of the dead Lord Osiris. And when she had found all of them, she performed the Black Rite, and eternity gave birth to Time again, and Osiris was alive.

And the secret of the Black Rite is the Secret of Secrets, and even those who know it do not know it fully; but it will be revealed when we pursue Isis and Osiris unto the heights, yea, into the starry infinity above us.

Sirius Rises Again

Three more bits of data have come to me recently. Alan Vaughn, a well-known West Coast occultist and editor of *Psychic* magazine, read a draft of this book and immediately phoned me in high excitement. Mr. Vaughn also had the impression of being contacted by Sirius in 1973 — January 1973, to be exact. Those who want to confirm this, or get more details, can contact Mr. Vaughn at *Psychic*, 680 Beach Street, San Francisco.

The second datum is most striking when we notice that, whether we approach the Sirius Mystery from the modern end and work backward from Aleister Crowley, or start from the ancient end and work forward from the Egyptians, we continually collide with the mysterious and enigmatic history of Freemasonry. I recently acquired *Morals and Dogma of the Ancient and Accepted Scottish Rite of Freemasonry*, by General Albert Pike 33°. Standard references agree in considering Pike the highest initiate in 19th century American freemasonry. Concerning Sirius, he says:

> To find in the BLAZING STAR of five points an allusion to Divine Providence is also fanciful; and to make it commemorative of the Star that is said to have guided the Magi is to give it a meaning comparatively modern. Originally, it represented SIRIUS, or the Dog Star.[92]

This blazing star appears in every Masonic lodge, needless to say.

My third new clue comes from a rather sensational book called *The Curse of the Pharaohs*, by Phillip Vandenberg. According to Vandenberg, an archeologist named Duncan Mac-Naughton discovered in 1932 that the long dark tunnels in the Great Pyramid of Cheops function as telescopes, making the stars visible even in the daytime. The Great Pyramid is oriented, according to MacNaughton, to give a view, from the King's Chamber, of the area of the southern sky in which Sirius moves throughout the year.[93]

Despite my skepticism and my alternative models, I can't help wondering: *but what if it's true?* What if Earth and Sirius do have some strange cosmic link? As Robert K.G. Temple says in his *Sirius Mystery*:

> I would even venture that we may be under observation or surveillance at this very moment, with an extraterrestrial civilization based at the Sirius system monitoring our development to see when we will *ready ourselves* for their contacting us . . . Would they think that [this book] was their cue? If what I propose in this book really is true, then am I pulling a cosmic trigger?[94]

Sirius is only 8.6 lightyears away. The British Interplanetary Society already has a design for a starship that could be sent to Barnard's Star (6 lightyears away) in 2000. The first O'Neill space cities will be orbiting the earth by then, and by 2004, according to Dr. Asimov's calculations, the biological revolution will be producing DNA for any purpose we want, possibly including immortality. In 2012, if the McKenna scenario is right, comes the Omega Point. In that case, Dr. Temple, we are all pulling a cosmic trigger.

Blood of the Gods?

Recently, *Ancient Astronauts* magazine printed an article claiming that a number of prominent occultists and consciousness-researchers were interstellar hybrids — descendants of the matings between normal humanity and von Daniken's space-gods. I was pleased to find myself on the list of Godlings. The article asserted that what all of us have in common, besides a proclivity for the higher states of consciousness, is Rh-negative blood.

It is a charming theory. The only thing wrong with it is that your humble Narrator happens to have Rh-positive blood. Sorry about that . . .

Weirdness and synchronicity continue to haunt me. ("Beyond a certain point," Crowley wrote, "the whole universe becomes a continuous Initiation.") When the psychic lady with the incredible name, Penny Loony, gave me the prophecies mentioned earlier, she added that within a year I would be traveling to Europe and diving into the ruins of Atlantis. I didn't put much faith in either of those forecasts, especially not the second, since I don't believe in Atlantis.

But on November 23, 1976 — a sacred Discordian holy day, both because of the 23 and because it is Harpo Marx's birthday — a most ingenious young Englishman named Ken Campbell premiered a ten-hour adaptation of *Illuminatus* at the Science-Fiction Theatre of Liverpool. It was something of a success (the Guardian reviewed it three times, each reviewer being wildly enthusiastic) and Campbell and his partner, actor

Chris Langham, were invited to present it as the first production of the new Cottesloe extension of the National Theatre, under the patronage of Her Majesty the Queen.

This seemed to me the greatest Discordian joke ever, since *Illuminatus*, as I may not have mentioned before, is the most overtly anarchistic novel of this century. Shea and I quite seriously defined our purpose, when writing it, as trying to do to the State what Voltaire did to the Church — to reduce it to an object of contempt among all educated people. Ken Campbell's adaptation was totally faithful to this nihilistic spirit and contained long unexpurgated speeches from the novel explaining at sometimes tedious length just why everything government does is always done wrong. The audiences didn't mind this pedantic lecturing because it was well integrated into a kaleidoscope of humor, suspense, and plenty of sex (more simulated blow jobs than any drama in history, I believe). The thought of having this totally subversive ritual staged under the patronage of H.M. the Queen, Elizabeth II, was nectar and ambrosia to me.

The National Theatre flew Shea and me over to London for the premiere and I fell in love with the whole cast, especially Prunella Gee, who emphatically has my vote for Sexiest Actress since Marilyn Monroe. Some of us did a lot of drinking and hash-smoking together, and the cast told me a lot of synchronicities connected with the production. Five actors were injured during the Liverpool run, to fulfill the Law of Fives. Hitler had lived in Liverpool for five months when he was 23 years old. The section of Liverpool in which the play opened, indeed the very street, is described in a dream of Carl Jung's recorded on page 223 of Jung's *Memories, Dreams, Reflections*. The theatre in Liverpool opened the day Jung died. There is a yellow submarine in *Illuminatus*, and the Beatles first sang "Yellow Submarine" in that same Liverpool Theatre. The actor playing Padre Pederastia in the Black Mass scene had met Aleister Crowley on a train once.

The cast dared me to do a walk-on role during the National Theatre run. I agreed and became an extra in the Black Mass, where I was upstaged by the goat, who kept sneezing.

Nonetheless, there I was, bare-ass naked, chanting "Do what

thou wilt shall be the whole of the law" under the patronage of Elizabeth II, Queen of England, and I will never stop wondering how much of that was programmed by Crowley before I was even born.

And so Penny Loony's prediction that I would travel to Europe came true, and Crowley and the Illuminati were involved in it.

As for the prediction that I would dive into the ruins of Atlantis: after I got back from England, an occultist named Alve Stuart contacted me and invited me to join an expedition to the Bermuda Triangle to investigate various legends, including the idea that part of Atlantis was down there, and reports from natives of the area that UFOs are often seen *rising from* the waters. I declined, partly because of competing projects that seemed even more bizarre and amusing, and partly because I wanted to see what would happen if I refused "Their" evident desire to get me to Atlantis.

A month later, Charles Berlitz claimed to have found a sunken pyramid in the Bermuda Triangle. He said it was twice the size of the pyramid of Cheops, and that was really amusing, because Shea and I had put a pyramid "twice the size of the pyramid of Cheops" right there, in *Illuminatus*, but we thought we were writing fiction at the time.

As we go to press, I hear from Carl Weschcke, an occult publisher who has printed many of my articles in his magazine, *Gnostica*, that Berlitz has joined forces with Alve Stuart, the man who wanted to take me to Atlantis. The two of them are down there now, hoping to bring back photos of that damned pyramid Shea and I think we invented, and of the UFOs rising into the stars. Lovely. I am still living in Jung-land. I turned on TV last night and picked up an ad for a film called *Airport 77*. The ad began with a radar operator shouting "Flight 23 is down in the Bermuda Triangle."

I have by now encountered the "real" Head of the "real" Illuminati several times. (The fellow who gave me $200 when I was on Welfare did not claim to be the Head of the Illuminati, only an agent.) The first real Head I met was Rev. Thomas Patrick McNamara of San Francisco. He is a charming and witty person.

The second real Head is Robert Shell of Roanoke, Virginia. I haven't met him in person yet, but we've corresponded quite a bit, and he seems charming and witty also. The third real Head is an individual in southern California who shall be nameless and who is neither charming nor witty. He threatened to sue me for a put-on letter I had written to an occult journal, *Green Egg*, in which I had jokingly pretended I was the real Head of the Illuminati. I sent him back a form saying his letter would not program into my computer and would he please resubmit it in Fortran; I haven't heard from him since. Another real Head of the Illuminati is a chap called Frater Paragranis, in Switzerland, who registered his claim to that title in Francis King's book, *Sexuality, Magick and Perversion.*

I have also been corresponding for a year now with a 33° freemason in Texas. Part of the time I think *he's* the real Real Head of the Illuminati. Part of the time I think that he thinks *I'm* the Real Head. And part of the time I think he just likes to correspond with professional writers about occult subjects.

Recently, English playwright Heathcote Williams sent me a Xerox of *There Is No More Firmament*, a one-act play written by the pioneer surrealist, Antonin Artaud, back in the early 1920s. This strange, weirdly suggestive drama certainly deserves to be mentioned as part of the Sirius Mystery.

There Is No More Firmament begins with discordant music indicating "a far-off cataclysm." The curtain rises on an ordinary street scene, with actors coming and going rapidly. There are bits of ordinary conversation ("Wines . . . window-glass . . . gold's going down"), suggestions of violence and insanity ("He's undressing me. Help, he's ripping my dress off . . ." "I'm on fire, I'm burning, I'm going to jump") and, finally, the word "Sirius" repeated in every tone of voice and every pitch of the scale: SIRIUS . . . SIRIUS . . . SIRIUS . . . SIRIUS . . . Then a loudspeaker thunders, "THE GOVERNMENT URGES YOU TO REMAIN CALM."

Actors rush about claiming that the sun is getting bigger, the plague has broken out, there is thunder without lightning, etc. A reasonable voice tries to explain: "It was a magnetic phenomenon . . ." Then the loudspeaker tells us:

"STUPENDOUS DISCOVERY. SKY PHYSICALLY ABOL-
ISHED. EARTH ONLY A MINUTE AWAY FROM SIRIUS. NO
MORE FIRMAMENT."

One actor claims it is the end of the world. Another says it is
two worlds ramming each other.

Tom-toms beat and a chorus sings the *Internationale*. Communist and anarchist slogans are shouted. One actor suggests,
"There, you see, it was the Revolution." There is a chant, hailing
the new ruler, King Mob.

A group of scientists appear and disagree with each other
vehemently about what is happening, while a Revolutionary objects, "It isn't science any more, it's immoral." Another promises
us, not very reassuringly, "We won't see the Antichrist yet." Finally, one scientist comes forth to explain to the audience, "The
molecular grouping in Sirius is everything. These two forces,
ours and theirs, had to be put in touch with each other."

The curtain falls and violent percussion instruments and
sirens create a din as the audience leaves.

(For the curious, the whole text of this play can be found in
Antonin Artaud, *Collected Works*, Vol. II. Calder and Boyars:
London, 1971.)

Artaud went "insane" about ten years after writing this play,
and spent the World War II years in a mental hospital. After the
war ended, he regained his "sanity" and lived his final years in
Paris as a hero to the young intelligentsia, who regarded him as a
prophet. The people who were allegedly "sane" during the years
of Artaud's hospitalization spent most of their time trying to
blow up as much as possible of the civilized world.

The Dark Companion

On July 23, 1976 — the third anniversary of my original Sirius experience — I made an attempt to duplicate the effect, which
is certainly interesting and suggestive, however one explains
it. This time I did a formal invocation of Hadit, the Intelligence

identified with Sirius in Crowley's symbology, using all the paraphernalia of ceremonial magick. I was assisted by Isaac Bonewits, author of *Real Magick*, and Charles Hixson, a computer programmer with an interest in Cabala.

Neither Isaac nor Charles experienced anything out of the ordinary. I got into a high, spaced-out "mystical" state, but with no objective phenomena immediately forthcoming, even though I had focused my energy on producing some sort of objective effect.

The next week, however. *Time* magazine ran a full-page review of Temple's *The Sirius Mystery*. I found this, quite simply, infuriating: it was so easy to see it as an answer to my ritual, and it was equally easy to dismiss it as a "mere coincidence." Somewhere, I seemed to hear a mocking laugh and a cryptic whisper, "We're going to keep you guessing a while longer."

Another full-page item that week, alas, was even more suggestive and even less conclusive. *Rolling Stone* had a display ad for a new rock group called Rameses, which came from Germany and featured *a singer named Winifred*. That was weird by itself, because in the novel *Illuminatus*, The Illuminati turn out to be run by a German rock group (called not Rameses but the American Medical Association) featuring a singer named Winifred. What was really provocative, however, was that this group was being promoted in this country by Annuit Coeptis records and the ad featured the eye-on-the-pyramid design which we have seen so many times linked with the Illuminati and with Sirius.

Several readers of *Illuminatus* actually cut the ad out of *Rolling Stone* and sent it to me, asking how I had "managed" this trick. I told them it was magick.

Saul-Paul Sirag has suggested recently, perhaps with some whimsy, that the SMI²LE scenario will eventually, as science works on the theory of interstellar propulsion, result serendipitously in time-travel. Some time in the 1990s, he told me, some of us will be involved in the first experiments on a time-machine. Like all prototypes, this will have some bugs in it, and it will create, unintentionally, a series of wrinkles or weirdnesses in the time-flow, which rolling backwards will create the "occult" events which drew so many of us into the Starseed scenario in the late 1960s and early 1970s. The Higher Intelligence behind all this is, then, *literally* ourselves-in-the-future.

Was all that Sirius material just a red herring then? Oddly enough, perhaps not; perhaps, if we are to have time-travel, Sirius will be intimately involved in it. Astronomer A.T. Lawton and journalist Jack Stonely, in their book *CETI*, point out that rotating Black Holes, produced by collapsing neutron stars, would theoretically make fine time-machines. The closest dwarf star we might use for this purpose, they point out, is the Dark Companion of Sirius.[95]

This reminds me that Osiris, the Dark Companion of Sirius in Egyptian mythology, was the God of Resurrection and of Eternal Life. I cannot help recalling a Hermetic treatise quoted by Temple which says that the Dark Rite of Osiris (granting Immortality) will not be fully understood until we "pursue the stars unto the heights." As Temple remarks, that does seem to mean going out there in spaceships.

Via Dolorosa

In September 1976, I was teaching a seminar on these ideas with physicists Sirag and Sarfatti, psychologist Jean Millay and mathematician Michael Mohle. Jean Millay, in the course of her presentation of bio-feedback instruments, demonstrated how to harmonize the brain-waves of all the participants. When we entered the alpha state simultaneously, I recognized it at once; it was the state in which I find myself whenever my ESP suddenly kicks into action. I wondered if I would get a flash of that sort, and immediately it told me that *my son, Graham, would die soon.*

Everybody who gets involved in parapsychology at all eventually realizes, with some anxiety, that you are likely to get that kind of precognition at any time. I threw myself, by concentration methods learned from Crowley, into a high-energy state and banished fear and anxiety.

The Dark Rite of Osiris (granting Immortality) will only be
understood when we pursue the gods to their home in the Stars.

Then, superstitiously, and feeling that I was finally succumbing to the gullibility I have seen capture many occult investigators, I set out on a course of rituals, in the following weeks, to protect Graham. Since I was aware that, according to magick theory, this might only deflect the calamity slightly, I included rituals to protect the rest of my family also.

I also prayed, for the first time in my adult life, for the strength to bear it, if I could not deflect it.

On October 2, Luna — she who had perhaps levitated once, and who had most certainly taught me much about the Wheel of Karma — came to my room while I was writing and asked me to recommend a novel for her to review for a class at school. While we were discussing this, I was suddenly moved to say to her, "I'm awfully busy these days and we hardly ever talk together. I hope you know I love you as much as ever."

She gave me that wonderful Clear Light smile of hers, and said, "Of course I know that."

That was our last conversation, and I will always be grateful for the impulse that led me to tell her one last time how much I love her.

On October 3, Luna was beaten to death at the store where she was working after school, in the course of a burglary.

I was sleeping (taking a very uncharacteristic afternoon nap) when Officer Butler, a Berkeley policeman, came to the door and asked to speak to both my wife and myself. It has occurred to me that, because I never nap in the afternoons normally, my unconscious might have known and was preparing me with extra rest.

"It's about your daughter, Luna," the. officer said. "Please sit down."

We sat down.

"I'm sorry," he said. He was black and had the most pained eyes I have ever seen. "Your daughter is dead."

"Oh, God, no," I said, starting to weep and thinking how trite my words were: the Author who writes is always watching the human who lives, in my case. Horribly, I empathized totally with Officer Butler's pity and embarrassment; I had lived this scene many times, 20 years ago, when I was an ambulance attendant and medical orderly. But in those cases I had played the role of the pitying and embarrassed witness to the grief of a suddenly bereaved family; now, abruptly and unbelievably, I was on the other side of the drama.

The next hour is very vague. I remember telling Arlen, "We were very, very lucky to have that Clear Light shining within our family for 15 years. We must never stop being grateful for that, even in our grief." I was thinking of Oscar Ichazo's luminous remark that "nobody is truly sane until he feels gratitude to the whole universe," and beginning to understand what Oscar meant.

I remember sitting in the living room, talking very rationally with Graham, my son, and Karuna, my oldest daughter, and thinking, "Hell, grief isn't so bad. I'll get through this"; and a minute later I was sobbing uncontrollably again.

Late in the evening, I realized fully with total horror that this was going to be worse, much worse, than any other bereavement I have known. Having lost my father, my brother and my best friend in the last few years, I thought I was acquainted with grief and could distance myself from it by the Crowley techniques of breaking any emotional compulsion. But this was of a different order of hellishness than other griefs: losing parents or brothers or friends just does not compare with losing a child you have adored since infancy. I am going to suffer as I have never suffered before, I thought, almost in awe; and I remembered Tim Leary's gallantry in prison and determined to bear my pain as well as he had borne his.

Then the phone rang and my dear friend, cyberneticist Michael McNeil asked me, gently, if we had considered cryonic preservation for Luna's body, in the hope that future science would be able to resurrect her.

I was off Welfare by then, and earning decent cash regularly from my writing, but it was impossible. "We don't have that kind of money," I said.

"We can raise it," Michael said. "Paul Segall and all the people at the Bay Area Cryonics Society will donate their labor free. I've got pledges for enough money to cover the first year's expenses . . ."

"Pledges? Who?" I said stupidly.

"People who appreciate your writings on longevity and immortality, and want to help you now."

I was stunned. It seemed to me that my writings were still, even with the success of *Illuminatus*, known only to small coteries in places like Texas and Missouri. By national standards, I was still very much an unknown.

"Hold on," I said, and went to talk to Arlen. It was an excruciating moment. We had both felt that cryonic preservation was impossible on our income, and we were trying to accept the death of Luna with all the stoicism and forbearance we could muster. Would it be an unnecessary cruelty to ask Arlen to consider the long-range hope of resurrection?

Within a few seconds, after I had stumbled through an explanation, Arlen said, "Yes. Even if it doesn't work for Luna, every cryonic suspension contributes to scientific knowledge. Somebody, some day, will benefit."

"Oh, my darling," I said, beginning to weep again. Like Luna, Arlen was teaching me one more time how to stop the Wheel of Karma, how to take bad energy and turn it into good energy before passing it on.

The next day was a melodrama, since Luna had not died naturally and we were creating a precedent: nobody, anywhere, had ever before tried to cryonically preserve a murder victim. Michael McNeil and Dr. Segall consulted a lawyer before confronting the coroner and the D.A. directly; one false move and we might have lost the gamble, snared in bureaucratic red tape and police business-as-usual. Fortunately, the coroner turned out to be a most broad-minded man and was immediately captured by the idea of the cryonic gamble. *

◆

* Prof. R.C.W. Ettinger has written a detailed mathematical proof of the obvious: *however* you calculate the odds on cryonic preservation, and whatever way you estimate scientific advances, you come out with a chance above zero. Burial or cremation give you a chance of exactly zero.

◆

Then, when all was going well, the next blow fell. Paul Segall called to inform me, haltingly, that Luna's body had decomposed so far between the murder and the time she was found that cryonic preservation seemed virtually pointless.

"I suggest preservation of the brain," he said.

I understood at once: that gave us two chances that were thinkable at this time (brain transplant and/or cloning), and who-knows-how-many other scientific alternatives in the future that we cannot imagine now.

"Do it," I said.

And so Luna Wilson, who tried to paint the Clear Light and was the kindest child I have ever known, became the first murder victim to go on a cryonic time-trip to possible resuscitation.

We are the first family in history to attempt to cancel the God-like power which every murderer takes into his hands when he decides to terminate life. Understanding fully the implications of what we were doing, I knew the answer to those who would ask me, as they did in later months, "Do you still oppose capital punishment?" The reply is, of course, that I oppose it more vehemently than ever. I have made a basic choice *for life* and *against death* and my whole psychology has changed in the process. If I still remember that all realities are neurological constructs and relative to the observer, I am nonetheless committed now to one reality above all alternatives: the reality of Jesus and Buddha, in which reverence for life is the supreme imperative.

I found myself remembering, over and over, the famous lines from *Macbeth*:

> Most sacrilegious murder hath broke ope
> The Lord's annointed temple

These lines had puzzled me once, in high school; Duncan was murdered in his bedroom, not in a church. Later, of course, I learned that Shakespeare was employing the medieval metaphor that the body is the temple of the soul. In that metaphor, all murder is sacrilegious: for the body is the Lord's dwelling and to kill it is to dispossess God, a bit, from the universe.

Sacrifice cattle, little and big: after, a child.

And I recalled poor John Keel when the bridge collapsed, killing one hundred Godlings, most of them asleep and not aware of their Godliness: "The lousy bastards have done it again. They knew this was going to happen."

Luna was so beautiful that she could tell *macho* adolescent hoods to stop shoplifting because stealing makes more bad Karma, and they would stop. Even the cops loved her.

And how many fathers and mothers, in this cruelly insane century, have wept over murdered children as Arlen and I wept that night, and the next day, and many days.

Most sacrilegious murder . . .

The most elegant formulation of Bell's Theorem, Saul-Paul Sirag was telling me the other day, is that there is *no true separation* anywhere. "Send not to ask for whom the bell tolls; it tolls for thee."

When the king of Wu sent Confucius into exile, many disciples followed the philosopher, but in later years one of them said he wished he could see his home again. "How is it far," Confucius asked, "if you can think of it?"

Those words ran through Ezra Pound's mind in the death-cells at Pisa, where he watched a man hanged every morning and waited to learn if he, too, would be sentenced to death. The words of Confucius appear, both in Chinese and English, in *The Pisan Cantos*, which Pound wrote in those horrible months, usually associated with the images of the diamond that is not destroyed in the avalanche and the "rose in the steel-dust," the visible form created by an invisible magnetic field.

How is it far, if you can think of it?

The police caught the killer in a few days. He was a Sioux Indian, well-known around Berkeley, given to threats of suicide, constant alcoholism and grandiose claims that he would do something "great" for his people some day. I suppose, in his mind, he was getting even for Wounded Knee when he beat my daughter to death. The guys who dropped the napalm on the Vietnamese children thought they were protecting their homes from the barbarian hordes of "gooks." Gurdjieff used to say. "Fairness? Decency? How can you expect fairness and decency on a planet of sleeping people?" And during the first World War, he said. "Of course, if they were to wake up, they'd throw down their guns and go home to their wives and families."

In the following week, I often found myself in a room, going somewhere, without knowing how I had gotten there, or what I was looking for. I would think, almost with humor, "Oh, yes, you're in Shock."

I spent hours sitting on the sundeck, looking down over the cities of Berkeley, Oakland, San Francisco and Daly City, and musing on the Zen paradox that every man, woman, and child down there thought they were as important as me, *and they were all correct.* I tried to write down or write out some of my feelings on the fourth day, but all I typed was "The murder of my child is no worse than the murder of anybody's child; it only *seems* worse to the Ego."

Meanwhile, literally hundreds of people came by, to express their own grief or to contribute to expenses. Over 100 merchants of Telegraph Avenue, where Luna was especially known and loved, contributed generously, without being asked.

Tim Leary offered to cancel his lecture tour and come stay with us for a week, to help. I told him that it was more important to spread the SMI²LE message; but he called frequently on the phone thereafter to offer words of help to each of us in the family. One day he sent a telegram saying:

YOU ARE SURROUNDED BY A NETWORK OF
LOVE AND GRATITUDE. WE ARE ALL WITH
YOU AND SUPPORT YOU.

A network of love . . . the phrase struck me hard; after all, I had spent at least ten years asking if the occult matrix in which I was embroiled was a conscious Network or just a quantum Net of synchronicity. A network of love was what the Christians mean by the Communion of Saints, the Buddhists by the Sangha, occultists by the Secret Chiefs, Gurdjieff by the Conscious Circle of Humanity.

The Berkeley *Barb* called and asked if I could pick out a few of Luna's poems for a memorial page they were doing. (Over and over, that first week, I was to be astonished to find how many people outside the family realized what I had thought only we knew: how *special* Luna was, how rare and loving . . .)

Going through Luna's notebook, I picked out five poems to send to the *Barb*. Among them was

The Network
Look into a telescope
to see what I can
see:
baffled by the sight of
constellations
watching me.

I was overwhelmed by the coincidence-synchronicity with Leary's telegram (YOU ARE SUPPORTED BY A NETWORK OF LOVE . . .) and my long years of speculation about the Net or the Network. I took a new imprint, Tim would say; I entered a belief system in which the Network of Love was not one hypothesis among many but an omnipresent Reality.

Once my eyes were truly open to it, the Network was everywhere, in every tree, every flower, in the sky itself, and the golden merry light that had been Luna was part of it. Once, such is the power of Will and Imagination, She spoke to me and said "Foot doot." That had been among Her first spoken words and we had heard it daily for about a year, in 1963; it meant "fruit juice," which She always preferred to milk.

It is absurd for a 45-year-old man to sit at a typewriter weeping over the words "Foot doot."

Among Luna's papers, Arlen found a note Tim Leary had sent Her from Vacaville Prison in 1974, when she asked for a personal message in Tim's handwriting. He had written:

Beloved Satellite,
We will be coming to join you in outer space

It is four months since Luna entered cryonic suspension. I am now a Director of the Prometheus Society, a Maryland-based group engaged in lobbying Congress to create a National Institute of longevity and immortality research. Tim Leary and I are both deeply involved with the L5 Society, a group of scientists who are determined to send out the first space-city (designed by Prof. Gerard O'Neill of Princeton) by 1990. Working also with the Physics Consciousness Research Group and Jean Millay and other bio-feedback investigators, I am convinced that Intelligence[2] — a planetary rise in intelligence — will also be achieved in our time. The Starseed Signals, however you explain them, did indeed contain the evolutionary imperative awaiting our generation.

Looking out my window down at the vast urban sprawl of the Bay Area, I sometimes recall that somewhere down there another young girl lies beaten to death, another poor cop is breaking the news to another pair of bereaved parents. We still have one murder every 14 minutes in this mad society.

I know, truly, that I have been a lucky man, and my family has been lucky, compared to what happened to the Jews (and most of Europe) in the 1930s and 1940s, or to the colored races on this continent for three centuries, or to the nightmare horror in Vietnam between 1940 and 1973. Or compared to most of human history, which is still, as Joyce said, a nightmare from which we are seeking to awake.

Tim Leary was here last week, lecturing at UC-Berkeley. The news arrived that his appeal had been rejected by the New Orleans court and he might have to go back to jail again. Tim didn't let anybody know about this (I found out from the only person in the room when the news came on the phone); Tim continued to radiate humor, cheer and optimism.

Arlen had a conversation with Tim, in which she expressed gratitude for the example he had given us during the last three years of his confinement. "You convinced us that it is possible to transcend suffering," she said, "and that helped us more than anything else in the first weeks after Luna's death."

Tim said, "That's the whole point of all my work on brain change!" He hugged her excitedly. "That's it! You've got it! *Positive energy is as real as gravity.* I've felt it."

Two hours later, at the door, Tim was stopped by one of our guests with a final question before he left.

"What do you do, Dr. Leary, when somebody keeps giving you negative energy?"

Tim grinned that special grin of his that so annoys all his critics. "*Come back with all the positive energy you have,*" he said. And then he dashed off to the car, to the airport, to the next lecture . . . and to God-knows-what fate in the fourteenth year of his struggle with the legal system.

And so I learned the final secret of the Illuminati.

THE END

AFTERWORDS

by Saul-Paul Sirag

I first met Uri Geller in Berkeley in April 1973. I was working on a story about Geller for *Esquire*, and I went to New York in May and June to pursue the story. After several interviews with Geller and Dr. Andrija Puharich, both in the city and at Puharich's house in Ossining (where Geller often stayed), they began mentioning the extraterrestrial aspects of their story. They spoke of a computer-like entity which had communicated with them and claimed it was "millions of light-years into the future" (and Puharich was quite aware that light-year is a distance, not a time). They showed me a typical UFO photo that Geller was supposed to have shot from a plane window over France. They told me of a red laser-like thing that identified itself as one form of the communicating entity. ("Now you can see how we look," it allegedly said.) They mentioned tapes that recorded themselves and, even more miraculously, subsequently erased themselves — a fantastic yam that weirdly foreshadowed the Watergate tape erasures many months later.

I was intrigued by these extraterrestrial claims, although I regarded them as pretty far-fetched. Finally, I asked Geller if it might be possible for me to see the communicating entity if I were in an expanded state of consciousness due to some psychedelic.

Puharich was already famous (or infamous if you will) for psychedelic research in the 1950s and had written a book on ESP experiments he had conducted with *Amanita muscaria*, called *The Sacred Mushroom*. Uri was wary of psychedelics, but he said he wondered what it would be like to see me in a psychedelic state. And so I came to spend a few hours with Uri Geller while tripping on LSD. The experiment was conducted in a friend's apartment in Manhattan, and the friend remained straight so we could compare notes later.

At one point in the evening, I felt that the time was right and asked Geller if it would now be possible for me to see the Entity. He told me to look into his eyes and tell him what I saw.

My first thoughts were, "This is no way to do it. I'll only see those red lights they've been telling me about. Doesn't he realize that's all I'll see? Of course, he does — it's just a psychological trick. When I see the red lights, he'll tell me I've seen the Entity too, but it won't prove a damned thing."

Instead, when I looked into Uri's eyes, they became quite bird-like, and suggested a bird of prey. Then his nose became a beak, and his entire head sprouted feathers, down to his neck and shoulders.

I jumped back a bit, startled. "Uri, you look just like an eagle!" I exclaimed, and I must have sounded awestruck.

Uri became very excited — as only Uri can. But he wouldn't comment about what I had seen; he was very mysterious about it. Instead, we became involved in telepathy and bending things. I had to put my Eagle experience into the IDUNNO file. I didn't know what to make of it — it was hardly how I expected an extraterrestrial to look.

My memory of the event went *active* again only in November of that year. I had returned to Berkeley in June and had become a research associate at the Institute for the Study of Consciousness. (To show how convoluted this whole business is, I might mention that Arthur Young, founder of the Institute, was the one who originally turned Robert Temple on to the idea of trying to find out how the Dogon tribe knew so much about the dark companion of Sirius. And Arthur Young, in turn, had first heard of this tribal lore from Harry Smith, a film maker, who claims to be a son of *Aleister Crowley* . . .)

Anyway, in November 1973 I started to hear about Ray Stanford's teleportation stories from Alan Vaughn, who had gone to Texas to interview Stanford for *Psychic* magazine. Stanford claimed to have been teleported in his car twice during the Fall of 1973. Each time the teleportation occurred, Stanford said, he had been driving to the airport to pick up Uri Geller.

Stanford attributed the teleportations to SPECTRA — the

name Geller and Puharich were now using to refer to the extra-terrestrial entity. By this time Puharich had written his book, *Uri*, which has a chapter on SPECTRA, but I had not heard either Geller or Puharich use this term nor refer to SPECTRA as a hawk. To Ray Stanford, SPECTRA was a very powerful being who came to him in the form of a hawk. Stanford, you must understand, is a psychic who has long been involved in UFO research and, long before hearing of Geller, had associated UFO experiences with hawk-like entities. In fact, before the teleporta-tions Stanford had some rather strange hawk-infested dreams in which he was invited to join forces with SPECTRA.

In this context, my "eagle" experience with Geller began to take on a certain significance.

Then in mid-December 1973, the January 1974 issue of *Ana-log* hit the stands with a cover story called "The Horus Errand." The cover illustration showed a man in a white-and-gold uniform with a hawk-like helmet and the Eye of Horus over his left breast pocket. Over his right breast pocket was his name tag, which was (are you ready?) *Stanford*.

This was, to me, an incredible Jungian synchronicity, and I called Alan Vaughn to tell him about it. He rushed out to buy that issue of *Analog* and called me back with the news that the figure on the cover even looked like Ray Stanford. The synchronicity was getting heavier — and we didn't know, yet, about Timothy Leary and Robert Anton Wilson and their synchronicitous links with all this.

Vaughn wrote to the artist who had done the "Horus" illustra-tion for *Analog* — Kelly Freas, one of the best in the science-fic-tion business. It turned out that Freas had never met Ray Stan-ford, and had not been consciously using Stanford's face in the illustration. There *was* a link, however. About ten years earlier, Freas had had a psychic reading done by Stanford via mail. In the reading, Stanford claimed that Freas had been some sort of illustrator in a past life in ancient Egypt. For that reason Freas uses Egyptian symbols whenever he gets the chance — as he did in illustrating "The Horus Errand." The Egyptian themes are very minor in the story itself, and the hero's helmet, for instance, is never described beyond its white and gold colors. Freas had turned it into a hawk's head because Horus, the hawk-headed Lord of Force and Fire, was the oldest known Egyptian god.

Freas also said that he hadn't made any conscious connection between the Stanford in the story and the Ray Stanford who had given him a psychic reading by mail ten years earlier. He emphasized that he didn't know what Ray Stanford looked like.

Another unusual feature of the *Analog* cover, Freas said, was that he usually paints human figures from either photos or live models, but in this case he had simply painted from imagination.

The *Analog* cover also shows a red laser-beam streaming off the top of a *pyramid-shaped* building directly behind the figure of Stanford. The story mentions no such laser-beam, but that was what I had *expected* to see in Uri Geller's eyes . . .

There is a further dimension to this whole story. Geller and Puharich had first described the extraterrestrial entity to me as a spacecraft computer. By November of 1973 I had learned that they were also describing the entity as a hawk and calling it SPECTRA. In Puharich's book, *Uri* (published in 1974), SPECTRA is described as a giant computer which occasionally projects a hawk-like entity onto this planet.

People tell me that the name, SPECTRA, smacks of grade B science-fiction. While that's true, it is also true that RCA used to manufacture a large computer called Spectra-70. RCA suddenly went out of the computer business entirely in October 1971 under mysterious circumstances. Two months later, in December 1971, SPECTRA came through to Geller and Puharich as a mechanical sounding voice claiming to be a spacecraft-computer "53,069 light-ages" away. Later SPECTRA came in the form of a hawk. Of course, Dr. Puharich has a long background in electronics and the name of the RCA computer, Spectra-70, was undoubtedly buried somewhere in his conscious or unconscious. But that does not explain my own bird-of-prey experience with Geller, or Ray Stanford's hawk-SPECTRA dreams, or the teleportations that Stanford (and others) have claimed occur around Geller.

Since meeting Robert Anton Wilson, I have been learning the occult lore of Horus, and have discovered that synchronicities are to be found everywhere. For instance, after *Illuminatus* was published, I half-jokingly told Wilson that he should have put San Francisco into his conspiracy-mythos since San Francisco, like the Illuminati, was founded in 1776. We both laughed about that. Then a few months later I came across the fact that Phi Beta Kappa was founded in 1776, and suggested that Wilson include that if he ever writes a sequel to *Illuminatus*.

Later, just to check, I looked into Heckethorn's *The Secret Societies of All Ages and Countries*. There was the flat statement that Phi Beta Kappa was a Bavarian Illuminati order introduced to the United States on December 5, 1776. Their motto, incidentally, was *Philosophy is the Rule of Life*.

The most comprehensive conspiracy theory I know of is the interpretation of quantum mechanics devised by Sir Arthur Eddington. (Remember that Wilson claims that every time he tells me something weird I can find a model in quantum theory that might explain it — so here goes . . .)

Eddington says that the lesson from physics and especially from quantum mechanics is that insofar as we can describe the world at all we are necessarily describing the structure of our own minds. In case you think I'm over-simplifying Eddington's view, let me quote from his *Philosophy of Physical Science*, page 148:

> The starting point of physical science is knowledge of the group-structure of a set of sensations in a consciousness. When these fragments of structure, contributed at various times and by various individuals, have been collated and represented according to the forms of thought that we have discussed [i.e. group structure] . . . we obtain the structure known as the physical universe.

In case Eddington's meaning is not perfectly clear to you, I will quote a slightly more poetic version, from an essay of his reprinted in *The World of Mathematics*, edited by James Newman, page 1104:

> We have found a strange foot-print on the shores of the unknown. We have devised profound theories, one after another, to account for its origin. At last, we have succeeded in reconstructing the creature that made the foot-print. And Lo! It is our own.

Recently, I have been using Eddington's approach to derive the proton-electron mass ratio. (Actually, I'm using a slight modification of Eddington's approach, to be exact.) From Eddington's group-theoretical point of view, creatures to whom space-time has four dimensions will find algebraic structures having 10 elements and 136 elements playing a very fundamental role.

Eddington attempted, unsuccessfully, to derive the proton-electron mass ratio from the two numbers 10 and 136, together with the number of unity, 1. I have pointed out that if you have 136 elements and want to order them two at a time (e.g., one for the proton, one for the electron), you will have 18,360 ways to order these 136 things. (This holds true, of course, whatever the 136 things are.) Since I want to do *something* with Eddington's 10, I divide our ways of ordering into 10 parts (for the 10 dimensions of curvature in space-time). We then obtain 1,836 — which is very close to the desired proton-electron mass ratio.

Like much of the data in this book, this might seem like "mere coincidence." But after making this calculation, I found in an old *Scientific American* (May 1963) an article by P.A.M. Dirac, which states that "The gravitational field is a tensor field with 10 components. One finds that six of the components are adequate for describing everything of physical importance and the other four can be dropped out of the equation. One cannot, however, pick out the six important components from the complete set of 10 in any way that does not destroy the four-dimensional symmetry."

Dirac, one of the founders of quantum theory, was here attempting to marry quantum mechanics to general relativity and was running into trouble. His extremity was my opportunity. I had gotten the proton-electron mass ratio by dividing 10 into 18,360. So from what Dirac proposed, I decided to see what would happen when I divided 18,360 by 9, by 8, by 7 and by 6. What I got was the electron mass numbers of the other Baryons, the Lambda, the Xi, the Sigma and the Omega.

Dirac had complained that when one uses fewer than 10 tensors one destroys space-time symmetry; but that is just what I want. The reason is that, since Dirac wrote in 1963, it has been discovered that mass splittings can come about by breaking an underlying gauge symmetry. This is how the weak force is gotten out of the electromagnetic force by Steven Weinberg and various other physicists much in vogue today. I am now preparing a paper in which I get the strong force out of the gauge symmetry of general relativity. (Actually, this has already been done by Abdus Salam and Jack Sarfatti. I'm just giving them more ammunition.)*

But things begin to look positively contrived when one notices that Eddington's 1, 10 and 136 are members of a well-known mathematical series that goes 1, 10, 45, 136, 325 . . . etc.

The next number in that series is 666.

Berkeley, California

Summer, 1977

◆

* For those who wish to see the entire mathematical derivation, see "A Combinatorial Derivation of Proton-Electron Mass Ratio," by Saul-Paul Sirag, Published in *Nature*, Vol 268, July 28, 1977.

◆

NOTES and INDEX

NOTES

Prologue: Thinking About the Unthinkable

1. The best single reference on the Illuminati in fact and legendry
   is The *Illuminoids*, by Neal Wilgus, Sun Press: Albuquer-
   que, New Mexico, 1977. Seventeen mutually contradictory
   and quite typical anti-Illuminati books or pamphlets are
   quoted in Volume I of *Illuminatus (The Eye in the Pyramid,*
   by Robert J. Shea and Robert Anton Wilson, Dell: New
   York, 1975).

2. *The Book of Lies* (falsely so called) by Aleister Crowley, Samuel Weiser: New York, 1952.

3. A typical work linking Crowley with the Illuminati conspiracy
   is *The Trail of the Serpent* by "Inquire Within," Christian
   Book Club of America: Hawthorn, Cal., 1969. "Inquire
   Within" was the pen name of Carolyn Stoddard who, like
   Crowley himself, was a former member of the Hermetic
   Order of the Golden Dawn, a secret occult order active in
   England and America from 1888 to the present. Crowley,
   Carolyn Stoddard and Dr. Israel Regardie (*The Eye in the
   Triangle*, Llewellyn: St. Paul, 1970) have all traced the
   Golden Dawn order back to a mysterious Anna Sprenger of
   Bavaria, possibly an initiate of the original Bavarian Illumi-
   nati.

4. The *Illuminoids*, op. cit., p. i.

5. *The Sirius Mystery*, by Robert K.G. Temple, St. Martin's
   Press: New York, 1976.

6. Simonton's pancakes are discussed in *The Edge of Reality*,
   by J. Allen Hynek and Jacques Vallee, Regnery: Chicago,
   1975, pp. 147-154.

7. The experience of the two Naval Intelligence officers is recounted in *The Invisible College*, by Jacques Vallee, Dutton:
   New York, 1976, pp. 12-16. A Pentagon official confirmed
   this story on a Rod Serling "UFO Report" on NBC-televi-
   sion during 1976. Both officers are still with Naval Intelli-

gence and regarded as sound and sane by their superiors.

8. The two visits to Lanalus are recounted in *The Mothman Prophecies*, by John Keel, Dutton: New York, 1975. Keel also reports several dozen other Contactees who got the same "message" as these two, but with dozens of conflicting details about the Contacting entities and their physical appearance, mode of transport, time elapsed, etc.

Part One. The Sirius Connection

9. *Gems from the Equinox*, by Aleister Crowley, Llewellyn: St. Paul, 1974, p. 277.

10. *The Teachings of Don Juan*, by Carlos Castaneda, Ballantine: New York, 1968, pp. 97-98 and 148 ff.

11. *The Peyote Cult*, by Weston LeBarre, Schocken: New York, 1969.

12. *The Secret Life of Plants*, by Peter Tompkins and Christopher Bird, Avon: New York, 1973. For Steiner and Goethe see pp. 293-300, 381-83,122-35.

13. *Secret Life of Plants*, op. cit., pp. 150-57, 135-40.

14. *Secret Life of Plants*, op. cit., pp. 43-44.

15. *The Roots of Coincidence*, by Arthur Koestler, Vintage: New York, 1973. *The Challenge of Chance*, by Koestler et al., Vintage: New York, 1975.

16. *Forum of Contemporary History*, July 2, 1973.

17. "Tim Leary: A Personal Appraisal," by Walter Huston Clark, *Association for Humanistic Psychology Newsletter*, April 1976, pp. 1-2. Dr. Clark also offers his professional opinion, as a theologian, on the case of Dr. Leary and his critics. Clark opines that Leary is unusually honest, contrary to his media image as a con-man, and has all four of the positive traits of sainthood, contrary to his image as a scoundrel. Dr. Clark possesses advanced degrees in both theology and psychology.

18. *Sex and Drugs*, by Robert Anton Wilson, Playboy Press: New York, 1973, pp. 230-232.

19. *The Invisible College*, op. cit., pp. 161-74.

20. *The Tao of Physics*, by Fritjof Capra, Shambhalla: Berkeley, 1975, pp. 286-299.

21. *Ten Faces of the Universe*, by Fred Hoyle, W.H. Freeman: San Francisco, 1977, pp. 120-128.

22. *The Challenge of Chance*, op. cit., pp. 215-216.

23. *Millbrook*, by Art Kleps, Bench Press: Oakland, Cal., 1977, pp. 137-138.

24. *LSD*, ed. by David Solomon, Putnam: New York, 1964.

25. Out of print. To be republished in *Neuro-Politics*, by Timothy Leary, 88 Books: San Diego, 1977.

26. *The Book of Lies*, op. cit., pp. 148-49. The book as a whole is simultaneously an account of Crowley's love affair with a mistress and a commentary of the Cabalistic Tree of Life, like Joyce, Crowley loved to pack seven levels of meaning into one sentence.

27. *Sex and Drugs*, op. cit., pp. 77-92, 110-42. See also my *Book of the Breast*, Playboy Press: New York, 1976, pp. 97-131.

28. *This Timeless Moment*, by Laura Archera Huxley, Celestial Arts: Millbrae, Cal., 1975, p. 236. The sentence was found in a book of literary criticism, *Coloquio de Buenas Aires*, edited and published by the P.E.N. Club of Argentina.

29. The source for Huxley's 1929 peyote trip with Crowley is *Sexuality, Magic and Perversion*, by Francis King, Citadel Press: New York, p. 118.

30. *In My Own Way*, by Alan Watts, Vintage Books: New York, 1973, pp. 141-42.

31. *The Sufis*, by Idries Shah, Jonathan Cape: London, 1969, pp. 244-48,380-81. Shah also links Sufism with Masonry proper; Crowley's Ordo Templi Orientis claimed to carry on the tradition of the Templars, to have the secret lost by other Masonic groups (including the mysterious Mason Word) and to have been founded by a Sufi, Mansur el Hallaj.

32. *Uri*, by Andrija Puharich, Bantam: New York, 1974. The extraterrestrial communications occur in nearly every chapter.

33. *The Center of the Cyclone*, by John Lilly, M.D., Bantam: New York, 1972,pp.23-25,37,231.

34. *Terra II*, by Timothy Leary and L. Wayne Benner, Imprinting Press: San Francisco, 1973. Chapter 19.

35. *Intuition*, by R. Buckminster Fuller, Anchor Books: Garden City, New York, 1973, pp. 159-65, 167-70.

36. "Faster than a Speeding Photon," *City* (San Francisco), October 7, 1975.

37. *The Magical Revival*, by Kenneth Grant, Weiser: New York, 1973, p. 15.

38. *Ibid.*, p. 50.

39. *Tantra: The Yoga of Sex*, by Omar Garrison, Avon Books: New York, 1973, pp. 69, 122.

40. "Life After Life," *Readers Digest*, January 1977, pp. 192-215.

41. *The Invisible College*, op. cit., p. 26.

42. *The Books of Charles Fort*, Henry Holt & Co.: New York, 1941, pp. 861-62. Fort's source is the New York World, July 27, 1908.

43. *Invisible College*, op. cit., pp. 122-23.

44. *Aleister Crowley and the Hidden God*, by Kenneth Grant, Weiser: New York, 1975, pp. 36-37.

45. *Ibid.*, p. 37.

46. *Flying Saucers*, by Carl Jung, Harcourt Brace: New York, 1959, p. xii. Jung says that the appearance of UFOs worldwide indicates "changes in the constellation of psychic dominants, of the archetypes, or 'gods' as they used to be called, which bring about, or accompany, long-lasting transformations of the collective psyche." He then compares them to the "signs and wonders" that accompanied the transition from paganism to Christianity 2,000 years ago.

47. *The Edge of Reality*, op. cit., pp. 63-65.

48. *History of Secret Societies*, by Akron Daraul, Pocket Books: New York, 1961. *Manual of Sex Magick*, by Louis Culling, Llewellyn: St. Paul, 1971. *Secret Rituals of the O.T.O.*, by Francis King, Weiser: New York, 1975. *The Sufis*, by Idries Shah, op. cit.

49. *The Dermis Probe*, by Idries Shah, Dutton: New York, 1971, p. 9.

50. *The Law is For All*, by Aleister Crowley, edited by Israel Regardie, Llewellyn: St. Paul, 1976; *The Eye in the Triangle*, by Israel Regardie, Llewellyn: St. Paul, 1970. See also *Confessions of Aleister Crowley*, Bantam: New York, 1971, pp. 413-27.

51. All quotations from the *Book of the Law* are from *The Law is For All*, op. cit., pp. 45-65.

52. *The Center of the Cyclone*, op. cit., p. 231.

53. The quotes from Senator Humphrey and the Abolish Death Committee are from undated newspaper stories in the Immortalist Archives of Mr. Carl Spann of San Francisco.

54. *San Francisco Phoenix*, July 11, 1974, article titled "Immortalist Revolution Wins the Bay Area."

55. *The Immortality Factor*, by Osborn Segerberg, Jr., Dutton: New York, 1974, pp. 358-63.

56. *The Eternal Man*, by Louis Pauwels and Jacques Bergier, Avon Books: New York, 1972, p. 14.

57. *Extended Youth: The Promise of Gerontology*, by Robert Prehoda, Putnam: New York, 1968, p. 86.

58. Quoted in *Prolongevity*, by Albert Rosenfeld, Knopf: New York, p. 5.

59. *Prolongevity, op. cit.*, p. 6.

60. *Prolongevity*, op. cit., p. 182.

61. Dr. Comfort is quoted in *No More Dying*, by Joel Kurtzman and Philip Gordon, Tarcher, Inc.: Los Angeles, 1976, p. 3.

62. *No More Dying*, op. cit., p. 3.

63. *Prodigal Genius: The Life of Nikola Tesla*, by John C. O'Neill, Neville Spearman: London, 1968, pp. 23-19.

64. *Kundalini*, by Gopi Krishna, Shambhalla: Berkeley, 1970.

65. *The Invisible Landscape*, by Terrence and Dennis McKenna, Seabury Press: New York, 1975, pp. 8-17.

66. *Secret Life of Plants*, op. cit., p. 61-65.

67. *Ibid.*, p. 73.

68. Details on the life of Jack Parsons are from the works of Francis King and Kenneth Grant, *op. cit*, and from personal reminiscences by Grady McMurty.

69. *Gurdjieff: Making A New World*, by J.G. Bennett, Turnstone Books: London, 1973, p. 274. On the following page, 275, Bennett defines Gurdjieff's goal as a writer: "to place the reader constantly in the unaccustomed perspective of an extraterrestrial observer."

70. *Other Tongues, Other Flesh*, by George Hunt Williamson, Amherst Press: Amherst, Wisc., 1953, p. 72.

71. *Other Tongues, Other Flesh*, op. cit., pp. 88, 219,227.

72. *A Study of Gurdjieff's Teachings*, by Kenneth Walker, Jonathan Cape: London, 1967, p. 167.

73. *Ghost Dance: Origins of Religion*, by Weston LeBarre, Doubleday: New York, 1970.

74. *Tales of Power*, by Carlos Castaneda, Simon & Schuster: New York, 1974, p. 270.

75. See "From Dallas to Watergate," by Peter Dale Scott in *Government by Gunplay*, ed. by Sid Blumenthal, American Library: New York, 1976, pp. 113-29.

76. *Magick*, by Aleister Crowley, Samuel Weiser: New York, 1974, p. 5.

77. *Uri*, op. cit., p. 116 ff.

78. *The Mothman Prophecies*, op. cit.

Part Two: Models and Metaphors

79. *Book of Lies*, op. cit., p. 100.

80. *The Sirius Mystery*, op. cit., p. 2-3.

81. *Sirius Mystery*, op. cit., p. 3.

82. *Sirius Mystery*, op. cit., p. 15.

83. *Sirius Mystery*, op. cit., p. 49.

84. *Sirius Mystery*, op. cit., p. 229.

85. *Sirius Mystery*, op. cit., pp. 55-100; The Book of Thoth, by Aleister Crowley, Level Press: San Francisco, 1974, p. 118.

86. *Sirius Mystery*, op. cit., pp. 79-81.

87. *The Invisible College*, op. cit., passim.

88. *Upwingers: A Futurist Manifesto*, by F.M. Esfandiary, John Day Co.: New York, 1973, p. 4.

89. *The Invisible Landscape*, op. cit.

90. *No More Dying*, op. cit., p. 4.

91. *The Invisible Landscape*, op. cit., p. 184.

Part Three: Trigger

92. *Morals and Dogma of the Ancient and Accepted Scottish Rite of Freemasonry*, by Albert Pike, Supreme Council of the Southern Jurisdiction: Washington, D.C., 1871, pp. 14-15.

93. *The Curse of the Pharoahs*, by Phillip Vandenberg, Pocket Books: New York, 1977, p. 205.

94. *Sirius Mystery*, op. cit., p. 221.
95. *CETI: Communication with Extra-Terrestrial Intelligence*, by Jack Stonely and A.T. Lawton, Warner Books: New York, 1976, p. 200.

INDEX

Einstein, Albert, 34, 38, 42, 103, 120,
124, 195, 206, 208, 210, 217
and ERP, 193
Einsteinian theory, 38, 206, 208, 217,
221
Electroencephalograms, 205
Eleusinian Mysteries, 70, 149, 191
el Hallaj, Mansur, 100
Energy, 214
negative and positive, 239
Enochian angels, 163, 188
Equinox (journal), 74
Eris, 55-9, 151, 158
ERP demonstration (Einstein-Rosen-
Podolsky), 193
Esalen, 166
Esfandiary, F.M., 209
ESP, 7, 73, 78, 80-94, 99, 101, 118,
140-1, 198, 220, 235
interstellar, 8, 79, 89, 94, 102, 119,
147, 198
see also Telepathy
Eternal Man (Pauwels and Bergier),
123
Ettinger, R.C.W., 121, 239
Euclidean geometry, 44, 118, 203-6,
213, 217
Exo-psychology, 57, 119
Extended Youth (Prehoda), 123
Extraterrestrial contacts, *see* UFO
contacts and contactees
Extraterrestrial migration, 212, 217
Extraterrestrial visitors, 7, 14, 24-8,
39-40, 79, 89, 91, 112, 119,
131, 162, 175-9, 188, 228
see also UFOnauts - 14
Eye in pyramid symbol, *see* Eye in
triangle symbol
Eye in the Triangle (Regardie), 65
Eye in triangle symbol, 65, 67, 76,
146, 188
Eye of Horus symbol, *see also* Horus,
115, 146, 188, 190, 249

F.A.B., 157

Fables,
Sufi, 17, 27, 57, 61, 71, 187
Zen, 17
Babylonian, 17
Jewish, 187
German, 187-8
Egyptian, 227
Fact (journal), 31-2
Fairies, 13, 24, 28
Fang the Unwashed, 157
Fatima, 41
FBI, 153, 158, 174-5
Fechner, Gustav, 23
Federation Trading Post, 206
Feiffer, Jules, 30
Fertility rites, 23
Festival of Yoga and Esoteric
Sciences, 145
Finnegans Wake (Joyce), 46
Firesign Theatre, 0, 181
First Sex (Davis), 79
Fitzhugh Ludlow Memorial Library,
105
Fives, law of, 57, 64, 230
Flash Gordon, 7
Flesh of the Gods (Furst), 148
Flessel, Peter, 218
Flying Saucers. See UFOs
Folsom Prison. *See* Leary, Timothy
and imprisonment
Fonda, Jane, 174
Fort, Charles, 93, 96, 140, 212
Fortean News (journal), 169
Foundation for Research on
Immortality, 123
Four hundred and eighteen (418),
102, 111
Frazer, James, 30, 76, 197
Freas, Kelly, 176, 249-50
Free fall, 118, 205-6, 215 *See also*
Gravity,
Freemasons, *see* Masons
Freud, Sigmund, 28, 30, 50, 52
Freudians and Freudianism, 35, 52,
98, 204

What Critics Say About
Robert Anton Wilson

A SUPER-GENIUS . . . He has written everything I was afraid to write

Dr. John Lilly

◎

One of the funniest, most incisive social critics around, and with a positive bent, thank Goddess.

Riane Eisler, author of *The Chalice and the Blade*

◎

A very funny man . . . readers with open minds will like his books.

Robin Robertson, Psychological Perspectives

◎

Robert Anton Wilson is a dazzling barker hawking tickets to the most thrilling tilt-a-whirls and daring loop-o-planes on the midway of higher consciousness.

Tom Robbins, author of *Even Cowgirls Get the Blues*

◎

STUPID

Andrea Antonoff

◎

The man's either a genius or Jesus

SOUNDS (London)

◎

A 21st Century Renaissance Man . . . funny, wise and optimistic . . .

DENVER POST

◎

The world's greatest writer-philosopher.

IRISH TIMES (Dublin)

◎

Hilarious . . . multi-dimensional . . . a laugh a paragraph.

LOS ANGELES TIMES

◎

Ranting and raving . . . negativism . . .

Neal Wilgus

◎

One of the most important writers working in English today . . . courageous, compassionate, optimistic and original.

Elwyn Chamberling, author of *Gates of Fire*

◎

Should win the Nobel Prize for INTELLIGENCE.

QUICKSILVER MESSENGER (Brighton, England)

◎

Wilson managed to reverse every mental polarity in me, as if I had been dragged through infinity. I was astounded and delighted.

Philip K. Dick, author of *Blade Runner*

◎

One of the leading thinkers of the modern age.

Barbara Marx Hubbard

◎

A male feminist. ..a simpering, pussy-whipped wimp.

Lou Rollins

◎

SEXIST

Arlene Meyers

◎

The most important philosopher of this century . . . scholarly, witty, hip and hopeful.

Timothy Leary

◎

What great physicist hides behind the mask of "Robert Anton Wilson?"

NEW SCIENTIST

◎

Does for quantum mechanics what Durrell's *Alexandria Quartet* did for Relativity, but Wilson is funnier.

John Gribbin, physicist

◎

OBSCENE, blasphemous, subversive and very, very interesting.

Alan Watts

◎

Erudite, witty and genuinely scary.

PUBLISHER'S WEEKLY

◎

Deliberately annoying,

Jay Kinney

◎

Misguided malicious fanaticism.

Robert Sheafer, Committee for Scientific Investigation of Claims of the Paranormal

◎

The man's glittering intelligence won't let you rest. With each new book, I look forward to his wisdom, laced with his special brand of crazy humor.

Alan Harrington, author of *The Immortalist*

◎

Mosbunall* Books By Robert Anton Wilson

1972 Playboy's Book of Forbidden Words
1973 Sex, Drugs and Magick: A Journey Beyond Limits
1973 The Sex Magicians
1974 The Book of the Breast (now 'Ishtar Rising')
1975 ILLUMINATUS! (with Robert Shea)
       The Eye in the Pyramid
       The Golden Apple
       Leviathan
1977 Cosmic Trigger I: Final Secret of the Illuminati
1978 Neuropolitique (with T. Leary & G. Koopman)
1980 The Illuminati Papers
1980-1 The Schrodinger's Cat Trilogy
       The Universe Next Door
       The Trick Top Hat
       The Homing Pigeon
1981 Masks of the Illuminati
1983 Right Where You Are Sitting Now
1983 The Earth Will Shake
     (Historical Illuminatus Trilogy - volume 1)
1983 Prometheus Rising

*Adaptation of "sombunall" — See reference in *Quantum Psychology*, Robert Anton Wilson

HILARITAS
PRESS

Publishing the Books of Robert Anton Wilson
and Other Adventurous Thinkers

www.hilaritaspress.com

CPSIA information can be obtained
at www.ICGtesting.com
Printed in the USA
LVHW022051170820
663418LV00014B/1174